W9-DHV-668

EQUAL
EMPLOYMENT ISSUES

EQUAL EMPLOYMENT ISSUES

Race and Sex Discrimination in the United States, Canada, and Britain

Harish C. Jain
Peter J. Sloane

PRAEGER

PRAEGER SPECIAL STUDIES • PRAEGER SCIENTIFIC

Library of Congress Cataloging in Publication Data

Jain, Harish C.
    Equal employment issues.

    Includes index.
    1. Discrimination in employment. 2. Discrimination
in employment—Law and legislation. I. Sloane, Peter J.
II. Title.
HD4903.J34   331.13'3   81-8833
ISBN 0-03-050836-3   AACR2

Published in 1981 by Praeger Publishers
CBS Educational and Professional Publishing
A Division of CBS, Inc.
521 Fifth Avenue, New York, NY 10175 USA

PREFACE

Minority employment has certainly been one of the most significant and complex human resource problems faced by policy-makers, managers, trade unionists, and society as a whole since at least the early 1960s. A growing number of studies have been published in the equal pay and equal employment areas. However, there does appear to be a vacuum in the literature in relation to comparative perspectives with an interdisciplinary focus.

This book is an attempt to fill that vacuum. A comparative perspective of three countries—the United States, Canada, and Britain—is utilised to examine the similarities and differences in their approaches in public policies and practises at both macro- and micro-levels, with a focus on both labour economics and behavioural (socio-psychological) aspects.

We are indebted to so many organisations and individuals for assisting us in this study that it is difficult to acknowledge all of them. Harish C. Jain is grateful to the Canada Council and the University-Research Committee of the Canada Department of Labour for providing him leave fellowship and research grants, respectively. He was research consultant to the Organization for Economic Cooperation and Development (OECD) during 1976-1978, and this experience, along with his study entitled Disadvantaged Groups on the Labour Market and Measures to Assist Them, published by the OECD in 1979, provided him with a useful comparative perspective. The study compared policy measures in Sweden, West Germany, France, the United States, Canada, and Great Britain. Jain is also thankful to the several institutions that offered him the use of their research facilities. These include the University of Glasgow, Paisley College, and the International Labour Organization (ILO). In these and other educational institutions, such as University of Aston (England), International Institute of Management (West Germany) the European Institute for Advanced Studies in Management (Belgium) and INSEAD (France), Jain conducted seminars which helped him to gain a better understanding of equal employment and personnel and industrial relations issues and practises in Western Europe in general and in Britain in particular.

Peter J. Sloane wishes to acknowledge research funding from the Social Science Research Council, Manpower Services Commission, and Training Services Agency, and also from the Association of Universities and Colleges of Canada for the provision of a Commonwealth Fellowship, which enabled him to familiarise himself with North American experience at close quarters.

We are very grateful to the following scholars who helped provide comments on earlier drafts of several chapters in this book: Professor Naresh C. Agarwal from McMaster University, Professor Morley Gunderson from University of Toronto, Alistair Young from Paisley College, Brian Chiplin from the University of Nottingham, and Stanley Siebert from the University of Birmingham. We also wish to acknowledge the services of Jean Craft in typing much of the manuscript, Lucy Docherty in preparing the index and checking over the footnotes and references, and Nick Javor in doing library work.

Finally, we wish to thank a number of individuals for permission to use or draw from published material, and in particular the editor of the International Journal of Social Economics for permission to draw from our paper 'The Structure of Labour Markets, Minority Workers and Equal Employment Opportunities Legislation', in Volume 7, No. 3, 1980, of that journal; the Industrial Relations Journal for permission to adapt our paper 'Race, Sex and Minority Group Discrimination Legislation in North America and Britain', in the Summer 1978 issue; and the MacMillan Press Limited for permission to draw from Chapter 4 of Women and Low Pay (edited by P. J. Sloane), 1980.

CONTENTS

LIST OF TABLES

EQUAL
EMPLOYMENT ISSUES

1

INTRODUCTION

Discrimination against minority groups has been a central issue of public policy in the United States, Canada, and Britain since the 1960s. Minority groups include women, coloured workers, immigrants, foreign workers, the handicapped, the young, and the elderly.[1] But in this book we concentrate on race and sex discrimination, which have tended to receive most attention from both academics and policy-makers.

In the book, attention is focused on the United States, Canada, and Britain partly because there is more information on the workings of equal-employment legislation in the United States than in any other country and partly because public policy developments in Canada and Britain appear to mirror those in the United States.[2] Today it is public policy in these three countries to eliminate discrimination in the workplace on the basis of race, colour, sex, and numerous other grounds. Affirmative-action programmes are increasingly coming into vogue to increase the employment, training, and promotion opportunities of minorities and women.[3] Such programs have raised questions as to whether the goal of public policy should be to promote equal treatment or equal achievement in the workplace.[4]

Canada is the only country that has incorporated the International Labour Organisation's (ILO) Equal Remuneration Convention (No. 100, adopted in 1951),[5] which requires equal pay for work of equal value at the federal level. This aspect of the Canadian Human Rights Act continues to be controversial.[6] The equal value or "comparable worth" issue has also generated a great deal of debate in the United States and Britain.[7]

For the purpose of this book, the most important and intriguing aspect of discrimination based on race and sex is that both its existence and proposed remedies have been defined to a considerable extent in terms of the internal and external labour markets.[8] Thus, such discrimination has been viewed, in part, as an economic phenomenon which lends itself to amelioration by legally mandated equal-employment policies and practices.[9]

Since variations in personal characteristics and establishments make it difficult, if not impossible, to isolate the precise extent of discrimination at the macro-level, detailed analysis of the operation of local labour markets and individual enterprises and establishments is crucial. A feature of recent empirical work has been the emphasis placed on the internal labour market (ILM) and the related concept of the dual labour market (DLM).[10] These concepts are discussed in Chapter 3. This emphasis is, in fact, highly relevant to equal-opportunity legislation not only because it is at the level of the individual organisation or unit of employment that the laws are to be applied but also because the pertinent legislation appears to have certain features consistent with a dualist interpretation of the operation of the labour market, while the emphasis on equality of training and promotion opportunities is most appropriate and significant in the context of a well developed internal labour market.

The significance of the labour market's structure for equal-employment legislation and the effectiveness of the legislation in dealing with these issues will be discussed in subsequent chapters. But first we will outline some of the key dimensions of race and sex in the labour market.

DEMOGRAPHIC ASPECTS OF RACE AND SEX

Rate of participation in the labour market is important because it reveals much about people's attachment to work and changes in that attachment as economic conditions vary. In 1978 women's participation rate in the labour force in the United States reached a record high of 50 percent, up from 43.4 percent in 1971 and 32 percent in 1948; in Canada the rate in 1978 was 47.8 percent, up from 36.5 percent in 1971 and 24 percent in 1951.[11] Similarly, in Britain the activity rate (excluding students) for all women was 47.4 percent in 1978 and 43.0 percent in 1971, and, on a different basis, the proportion of women in the working population rose from 30.8 percent in 1951 to 36.6 percent in 1971.

Changes in the participation rates over time also indicate that the participation of men has declined while that of women has increased in the three countries. The participation rates of men have declined from 87 percent in 1948 to 77.9 percent in 1978 in the United States, while in Canada men's rates declined from 84 percent in 1951 to 77.9 percent in 1978.[12] In Great Britain, too, the activity rate for men declined, from 86.9 percent in 1961 to 85.8 percent in 1971 and 84.1 percent in 1978.

LABOUR-FORCE PARTICIPATION RATES OF MARRIED WOMEN

Rates of labour-force participation for married women have increased dramatically over time in each of the three countries. In Canada, in 1951 just over 10 percent had entered the labour market; in 1978 the rate had climbed to over 46 percent. Similarly, in the United States, in April 1951, 25.2 percent of married women (with spouse present) participated in the labour market, but in March 1978 their participation rate had reached 47.6 percent;[13] the participation rates for widowed, divorced, and separated women for these two dates in the United States were 39.3 percent and 42.8 percent, respectively.[14] Likewise, in Britain the proportion of married women who were economically active rose from 21.7 percent in 1951 to 42.3 percent in 1971 and reached 50.8 percent in 1978.

It is clear that more women are opting for careers than for having families. Moreover, more women are combining jobs (or careers) and child-rearing. Both economic considerations and changes in societal attitudes account for these developments.

RACIAL DIFFERENCES IN LABOUR-FORCE PARTICIPATION BY MALES IN THE UNITED STATES AND BRITAIN

Since no data are available for Canada by race, it is necessary here to concentrate on the United States and Britain. In the former, in 1948 the overall participation rate for males was slightly higher for non-whites (87.3 percent) than for whites (86.5 percent), and the rates for the two groups were quite similar between the ages of 20 and 44 years. By 1978 the overall participation rate of white males exceeded that of non-white males by about 6.5 percent (78.6 percent vs. 72.1 percent), and notable racial differences in participation rates existed in the groups aged between 20 and 44 years. Indeed, as Chamberlain et al. point out, participation rates of white males exceeded those of non-white males in all age categories, with the differential most pronounced in the younger groups. The authors suggest that this may be due to black men dropping out of labour force and to discriminatory hiring practises.[15]

In Britain an analysis has been made of the economic activity of the coloured population using the 1971 Census of Population.[16] For all men aged 15 and over, the total of those economically active was 81.4 percent of the population; the corresponding figure for those born in New-Commonwealth America or with one or both parents born in the New-Commonwealth was 91.7 percent; for those born in New-Commonwealth Africa or with one or more parents born in the New-Commonwealth, 71.5 percent; for those born in India or with one or both parents born in the New-Commonwealth, 89.5 percent; and for those born in Pakistan or with one or both parents born in the New-Commonwealth, 91.6 percent. Thus, in Britain activity rates for males born overseas are significantly greater than those for the indigenous population in the case of West Indians and Asians, but lower for Africans.[17]

RACIAL DIFFERENCES IN LABOUR FORCE PARTICIPATION BY FEMALES IN THE UNITED STATES AND BRITAIN

In the United States in 1948 some 45 percent of the non-white women but fewer than one-third of the white women were in the workforce. By 1978 about half the non-white and white women were in the labour force—53.3 percent and 49.5 percent, respectively. The participation rates of younger (16 to 24 years old) white women exceeded those of younger non-white women, but the reverse is true among women aged 25 to 44. According to Chamberlain et al., this may be because of the relatively inferior position of black families, which are more often headed by women than white families are, compelling higher participation rates among older black women than those of older white women.[18] In Britain the overall female work activity rate in 1971 was 42.7 percent, as opposed to 67.0 percent for women originating from New-Commonwealth America, 58.3 percent for women from Africa, 40 percent for women from India, and 17.1 percent for women from Pakistan. This shows that the immigrant population cannot be treated as a homogeneous entity. Pakistani females' participation rates in particular are less for cultural reasons.[19]

UNEMPLOYMENT BY RACE AND SEX

Women continue to experience higher unemployment than men in both the United States and Canada, as is evident in Table 1.1. In the United States women experience much lower rates of unemployment than non-whites. At more than 12 percent in 1978, the unemployment rate for non-whites was more than double the rate for whites. This relationship has been

TABLE 1.1

Unemployment Rates by Sex for Canada and by Race and Sex for the United States, 1975-1978

	Canada[a]			United States[b]		
	Males (percent)	Females (percent)	Average Rate	Males (percent)	Females (percent)	Average Rate
1975	6.2	8.1	6.9	7.9	9.3	8.5
1976	6.3	8.4	7.1	7.0	8.6	7.7
1977	7.3	9.4	8.1	6.2	8.2	7.0
1978	7.6	9.6	8.4	5.2	7.2	6.0
				White		
1975	—	—	—	7.2	8.6	—
1976	—	—	—	6.4	7.9	—
1977	—	—	—	5.5	7.3	—
1978	—	—	—	4.5	6.2	—
				Black		
1975	—	—	—	14.7	14.8	14.7
1976	—	—	—	13.5	14.2	13.8
1977	—	—	—	13.1	14.8	13.9
1978	—	—	—	11.6	13.7	12.6

Sources:
[a]Labour Force Annual Averages 1975-1978. Ottawa: Statistics Canada, February 1979, Cat. 71-529, pp. 131-134.
[b]Employment and Training Report of the President, 1979. Washington, D.C., U.S. Government Printing Office, 1979, Table A-20, p. 169; Table A-22, p. 172.

relatively stable over time, as shown in Table 1.1 despite a variety of manpower programmes and other measures.

In Britain recorded unemployment rates for women are actually lower than for men (Tables 1.2 and 1.3), but this reflects the fact that many women choose not to register as unemployed, rather than a lower propensity to become unemployed on the part of women. Further, it is clear that women's unemployment has in recent years been rising faster than that of men, and this is only in part a consequence of an increasing propensity on the part of women to register as unemployed. It is also clear from Table 1.4 that racial minorities suffer more than proportionate unemployment. Although data are not available on the rate of unemployment within minority groups, [20] racial minority unemployment as a percentage of total unemployment varies between 3.6 percent and 4.1 percent, while its share of total employment is only approximately 2.5 percent.

TABLE 1.2

Percentage of Registered Unemployment by Sex for Great Britain, 1965-1975

	Women	Men	All
1965	0.9	1.6	1.3
1966	0.9	1.8	1.4
1967	1.3	3.0	2.4
1968	1.0	3.2	2.4
1969	1.0	3.1	2.3
1970	1.1	3.4	2.5
1971	1.6	4.8	3.6
1972	1.8	5.0	3.8
1973	1.1	3.2	2.4
1974	1.3	3.8	2.8
1975	3.2	6.6	5.2

Source: W. Daniel, 'Survey of the Structure of Unemployment in the United Kingdom', Programme of Research and Actions on the Development of the Labour Market, Study 75/1. Commission of the European Communities, Brussels.

TABLE 1.3

Number of Registered Unemployed by Sex
for Great Britain, 1976-1979

	Women		Men	
	Registered Unem- ployed (thou- sands)	Employed (thou- sands)	Registered Unem- ployed (thou- sands)	Employed (thou- sands)
January 1976	270.5	8, 997	981.3	13,161
January 1977	356.2	9, 033	1,034.0	13, 121
January 1978	414.5	9, 089	1,070.2	13, 071
January 1979	401.3	9, 262	989.9	13, 091

Source: Equal Opportunities Commission, Fourth Annual
Report, 1979.

TABLE 1.4

Unemployed Persons in Great Britain Who Were Born or Whose
Parents Were Born in Certain Countries of the Commonwealth
and Pakistan

	Number Unemployed	Percentage of All Persons Unemployed
Nov. 13 1975	41,601	3.7
Feb. 12 1976	46,942	3.7
May 13 1976	49, 656	4.1
Aug. 12 1976	59, 070	4.1
Feb. 10 1977	49,797	3.6
May 12 1977	48,591	3.8
Aug. 11 1977	62,438	4.0
Nov. 10 1977	53, 100	3.7
Feb. 9 1978	51,657	3.6
May 11 1978	49,358	3.7
Aug. 10 1978	59,141	3.9
Nov. 9 1978	48,122	3.6

Source: Department of Employment Gazette. Data on
minority groups unemployed are provided in the March, June,
September, and December issues each year.

OCCUPATIONAL DISTRIBUTION BY SEX

As Tables 1.5, 1.6, and 1.7 indicate, women continue to
be concentrated in the clerical, sales, and service sectors of
the economy in all three countries. Over 62 percent of all female
workers in the United States and Canada were concentrated in
these occupations, compared to 20.8 percent of all males in the
United States and 26.9 percent in Canada during the same year.
In both countries men were much more evenly distributed throughout the occupational structure than women. In Canada, in 1978
4.5 percent of all women were in the managerial and administrative category, compared with 8.7 percent of all men, while in
the United States 6.1 percent of all women, compared with 14
percent of all men, were in the same category during that year.
A similar pattern prevails in Britain, where approximately two-
thirds of women, compared with one-third of men, are employed
in non-manual occupations. In 1978, 46.7 percent of women were
employed in just two occupational groups—clerical and related,
and selling. Hakim[21] notes that while there is considerable
vertical occupational segregation (i.e., among job levels) in the
United States and Britain, there is a stronger trend towards
the reduction of horizontal occupational segregation (i.e. among
types of job) in the former.

OCCUPATIONAL DISTRIBUTION OF WHITES AND
NON-WHITES IN THE UNITED STATES AND BRITAIN

In the United States blacks have made a considerable improvement from 1958 to 1978 in their relative occupational
position; they continue to be over-represented compared to
whites in the relatively low paying service and labouring jobs
and under-represented in the relatively high paying craft,
professional and technical, and managerial and administrative
positions. Blacks have made progress in the labour market in
the last two decades, as shown in Table 1.8, in white-collar
jobs, especially in professional, technical, and sales categories,
and in craft positions while decreasing their shares of service,
labouring, and farm jobs. However, within the former occupational categories blacks tend to be over-represented in lower
paying jobs and under-represented in higher paying ones. In
Britain too, racial minorities appear to be under-represented in
higher-level occupations as shown in Table 1.9. While both the
Census and National Dwelling and Household Survey (NDHS)
surveys suggest that overseas-born males of Indian and African

TABLE 1.5

Percentage Distribution of the Labour Force by Occupation and Sex for Canada, 1961–1978

	1961		1971		1978	
	Males	Females	Males	Females	Males	Females
Managerial	10.2	3.3	10.5	2.9	8.7	4.5
Professional	7.6	15.4	10.7	16.1	13.0	18.8
Clerical	6.9	28.8	6.5	30.5	6.5	34.0
Sales	5.6	8.3	5.6	7.0	10.4	10.0
Service	8.5	22.4	8.6	17.4	10.0	18.3
Primary	16.1	4.3	9.6	3.4	8.5	2.9
Blue Collar	35.0	12.8	33.8	9.8	—*	—

*Data not available.

Sources: S. Ostry and M. Zaidi, Labour Economics in Canada. Toronto: Macmillan of Canada, 1979, pp. 113–114; Women in the Labour Force, 'Basic Facts'. Toronto: Ontario Ministry of Labour, Women's Bureau, 1979, p. 4. Courtesy of Women's Bureau, Ontario Ministry of Labour.

TABLE 1.6

Occupational Distribution of Men and Women, 1958 and 1978

Occupational Category	Men, percent		Women percent		Ratio of Women to Men	
	1958	1978	1958	1978	1958	1978
White collar	36.5	40.8	55.1	63.2	1.51	1.55
Professional and technical workers	10.4	14.7	12.3	15.6	1.18	1.06
Managers and administrators	13.6	14.0	5.0	6.1	0.37	0.44
Sales workers	5.7	5.9	7.6	6.9	1.33	1.17
Clerical workers	6.9	6.2	30.1	34.6	4.36	5.58
Blue collar	46.8	16.4	17.1	14.8	0.37	0.32
Craft and kindred workers	19.4	21.1	1.1	1.8	0.06	0.09
Operatives	19.4	17.7	15.5	11.8	0.80	0.67
Nonfarm laborers	8.0	7.6	0.5	1.2	0.06	0.16
Service	6.4	8.7	23.2	20.7	3.63	2.38
Private household workers	0.1	0.1	9.4	2.9	94.0	29.0
Others	6.3	8.6	13.8	17.8	2.19	2.07
Farm	10.4	4.1	4.7	1.5	0.45	0.32
Farmers and farm managers	7.0	2.4	0.6	0.3	0.09	0.13
Farm laborers and supervisors	3.4	1.7	4.1	1.0	1.21	0.59

Source: Reprinted from Neil W. Chamberlain, Donald E. Culler, and David Lewin, The Labor Sector. New York: McGraw-Hill, © 1980, Table 8-6, p. 383. Used with permission of the McGraw-Hill Book Company.

origin are found in professional and managerial occupations in roughly the same proportion as whites, the representation of males of Pakistani-Bangladeshi origin, and West Indian origin in particular, is much lower. West Indian males, however, hold a high proportion of skilled manual occupations.

SEX AND RACE DIFFERENTIALS IN EARNINGS

In 1976 the average earned income of women employees in Canada who worked 50 to 52 weeks was 54.9 percent of men's earnings, as shown in Table 1.10. In Britain female manual workers attained over 70 percent of the male earnings level and non-manual workers over 60 percent, representing a significant improvement over the respective figures at the start of the 1970s. In the United States in 1975 white men earned about two-thirds more income than white women, while among blacks and others the earnings differential was about one-third between men and women. Table 1.11 also shows differences by occupation and education between men and women and between whites and blacks. In every occupational category white men earned more than non-white men, the differentials ranging between 4 percent and 25 percent. Among women, whites earned more than blacks in most occupational groupings, but the differences were quite small. Education has, in general, a positive effect on earnings. However, for most of the occupational categories in the table, earnings differentials in sex and race are not narrowed as a result of greater educational attainment. While more education does result in higher absolute earnings levels for all types of workers, attainment of higher education on the part of blacks and women does not seem to reduce earnings differential in the labour market.[22]

SOCIO-PSYCHOLOGICAL DIFFERENCES BY RACE AND SEX

Inequality in employment by race and sex has been explained not only in terms of the demographic variables discussed above but also in terms of structural, cultural, and socio-psychological differences.[23]

Structural factors center around systematic differences in how employees of different race and sex are treated by the organisation or by their superiors. For instance, Brown and Ford reference research showing the relative lack of promotional oppor-

TABLE 1.7

Percentage Distribution of the Labour Force by Occupation and Sex for Great Britain, All Industries and Services, Full-Time Adult Employees

Occupational Group	1970 Percent Distribution	
	Men	Women
Non-Manual		
Managers	6.33	1.42
(part*) Supervisors and foremen	2.03	1.36
Engineers, scientists and technologists	3.61	0.19
Technicians	3.19	1.21
Academic and teaching	2.33	5.60
(part) Medical, dental, nursing and welfare	0.71	7.71
Other professional and technical	3.17	0.70
(part) Office and communications	7.04	35.92
(part) sales	3.42	6.88
(part) security	1.10	0.12
All Non-Manual	32.85	61.11

Occupational Group	1978 Percent Distribution	
	Men	Women
Non-Manual		
Managerial (general management)	1.78	0.24
Professional and related supporting management and administration	6.31	1.96
Professional and related in education, welfare, and health	4.91	17.41
Literary, artistic and sports	0.74	0.47
Professional and related in science, engineering, technology, etc.	7.15	1.10
Management (excluding general management)	6.16	1.94
Clerical and related	7.12	40.40
Selling	3.15	5.64
Security and protective services	1.78	0.33
All Non-Manual	39.10	69.48

(part) Supervisors and foremen	4.13	1.32
(part) Medical, dental, nursing, and welfare	0.21	0.21
(part) Office and communications	1.24	0.16
(part) Sales	0.79	0.18
(part) Security	0.99	0.10
Catering, domestic, and other services	1.63	10.24
Farming, forestry, and horticulture	1.69	0.37
Transport	7.83	0.73
Building, engineering, etc.	25.66	5.63
Textile, clothing, and footwear	1.80	8.08
Other occupations	21.18	11.87
All Manual	67.15	38.89
Total	100.00	100.00

Manual

(part) Clerical and related	1.50	0.26
(part) Selling	0.49	0.16
(part) Security and protective services	0.54	0.04
Catering, cleaning, hairdressing, and other personal services	3.69	10.42
Farming, fishing, and related	1.95	0.26
Material processing (excluding metals)	3.75	2.15
Making and repairing (excluding metals and electrical)	4.98	5.54
Processing, making, repairing, and related (metals and electrical)	19.98	2.19
Painting, repairing, assembling, producing, inspecting, packaging, and related	4.98	8.18
Construction, mining, and related not indicated elsewhere	5.19	0.01
Transport operating, materials moving, storing, and related	11.99	1.10
Miscellaneous	1.85	0.20
All Manual	60.90	30.52
Total	100.00	100.00

*Part means a section of the occupational group appears under the non-manual heading and part under the manual heading.

Source: New Earnings Survey, HMSO, 1970 and 1978. Note that the occupational classification was changed between these two dates and the two sets of occupational groups are not comparable. Where there are fewer than 100 in the sample in any group, no figure of employment is provided.

TABLE 1.8

Occupational Distribution of Whites and Non-Whites, 1958 and 1978

Occupational Category	Whites (percent)		Non-Whites (percent)		Ratio of Non-Whites to Whites	
	1958	1978	1958	1978	1958	1978
White collar	45.8	51.8	13.8	36.2	0.30	0.70
Professional and technical workers	11.8	15.5	4.1	11.7	0.35	0.75
Managers and administrators	11.6	11.4	2.4	4.8	0.21	0.42
Sales workers	6.9	6.7	1.2	2.8	0.17	0.42
Clerical workers	15.4	18.0	6.1	16.9	0.40	0.94
Blue collar	36.6	32.9	40.7	37.2	1.11	1.13
Craft and kindred workers	13.4	13.7	5.9	8.8	0.44	0.64
Operatives	14.3	14.6	20.1	20.5	1.41	1.40
Nonfarm laborers	4.5	4.6	14.7	7.9	3.27	1.72
Service	9.5	12.3	33.0	24.1	3.47	1.95
Private household workers	1.7	0.8	15.4	3.6	9.06	4.00
Others	7.7	11.4	17.7	20.5	2.30	1.80
Farm	8.0	3.0	12.5	2.4	1.56	0.80
Farmers and farm managers	5.0	1.7	3.7	0.4	0.74	0.24
Farm laborers and supervisors	3.0	1.3	8.5	2.0	2.93	1.54

Source: Reprinted from Neil W. Chamberlain, Donald E. Cullen, and David Lewin, The Labor Sector, New York: McGraw-Hill, © 1980, Table 8-5, p. 382. Used with permission of McGraw-Hill Book Company.

TABLE 1.9

Percentage Distribution, by Socio-Economic Group, of Males Aged Sixteen and Over of Different Origin, Not Born in U.K., Who Have Worked in 1971 and 1977-1978

Ethnic Origin	West Indian[a]	American New-Commonwealth (both parents)[b]	Indian[a]	Indian[b]	Pakistani/ Bengali[a]	Pakistani[b]	African[a]	African New-Commonwealth[b]
Professional	0.8	1.0	10.3	9.6	4.2	3.2	8.0	9.3
Employers and managers	2.5	1.7	9.5	6.3	4.8	3.8	7.2	5.2
Junior non-manual	8.5	7.6	14.9	15.2	6.6	5.1	31.6	32.8
Skilled manual	48.8	45.1	35.0	32.1	30.7	25.2	34.6	26.4
Semi-skilled manual	26.2	27.2	20.1	23.9	37.3	38.1	14.1	21.3
Unskilled manual	13.2	17.3	10.2	12.9	16.4	24.6	4.6	6.0
All occupations	100.0	100.0	100.0	100.0	100.0	100.0	100.0	100.0
Number in sample	588	11,681	721	12,186	401	7,411	93	3,935

[a]National Dwelling and Housing Survey data.
[b]Census data.

Note: The 1971 Census figures relate to Great Britain, whereas the NDHS figures relate to England. However, in 1971 more than 96 percent of the people in Great Britain born in the New-Commonwealth lived in England. The Census figures are classified by birthplace of one or both parents, whereas those from the NDHS are split by ethnic origin.

Source: National Dwelling and Housing Survey, HMSO, 1978; and Lomas and Monck 'The Coloured Population of Britain', The Runnymede Trust, September 1977. In Barber, 'Ethnic Origin and the Labour Force', Employment Gazette, August 1980.

15

TABLE 1.10

Average Earned Income of Women and Men Employees by Weeks Worked, Canada, 1971 and 1976

Weeks Worked	Women (dollars)	Men (dollars)	Women/Men (percent)	Difference between Women's and Men's Earnings (dollars)	(percent)
_1971_					
50-52	4,785	8,646	55.3	3,861	80.7
40-49	3,416	6,235	54.8	2,819	82.5
30-39	2,507	4,497	55.7	1,990	79.4
20-29	1,794	3,167	56.6	1,373	76.5
10-19	1,195	1,766	67.7	571	47.8
0-9	543	711	76.4	168	30.9
_1976_					
50-52	8,447	15,394	54.9	6,947	82.2
40-49	6,153	11,109	55.4	4,956	80.5
30-39	4,687	8,160	57.4	3,473	74.1
20-29	3,253	5,226	62.2	1,973	60.7
10-19	2,037	3,133	65.0	1,096	53.8
0-9	1,098	2,656	41.3	1,558	141.9

Source: Women in the Labour Force: Facts and Figures, 1977 edition, Part II. Ottawa: Women's Bureau, Labour Canada, 1979, Table 7A, p. 40.

TABLE 1.11

Median Earnings in 1975 of Year-Round, Full-Time Wage and Salary Workers 16 Years Old and Over, by Educational Attainment, Sex, and Race, March 1976

Occupation and Race	Men					Women				
	Total	Less than 4 Years of High School	High School 4 Years Only	College 1 to 3 Years	College 4 or More Years	Total	Less than 4 Years of High School	High School 4 Years Only	College 1 to 3 Years	College 4 or More Years
All Persons										
Total	$12,680	$10,205	$12,289	$13,599	$17,118	$7,598	$5,835	$7,150	$8,284	$10,502
Professional and technical workers	15,682	12,480	13,385	14,607	16,775	10,501	7,222	9,308	10,343	10,896
Engineers	19,224	—*	17,631	18,216	19,910	—	—	—	—	—
Physicians	25,000	—	—	—	25,000	—	—	—	—	—
Health workers, except practitioners	11,440	—	—	—	12,570	10,552	—	9,664	10,676	12,029
Teachers, except college	12,483	—	—	—	12,873	10,255	—	—	—	10,382
Engineering and science technicians	12,813	—	12,644	12,941	—	8,805	—	—	—	—
Other professional, salaried workers	15,832	—	12,939	14,963	16,755	10,890	—	9,310	10,201	11,953
Managers and administrators, except farm	16,734	13,270	14,377	16,327	20,592	9,425	5,938	8,724	9,791	13,112
Sales workers	13,710	10,320	12,745	14,148	16,470	5,682	5,009	5,266	6,546	—
Retail trade	10,051	9,302	9,988	10,763	9,893	4,829	4,907	4,606	5,499	—
Other	15,750	11,381	14,624	16,060	17,352	9,028	—	8,424	—	—
Clerical workers	12,019	11,145	11,936	12,231	13,110	7,594	6,784	7,463	7,934	8,295
Craft and kindred workers	12,732	11,645	13,127	13,514	14,797	7,416	—	7,483	—	—
Operatives, except transport	10,962	10,027	11,516	12,146	—	6,295	6,134	6,459	—	—
Transport equipment operatives	11,150	10,439	11,798	12,261	—	—	—	—	—	—
Laborers, except farm	9,140	8,260	9,683	10,335	—	6,977	—	7,192	—	—
Private household workers	—	—	—	—	—	2,481	2,204	—	—	—
Service workers, except private household	9,628	8,112	10,047	12,075	10,522	5,542	5,085	5,609	6,771	—
Farmers and farm managers	—	—	—	—	—	—	—	—	—	—
Farm laborers and supervisors	5,539	5,365	5,066	—	—	—	—	—	—	—

(continued)

Table 1.1 (continued)

Occupation and Race	Men					Women				
	Total	Less than 4 Years of High School	High School 4 Years Only	College, 1 to 3 Years	College, 4 or More Years	Total	Less than 4 Years of High School	High School 4 Years Only	College, 1 to 3 Years	College, 4 or More Years
Whites										
Total	$12,961	$10,544	$12,473	$13,839	$17,351	$7,617	$5,932	$7,133	$8,236	$10,575
Professional and technical workers	15,787	12,607	13,531	14,736	16,867	10,521	—	9,265	10,333	10,922
Health workers, except practitioners	11,477	—	—	—	—	10,576	—	9,892	10,602	11,992
Teachers, except college	12,636	—	—	—	12,697	10,237	—	—	—	10,370
All other professional salaried workers	16,587	12,852	13,708	15,095	18,070	10,974	—	9,077	10,182	12,326
Managers and administrators, except farm	16,856	13,248	14,402	16,403	20,845	9,433	5,969	8,771	9,570	13,428
Sales workers	13,900	10,345	12,827	14,318	16,866	5,647	5,017	5,209	6,506	—
Clerical workers	12,074	11,056	11,975	12,276	13,264	7,511	6,610	7,409	7,806	8,387
Craft and kindred workers	12,875	11,758	13,278	13,822	14,852	7,304	—	7,363	—	—
Operatives, except transport	11,099	10,186	11,638	12,148	—	6,363	6,214	6,550	—	—
Transport equipment operatives	11,661	11,168	12,080	12,497	—	—	—	—	—	—
Laborers, except farm	9,553	8,578	10,000	10,480	—	7,102	—	—	—	—
Private household workers	—	—	—	—	—	2,806	—	—	—	—
Service workers, except private household	9,927	8,355	10,356	12,408	10,449	5,441	5,018	5,426	6,646	—
Farmers and farm managers	—	—	—	—	—	—	—	—	—	—
Farm laborers and supervisors	5,930	5,976	5,019	—	—	—	—	—	—	—

Blacks and Others covers the right-hand columns of the table below.

						Blacks and Others				
Total	$10,000	$8,413	$10,325	$11,602	$13,801	$7,486	$5,384	$7,265	$8,547	$10,061
Professional and technical workers	14,009	—	—	—	15,722	10,386	—	—	—	10,748
Health workers, except practitioners	—	—	—	—	—	10,440	—	—	—	—
Teachers, except college	—	—	—	—	—	10,354	—	—	—	10,449
All other professional, salaried workers	15,479	—	—	—	16,771	10,444	—	—	—	11,000
Managers and administrators, except farm	13,779	—	—	—	—	—	—	—	—	—
Sales workers	—	—	—	—	—	—	—	—	—	—
Clerical workers	11,622	—	11,424	—	—	8,212	—	7,949	8,797	8,007
Craft and kindred workers	10,969	10,319	11,101	11,352	—	—	—	—	—	—
Operatives, except transport	10,007	9,115	10,620	—	—	5,802	5,569	5,790	—	—
Transport equipment operatives	9,264	8,564	9,968	—	—	—	—	—	—	—
Laborers, except farm	7,866	7,619	7,947	—	—	—	—	—	—	—
Private household workers	—	—	—	—	—	2,202	—	—	—	—
Service, except private household	8,379	7,346	8,368	—	—	5,798	5,214	6,181	—	—
Farmers and farm managers	—	—	—	—	—	—	—	—	—	—
Farm laborers and supervisors	—	—	—	—	—	—	—	—	—	—

*Median not shown where base is less than 75,000.

Source: Adapted from U.S. Bureau of Labor Statistics, Year-Round Full-Time Earnings in 1975, Special Labor Force Report 203, 1977, p. 37. Reprinted from Neil W. Chamberlain, Donald E. Cullen, and David Lewin, The Labor Sector, New York: McGraw-Hill, ©1980, Table 8-1, p. 368. Used with permission of the McGraw-Hill Book Company.

TABLE 1.12

Female/Male Hourly Earnings Ratios, Aggregate Data for Great Britain, 1971–1976

	Hourly Earnings Ratio Excluding Overtime			Hourly Earnings Ratio Including Overtime		
	Manual	Non-Manual	All Employees	Manual	Non-Manual	All Employees
1971	61.3	52.2	63.7	59.8	53.4	63.7
1972	61.8	54.0	64.5	60.4	54.1	64.4
1973	62.0	54.3	64.4	60.7	54.4	64.2
1974	64.4	55.5	65.9	63.4	55.8	65.8
1975	68.0	60.7	70.6	66.8	60.9	70.4
1976	71.1	62.6	73.5	70.1	62.8	73.5

Source: New Earnings Survey, HMSO, 1971–1976.

tunities and upward mobility for blacks; these authors also suggest that differential levels of job satisfaction may also be attributed to supervisor bias in performance evaluation.[24] Sex structuring of organisations via differences in recruitment and control is also suggested by Acker and Van Houten's reinterpretation of Hawthorne's studies and Crozier's study of two French bureaucracies.[25]

Cultural factors such as beliefs, values, or psychological states pre-dispose members of different races to respond differently to their experience in the organisation. Bhagat reviewed the behavioural literature discussing the social role training and occupational readiness of American blacks to determine their propensity to identify with the U.S. work ethic. The evidence indicated that black ethnic values prevented a majority of the black population from strongly identifying with some themes of the American work ethic: (a) the good-provider theme, (b) the independence theme, (c) the success theme, and (d) the self-respect theme.[26] Several researchers have argued that cultural factors are important determinants of differential job satisfaction by race.[27]

Similarly, in the case of women, preferences, cultural patterns, and a number of other factors other than overt discrimination against them tend to maintain occupational segregation. Pressures from home and schools, i.e. from family members and vocational counsellors, might discourage them from fulfilling their career aspirations in non-traditional occupations.[28] Social factors relate to how employees of different race and sex are treated by their co-workers, customers, etc., and to their self-perceptions.[29]

PLAN OF THE BOOK

Chapter 2 in this book briefly surveys theories of labour market discrimination in order to provide a basis for the analyses of employer and trade union discrimination which follow. Chapter 3 focuses on the ILM, the DLM, and the human-capital approach as they relate to discriminatory behaviour. The empirical evidence on these theoretical concepts as well as psychological literature pertaining to pre-employment and post-employment discrimination is summarised.

In Chapter 4 we discuss (a) the rationale for equal employment legislation; (b) the number of women and coloured workers the legislation in the three countries is designed to assist; (c) the legal definitions of employment discrimination; (d) enforce-

ment mechanisms such as the incidence and disposition of cases
of discrimination by tribunals and courts in Britain and by
Boards of Inquiry and courts in Canada, and class-action suits,
affirmative-action programmes, court cases, and so forth, in
the United States; (e) guidelines issued by administrative agencies in the three countries; and (f) the effectiveness of these
legal and administrative instruments.

Chapter 5, contributed by Professor Naresh Agarwal, reviews the evidence on the extent of pay discrimination in the
three countries, analyses the major approaches that can be
employed in establishing equitable pay systems, and describes
and reviews the public policies dealing with equal pay in the
three countries.

Chapter 6, on trade unions and discrimination, outlines
(a) the legislation pertaining to discrimination by trade unions
in the three countries; (b) minority-group membership of trade
unions in North America and Britain; (c) patterns of union discrimination by industrial and craft unions, in the apprenticeship
systems, and in seniority and promotion systems; (d) legal cases
in the three countries; and (e) empirical studies of the effects
of unions on race/sex wage differentials.

Chapter 7 contains conclusions and policy implications.

NOTES

1. For a comprehensive discussion of concepts and evidence
relating to minority groups, see Harish C. Jain, Disadvantaged
Workers on the Labour Market and Measures to Assist Them.
Paris, France: OECD, 1979, p. 68.
2. For a discussion of this point, see Harish C. Jain,
'Discrimination in employment: Legal approaches are limited',
Labour Gazette, vol. 78 (1978) pp. 284-288.
3. See Chapter 4 of this book on equal employment legislation. Also see New Equals, vol. 12 (1980) p. 12.
4. See Arthur B. Smith, Jr., 'The law and equal employment opportunity: What's past should not be prologue', Industrial
and Labor Relations Review', vol. 33 (1980) pp. 493-505.
5. See Naresh C. Agarwal and Harish C. Jain, 'Pay discrimination against women in Canada: Issues and policies', International Labour Review, vol. 117 (1978) pp. 169-178. Also see
Chapter 5 in this book by Naresh Agarwal.
6. Race and Sex Equality in the Workplace: A Challenge
and an Opportunity, Proceedings, Harish C. Jain and Diane
Carroll, eds., Ottawa: Minister of Supply and Services, Canada,

1980, p. 236. See, in particular, the papers on equal pay by A. E. Richards, Naresh Agarwal, and D. Gallagher, pp. 45-62.

7. See testimony of employer and union witnesses at the hearings of the Equal Employment Opportunity Commission on Job Segregation and Wage Discrimination under Title VII and the Equal Pay Act, April 28-29, 1980, Washington, D.C.

Also see George T. Milkovich, 'Wage differentials and comparable worth: The emerging debate', December 1979, mimeographed paper; and 'Pay inequalities and comparable worth', paper presented at the Industrial Relations Research Association 33rd Annual Conference, Denver, Colorado, September 5-7, 1980.

For Britain, see The Annual Reports of The Equal Opportunities Commission 1976-1979.

8. For a thorough discussion of these concepts, see Harish C. Jain and Peter J. Sloane, 'The structure of labour markets, minority workers and equal employment opportunity legislation', International Journal of Social Economics, vol. 7 (1980) pp. 95-121. Also see Chapter 3 in this book.

9. See Neil Chamberlain, Donald Cullen, and David Lewin, The Labor Sector, third edition. New York: McGraw-Hill, 1980, p. 366.

10. The two concepts are related because dualism implies that minority groups are denied access to ILMs as well as primary markets. The distinction between the two is discussed more fully in Jain and Sloane, op. cit., and in Chapter 3 in this book.

11. See Chamberlain et al., The Labor Sector, p. 3, for the United States and The Current Industrial Relations Scene in Canada 1979, W. D. Wood and Predeep Kumar, eds., Kingston, Ontario: Queen's University Industrial Relations Centre, July 1979, p. 136, for Canada.

12. Ibid., p. 8 for U.S. and p. 136 for Canadian figures, respectively.

13. See Sylvia Ostry and M. Zaidi, Labour Economics in Canada, third edition. Toronto: Macmillan, 1979, p. 42. Also see The Current Industrial Relations Scene in Canada, 1979, p. 139. For the U.S. figures, see Employment and Training Report of the President, 1979. Washington, D.C.: U.S. Government Printing Office, 1979, Table B-2, p. 292.

14. Employment and Training Report of the President, Table B-2, p. 293.

15. Chamberlain et al., The Labor Sector, p. 9.

16. See G. B. Gillian Lomas and Elizabeth Monck, The Coloured Population of Great Britain: Employment and Economic Activity, 1971. London: The Runnymede Trust, September 1977.

17. A survey carried out in 1977-1978 suggests that activity rates of males of minority ethnic origin differ little from those of white males for those aged 35 and over, but are lower in the younger age groups because of the large number of students. See Ann Barber, 'Ethnic origin and labour force', Department of Employment Gazette, August 1980.

18. Most of the discussion on racial differences in labour force participation in the United States has been based on Chamberlain et al., The Labor Sector, p. 9.

19. See Lomas and Monck, The Coloured Population of Great Britain.

20. Barber's 1977-1978 survey, 'Ethnic origin and labour force', reports that for males in the National Dwelling and Housing Survey unemployment for whites born in the United Kingdom was 5.3 percent, while for non-white males born abroad unemployment was 7.3 percent; for women born in the United Kingdom unemployment was 4.6 percent and for non-white women born abroad 8.1 percent.

21. Catherine Hakim, 'Occupational segregation; A comparative study of the degree and pattern of the differentiation between men's and women's work in Britain, the United States and other countries', Department of Employment, Research Paper No. 9, London, November 1979.

22. For a thorough discussion relating to measurement of pay discrimination, see Agarwal and Jain, 'Pay discrimination against women in Canada', pp. 169-178, and Naresh Agarwal's contributed Chapter 5 in this book.

23. See Michael K. Moch, 'Racial differences in job satisfaction: Testing four common explanations', Journal of Applied Psychology, vol. 65 (1980) pp. 299-306.

24. H. A. Brown and D. L. Ford, 'An explanatory analysis of discrimination in the employment of black MBA graduates', Journal of Applied Psychology, vol. 62 (1977) pp. 50-56.

25. Joan Acker and Donald R. Van Houten, 'Differential recruitment and control: The sex structuring of organizations', Administrative Science Quarterly, vol. 19 (1974) pp. 152-163. The authors explain differential sex control in this way. For instance, they suggest that in the Hawthorne studies the sex power hierarchy in the home and in the factory were congruent; this congruence acted as a power multiplier, enhancing the authority of male superiors in the workplace. Similarly, differential recruitment of women into organisations was done by recruiting them into organisational roles demanding passivity and compliance.

26. Rabi S. Bhagat, 'Black-white ethnic differences in identification with the work ethic: Some implications for organizational integration', Academy of Management Review, vol. 4 (1979) pp. 381-391.

27. See, for example, W. S. Alper, 'Racial differences in job and work environment priorities among newly hired college graduates', Journal of Applied Psychology, vol. 60 (1975) pp. 132-134.

R. Bloom and J. Barry, 'Determinants of work attitudes among Negroes', Journal of Applied Psychology, vol. 51 (1967) pp. 291-294.

J. W. Slocum and R. H. Strawser, 'Racial differences in job attitudes', Journal of Applied Psychology, vol. 56 (1972) pp. 28-32.

28. James R. Terborg, 'Women in management: A research review', Journal of Applied Psychology, vol. 62 (1977) pp. 647-664. In this review of the literature, Terborg examines studies dealing with the entry of women into business and factors influencing the socialisation of women once they have gained entry; he questions the validity of stereotypes as explanations for hiring discrimination and provides alternative explanations, such as women's self-concepts.

Also see George Stevens and Angelo DeNisi, 'Women as managers: Attitudes and attributions for performance of men and women', Academy of Management Journal, vol. 23 (1980) pp. 355-361.

Myron D. Fottler and Trevor Bain, 'Sex differences in occupational aspirations', Academy of Management Journal vol. 23 (1980) pp. 144-149.

29. See Michael K. Moch, 1980, op. cit., and James R. Terborg, 1977, op. cit.

2

THEORIES OF DISCRIMINATION

> Discrimination is a phenomenon which is so pervasive
> in all human societies that there is no doubt at all
> that it exists. It is not, however, a unitary phenome-
> non but a complex of a number of related forms of
> human behaviour, and this makes it not only hard
> to define but frequently difficult to comprehend
> fully.—K. E. Boulding[1]

As the above quotation implies, there are a large number
of reasons for the existense of wage differentials among different
groups in the labour force, such as men and women or blacks
and whites. Broadly speaking, we may distinguish between
those factors which influence the demand side of the labour
market, including personal characteristics and the preferences
of the employers, and those which influence the supply side,
including preferences of the workers themselves and their availability for particular jobs. In general it is assumed that discrimination manifests itself on the demand side of the market,
though it is recognised that there may also be feedback effects
which influence supply.

In a sense all pricing is discriminatory,[2] so that "discrimination" as a term of opprobrium must include the notion of prejudice,
inequity, or the use of irrelevant criteria in the treatment of
particular individuals or groups in the labour market. Discrimination may be most simply defined as the receipt of lower pay
for given productivity,[3] but this obscures the fact that equally
productive workers may receive different levels of pay because
of differences in supply conditions (e.g., monopsony) which

have nothing to do with the prejudices of the employer other than a desire to maximise profits. A further step would be to define discrimination as any form of unequal treatment of different groups of employees which does not <u>directly</u> result in cost minimisation in relation to labour utilisation or, as far as discrimination on the part of employees is concerned, which does not <u>directly</u> result in the maximisation of the total wage income.[4] However, even this definition may be regarded as failing to ensure an equitable outcome, as it leaves open the possibility of "statistical" discrimination. The latter may be defined as a situation in which potential employees are screened on the basis of the characteristics of the groups of which they are members. Let us suppose, for instance, that men are preferred to women because they are as a group less prone to absenteeism or are more productive than the latter, but that a priori it is not possible to assess the potential absenteeism or productivity of a particular man or woman. Then an individual woman with a high potential attendance rate or level of performance may be excluded from employment on grounds which are quite rational in terms of cost minimisation but inequitable in terms of her own potential performance. Discrimination under the law may, of course, be defined, and has been in practise, to make unlawful such statistical discrimination despite the fact that enforcement of this policy may be inefficient from the point of view of maximising potential output. There is no reason, therefore, to expect that economic and legal definitions of discrimination will be consistent with each other. This is also seen in relation to affirmative action, where the need to attract more employees of minority groups may inflate employers' costs and, following the <u>Griggs v. Duke Power Co.</u> case, in the requirement to validate any recruitment test in which blacks and whites pass at different rates, with the same effect on costs.[5]

From both legal and economic viewpoints, it seems necessary to understand the sources of discrimination if appropriate policies are to be found to deal with the problem. The neo-classical theory developed by Gary Becker[6] is based on the notion of personal prejudice or aversion. Thus, it is assumed that an employer is prepared to pay a premium (or sacrifice profits) in order to avoid associating with members of disfavoured groups. Similarly, discriminatory employees will be prepared to accept a lower wage to avoid employment with such minorities or, perhaps more realistically, to require a higher wage where workforces are mixed than where they are segregated. An important prediction of Becker's model is that discrimination is likely to prevail only where market structures are monopolistic, for where competition prevails discriminators will be unable to compete with non-discriminating employers, who will have lower costs. Tests of this theory have been carried out both in terms of relative wages, assuming labour supply curves to individual industries slope upward, and in terms of relative minority/majority employment ratios, assuming perfectly elastic labour-supply curves, but results have been mixed. Becker himself, Shepherd (1970),[7] Comanor (1973),[8] Haessel and Palmer (1978)[9] (for race but not for sex), and Medoff (1980)[10] report findings which are consistent with the theory, but Franklin and Tanzer (1968),[11] Oster (1975),[12] Johnson (1978),[13] and Fujii and Trapani (1978)[14] find no such support. The diversity of results may be due in part to variations in the specification of the equation and omitted variables in some of the studies, though Shepherd and Levin (1973)[15] have argued that all firms of any size possess a certain degree of discretion which may result in "positive" as well as negative discrimination, so that there is no a priori determinate relationship between market structure and discrimination.

Such factors may also explain conflicting findings in regulated structures and government employment. In the former case Sowell[16] finds that regulated industries have historically shown themselves to be more discriminatory than unregulated ones, though political factors such as the introduction of new anti-discrimination legislation means that they are more prone to make rapid changes in eliminating discrimination than is normal (as in the telephone industry in the 1960s). As far as federal government is concerned, Smith (1976)[17] finds that discrimination against blacks was slightly greater than in private industry in 1970. In contrast, Long (1976)[18] finds that the adjusted black/white earnings ratio in 1969 was 6 percent higher in federal than in private employment and the corresponding figure for women some 25 percent higher. This finding is confirmed with respect to race by Johnson, who reports that there is a general tendency for wage discrimination to fall as an industry's freedom from competitive forces rises. More specifically, the government appears to discriminate in favour of blacks, non-profit firms and regulated industries are relatively neutral, and competitive and oligopolistic industries are the most discriminatory.

These studies have served, despite their conflicting results, to clarify and expand certain parts of Becker's theory and to provide some interesting data for equality-of-opportunity policies. For instance, Shepherd and Levin's and Medoff's studies suggest that it is more appropriate to test physical distance models by concentrating on white-collar employment patterns, since it is this group that is in closest contact with management and it is hard to see why managements should be concerned about the employment of minorities in blue-collar occupations (other than as a response to employee segregation). Shepherd and Levin, using a sample of 200 of the largest U.S. enterprises, find for both black and female white-collar workers only a weak association between individual elements of market structure and employment, but Medoff, examining certain white-collar occupations in 21 industries categorised at the two-digit level, finds that market-power coefficients are significantly negative (in line with Becker) for all four white-collar occupations analysed. There is a similar argument in relation to firm size. Since small establishments have fewer production processes, we would expect relationships between managers and employees to be closer than in large establishments with relatively impersonal industrial relations. Support for the view that large establishments discriminate less than small ones can be found in Shepherd and Levin, Medoff, and Medoff and Dick (1978).[19] We must distinguish, therefore, between the adverse effects of growing industrial concentration and the positive effects of increasing establishment size. It should also follow that capital intensive modes of production which involve low levels of personal interaction (Franklin and Tanzer) will result in low levels of discrimination relative to labour intensive production processes, and support for this is found in Medoff. Further, if physical proximity is important, we would expect market discrimination to be greatest against the most highly educated blacks and women. As Johnson notes, several studies have found that black/white wage differences widen with the level of schooling; strong support for this is found in Medoff and Dick. For women, in contrast, it has been found that male/female earnings differentials vary inversely with educational level (Phelps Brown).[20]

The above finding raises the question of whether Becker's approach applies equally to racial and sex discrimination. As Thurow[21] and Chiplin and Sloane[22] have noted, there are some crucial differences between the two phenomena. Why, for instance, should men discriminate against their own or other men's wives, and in what sense do men seek physical distance from women at work? As Marshall[23] has argued with respect to race, status considerations appear to be more relevant and will come to the fore, particularly where issues of women supervising men arise. More crucially, many women have discontinuous labour-force experience because of family responsibilities which influence their potential return to on-the-job training. Thus, one estimate is that differences in experience may account for

as much as 85 percent of the white male/white female wage gap.[24]
Another question that arises is whether discriminators practise
their preferences with respect to both race and sex or whether
the two are substitutes for each other.[25] Haessel and Palmer
find that firms that discriminate in employment tend to do so on
the basis of both race and sex. Thus, while there are some
similarities between race and sex discrimination, there are also
certain important differences.

For policy purposes it is important to know whether discriminators benefit financially from discrimination or whether it
costs them money to indulge their tastes. According to Becker,
not only is national income reduced by discrimination but groups
both responsible for and subject to discrimination are made worse
off as a consequence. However, if optimal tariff theory is applied
to Becker's international trade model, it can be demonstrated
that is is possible for a majority group to gain at the expense
of a minority (Thurow and Krueger),[26] and Thurow contends
that in most cases whites, for instance, will indeed gain from
practising discrimination.[27] This is best illustrated by bargaining or monopoly-power models of discrimination rather than by
individual-taste-for-discrimination models such as that of Becker.
As Boulding notes, monopoly power in the labour market may
be exercised in a number of ways, including occupational licensing
trade union restrictions on entry, and informal hiring practises,
but its main purpose is to obtain job control and higher incomes.
In this respect it matters little which group is the subject of
discrimination, provided only that sufficient numbers are excluded from employment in the selected occupation or group.
Marshall proposes a bargaining model along the lines of Dunlop's
industrial relations system approach, in which racial employment
patterns are seen to emerge from the power relationship between
the actors (managers, white workers, black workers, and government agencies) and specific environmental contexts in which they
work (economic and labour market conditions, the distribution
of power in society, and so on). While this would add a great
deal of realism to the analysis of discrimination, considerable
theoretical development is required if it is to offer a major challenge to the established neo-classical theory.

An alternative approach, which has certain elements in
common with the above, is the dual labour market theory, which
sees prime-age white males (normally defined as ages 25 to 54)
as being concentrated in high paying, stable primary-market
jobs that offer on-the-job training and prospects of promotion
and most coloured workers, women, and youths as trapped in
low paying, insecure secondary-market jobs that offer no pros-

pect of advancement. The problem will be exacerbated to the extent that confinement to secondary jobs adversely affects the motivation of workers with respect to factors such as job performance, time-keeping, and attendance. The dual approach may be seen as one formulation of the crowding hypothesis, which has been frequently applied to female employment. Thus, it is held that a major reason for the relatively low pay of women is the fact that their exclusion from male jobs causes them to be overcrowded into a limited range of occupations, where the increase in the supply of labour tends to depress productivity. Yet empirical studies in both North America and Britain suggest that there is considerable mobility between allegedly secondary and primary jobs and that even in the former additional years of education lead to improved pay. Reality seems to accord with a segmented rather than a dichotomous labour market.[28] To the extent that labour market segmentation is significant, equal-opportunity and affirmative-action programmes may still have a part to play, but stimulating the economy in order to achieve full employment may contribute more to raising the relative pay of, and creating job opportunities for, minority workers.

Radical economists hold that capitalists deliberately segment labour markets in order to divide workers so that they do not form a cohesive group to challenge management. According to Roemer (1979),[29] such a divide-and-conquer strategy will force down the wages of both black and white workers, and in his model individual employers, in contrast to Becker's assumption,[30] deliberately integrate their workforces in order to prevent unity among their workers and the consequent capability to strike. The model also depends on employee discrimination, which allows a wage differential to emerge in mixed workforces. Thus, again in contrast to Becker's model, the assumption is that discrimination is a function of profit-maximising behaviour on the part of the employer, together with non-wage-income-maximising behaviour on the part of workers. An important empirical question that remains to be answered is to what extent integration does in practise weaken the workers' cohesion. Marshall feels, too, that employers would be foolish to promote racial antagonism, which may bring them into conflict with the law or lose them government contracts. The assertion that discrimination is a function of capitalism as such should not be accepted uncritically. Moroney (1979),[31] for instance, finds in the case of male/female relative earnings in those countries where data are available that women do not on the whole fare noticeably better in centrally planned than in capitalist economies. However, the earnings gap does appear to be wider in the predominantly English-speaking countries (the United States, Canada, the United Kingdom, and Australia), a finding he attributes to social and legal traditions.

A major problem in testing all these theories is in isolating the component of gross earnings differences which is discriminatory. This is due in part to the fact that we cannot estimate discrimination directly but only as a residual after all other variables which are thought to influence earnings have been accounted for. Since few, if any, data sets contain adequate information for this purpose, there is a considerable possibility of omitted-variable bias. Further, even specific variables on which information is available may have different implications for the various groups. Thus, measuring characteristics such as education by years of schooling may obscure variations in the quality of education received by each race or sex. Here, Welch (1973)[32] has found that lower-quality schooling for blacks is a major explanation for the black/white earnings differential. Similarly, a year of experience may imply less acquisition of human capital in the case of women than in that of men. Measuring sex discrimination compounds sex and marital-status effects. For instance, does the finding of higher earnings for married men for given characteristics represent discrimination in their favour or higher levels of motivation induced by family responsibilities? A more accurate measure of sex discrimination is probably obtained by concentrating on corrected earnings differentials between single men and single (never married) women. Generally, it is possible to give with any degree of confidence only upper and lower bounds for the effect of discrimination on earnings differences between majority and minority workers. These difficulties of economic analysis point to the fact that it will often be no easy matter for the courts to determine whether unlawful discrimination has been practised by particular employers, unions, or groups of employees.

NOTES

1. K. E. Boulding, 'Toward a Theory of Discrimination', in Phyllis A. Wallace, ed., Equal Employment Opportunity and the A.T. & T. Case. Cambridge, Mass., and London: The M.I.T. Press, 1976.

2. D. Mermelstein, ed., Economics: Mainstream Readings and Radical Critiques. New York: Random House, 1970, Section B, 'The Economics of Discrimination'.

3. D. J. Aigner and Glen G. Cain, 'Statistical theories of discrimination in labor markets', Industrial Labor Relations Review, vol. 3, no. 2 (1977).
W. S. Siebert and P. J. Sloane, 'Shortcomings and Problems in Analyses of Women and Low Pay', in P. J. Sloane, ed., Women and Low Pay. London: Macmillan 1980.
4. B. Chiplin and P. J. Sloane, 'Sexual discrimination in the labour market', British Journal of Industrial Relations, vol. XII, no. 3 (November 1974), reprinted in Alice H. Amsden, ed., The Economics of Women and Work, Middlesex: Penguin Books, 1980.
5. Nathan Glazer, Affirmative Discrimination: Ethnic Inequality and Public Policy. New York: Basic Books, 1975.
6. Gary Becker, The Economics of Discrimination. Chicago: University of Chicago Press, 1957.
7. W. G. Shepherd, Market Power and Economic Welfare. New York: Random House, 1970.
8. W. S. Comanor, 'Racial discrimination in American industry', Economica, vol. 40 (November 1973).
9. W. Haessel and J. Palmer, 'Market power and employment discrimination', Journal of Human Resources, vol. XIII, no. 4 (Fall 1978).
10. J. L. Medoff, 'On estimating the relationship between discrimination and market structure: A comment', Southern Economic Journal, vol. 46, no. 4 (April 1980).
11. R. Franklin and M. Tanzer, 'Traditional micro-economic analysis of racial discrimination: A critical view and alternative approach', Industrial and Labor Relations Review, vol. 21, no. 3 (April 1968).
12. S. M. Oster, 'Industry differences in the level of discrimination against women', Quarterly Journal of Economics, vol. LXXXIX, no. 2 (May 1975).
13. W. R. Johnson, 'Racial wage discrimination and industrial structure', The Bell Journal of Economics, vol. 9, no. 1 (Spring 1978).
14. E. T. Fujii and J. M. Trapani, 'On estimating the relationship between discrimination and market structure', Southern Economic Journal, vol. 44, no. 3 (January 1978).
15. W. G. Shepherd and S. G. Levin, "Managerial Discrimination in Large Firms', Review of Economics and Statistics, vol. LV, no. 4 (November 1973).
16. T. Sowell, Race and Economics. New York: David McKay, 1975.
17. S. Smith, 'Pay differentials between federal government and private sector workers', Industrial and Labor Relations Review, vol. 29, no. 2 (January 1976).

18. J. E. Long, 'Employment discrimination in the federal sector', Journal of Human Resources, vol. XI, no. 1 (Winter 1976).

19. M. H. Medoff and P. T. Dick, 'A test for relative racial demand functions in American manufacturing', Applied Economics, vol. 10 (1978).

20. Phelps Brown, The Inequality of Pay. Oxford: Oxford University Press, 1977.

21. L. C. Thurow, Generating Inequality. United States: Basic Books, 1975; London: Macmillan, 1976.

22. B. Chiplin and P. J. Sloane, Sex Discrimination in the Labour Market. London: Macmillan, 1976.

23. R. Marshall, 'The economics of racial discrimination: A survey', Journal of Economic Literature, vol. 12, no. 3 (September 1974).

24. A. Blinder, 'Wage discrimination: Reduced form and structural estimates', Journal of Human Resources, vol. 8 (Fall 1973).
G. J. Duncan and S. Hoffman, 'On-the-job training and earnings differences by race and sex', Review of Economics and Statistics, vol. LXI, no. 4 (November 1979).

25. Similarly, it could be argued that employers have no aversion to minority workers but simply reflect the taste for discrimination of their employees.
K. Arrow, 'The theory of discrimination', in O. Ashenfelter and A. Rees, eds., Discrimination in Labor Markets. Princeton, New Jersey: Princeton University Press, 1974.

26. L. C. Thurow, Poverty and Discrimination, Studies in Social Economics. Washington, D.C.: The Brookings Institution, 1969.
Anne O. Krueger, 'The economics of discrimination', Journal of Political Economy, vol. 71 (1963).

27. M. Silver, 'Employee tastes for discrimination, wages and profits', Review of Social Economy, vol. 26, no. 2 (September 1968). Silver argues that the result of employee discrimination will be a gain for the employer at the expense of both black and white workers, for discriminatory attitudes on the part of white workers increase the real costs of collusion for each group of workers in undertaking joint action against the employer.

28. A fuller discussion is contained in Sloane, Women and Low Pay, London: Macmillan, 1980; and in H. C. Jain and P. J. Sloane, 'The structure of labour markets, minority workers and equal employment opportunities legislation', International Journal of Social Economics, vol. 7, no. 3 (1980).

29. J. E. Roemer, 'Divide and conquer: Micro-foundations of a Marxian theory of wage discrimination', The Bell Journal of Economics, vol. 10, no. 2 (Autumn 1979).

30. While it seems reasonable to suppose that, as in Roemer's model, wages would be relatively higher in a wholly white establishment, would they in practise be higher too in a wholly black establishment, as his model also suggests?

Becker's model suggests that there will be an inverse relationship between the black/white wage differential and the proportion of black workers in the labour force. Attempts to estimate such relative demand functions have been made in the following articles:

W. Landes, 'The economics of fair employment laws', Journal of Political Economy, vol. 76 (1968);

O. Ashenfelter, 'Racial discrimination and trade unions', Journal of Political Economy, vol. 80 (1972);

R. J. Flanagan, 'Racial discrimination and employment segregation', Journal of Human Resources, vol. 3 (1973); and

Johnson, 'Racial wage discrimination and industrial structure'.

Such attempts have, however, produced rather mixed results. Johnson suggests this is due to an incorrect formulation of the model and himself produces results consistent with the model, though the relevant coefficient is significant at only the 10 percent level.

31. J. R. Moroney, 'Do women earn less under capitalism?', Economic Journal, vol. 89, no. 355 (September 1979).

32. F. Welch, 'Black/white wage differences in the return to schooling', American Economic Review, vol. 63, no. 5 (December 1973).

3

EMPLOYERS AND THE STRUCTURE OF LABOUR MARKETS

Both from the viewpoint of equal employment legislation and from that of the operation of the labour market, it is important to undertake a detailed analysis of the operation of local labour markets and individual enterprises and establishments. This is because it is at the level of the individual organisation or unit of employment that the laws are applied and because it is difficult, if not impossible, to isolate the precise extent of discrimination at the macro-level, on account of variations in personal characteristics and establishment variables. Here a feature of recent empirical work, as outlined in the previous chapter, has been the emphasis placed on the internal labour market (ILM) and the related concept of the dual labour market (DLM).[1] This is, in fact, highly relevant to equal-employment legislation,[2] because the legislation appears to have certain features consistent with a dualist interpretation of the operation of the labour market and because the emphasis on equality of training and promotion opportunities is most appropriate and significant in the context of a well developed ILM.[3]

This chapter is divided into four parts. In the first three parts the ILM, DLM, and the human-capital approaches are examined in turn as they relate to discriminatory behaviour. It is necessary to discuss the ILM and DLM concepts in some detail, because they have been rather loosely defined in much of the literature and this hinders analysis of their implications for the question of discrimination, viewed in a legal context. The empirical evidence relating to these concepts and to that of human capital is also summarised, and where possible, an attempt is made to point out any differences between North

American and British experiences. In the final part, we consider the policy implications of the analysis.

THE INFLUENCE OF ILMs ON EMPLOYMENT OPPORTUNITIES FOR MINORITY GROUPS

Building on earlier work by Smith, Mill, Cairnes, Dunlop, and Kerr relating to imperfections in the labour market, Doeringer and Piore[4] defined the ILM as 'an administrative unit within which the pricing and allocation of labour is governed by a set of administrative rules and procedures'. This is distinguished from the external labour market (ELM), where wages are determined by market forces. The two markets are, however, linked at various job levels which constitute ports of entry to and exit from the ILM, while other job levels are reached by transfer and promotion of current employees. The distinction is crucial as far as the disadvantaged or minority worker is concerned, because current employees are likely to be given preferential treatment over outside job applicants on account of factors such as possession of specific skills and knowledge of the enterprise. Workers in the ELM may not be aware of the existense of job opportunities in the ILM, even if they possess the requisite skills. Further, if they succeed in gaining entry to the ILM, such workers may remain disadvantaged because of their lack of seniority. This suggests a potential clash between seniority systems and equal-employment opportunity, since any gains made by members of disadvantaged groups when economic conditions are buoyant may be lost in a recession.[5] In turn, this situation has led to suggestions for more inverse seniority as contained in some U.S. collective-bargaining agreements,[6] whereby senior workers may be temporarily laid off first in the recession with appropriate financial compensation and protection of long term job security rights (see Friedman, Bumstead, and Lund).[7]

The distinction between the ILM and ELM is, however, an over-simplification, and following Kerr[8] and Alexander[9] we may adopt the following classification of labour markets:

(1) open-markets, which are unstructured, subject to competitive forces, and characterised by lack of skill, low capital/labour ratios, and an absence of firm specific training.
(2) 'guild' or craft markets, which are structured horizontally by means of occupational licencing such that there is considerable mobility of labour between firms but little between

industries or crafts. General training is more important than specific training.

(3) 'manorial' or enterprise markets, which are structured vertically by means of promotion ladders with relatively little mobility between firms. Training specific to the firm, in part a function of technology, is all-important. For manual employees the ILM will generally correspond to the plant, but for managerial staff it will be companywide, while other white-collar employees will tend to either pole, clerical workers and technicians being closer to the manual and professionals to the managerial extreme.

Most of the discussion in the literature has centred on the third market category, which can be regarded in part as an employer response to the state of the labour market, for if there is abundant labour in the ELM there is little inducement to concentrate on internal recruitment. As Taira[10] has suggested, there is an incentive for the employer to develop an ILM where it can contribute to profitability, which will be a function of the speed of adjustment of labour supply to demand, the cost of having unfilled vacancies and of labour turnover, and the transactions costs of hiring a worker from the ELM.[11]

There is some suggestion that ILMs predominate in high-paying, large, well-organised firms, but it has been claimed[12] that ILMs are a function not only of size of firm but also of bureaucratic control and the need for stability in the employment relationship. Size is important because the number of levels in a well developed career hierarchy pre-supposes a certain minimum size, and as size increases the possibilities for satisfactory career development multiply. Size also tends to go hand in hand with high capital intensity, which increases the need both for bureaucratic control and for predictability and dependability on the part of the workforce, and also with unionisation.[13] It is in this sort of enterprise, also, that specific skills are required and that experience over the working lifetime is important. It has recently been suggested that females in particular tend to be found more than proportionately in small firms,[14] so that many of them will be excluded from the benefits of the ILM. It is therefore important to establish, at least as far as equality of opportunity is concerned, the extent to which ILMs predominate. Unfortunately, empirical evidence on this question is rather limited. For the United States, Doeringer and Piore[15] estimate the proportion of the labour force within the two types of ILM outlined above from data on employment by size and type of enterprise and by craft union membership. They conclude that about 80 percent of the employed labour force works in ILMs, while the rest are engaged in agriculture or service occupations. The way in which they define an ILM in this case seems, however, to be far from adequate for most purposes. For instance, they include under the heading of structured markets 27 percent of workers employed in small enterprises, where administrative rules could well be relatively unimportant. In comparison to the United States little empirical work has been undertaken in Britain on the operation of the ILM. However, Bosanquet and Doeringer[16] report that a small survey that they undertook of British hiring and promotion practises generally confirmed the significance of the distinction between open and structured markets. By contrast Mackay et al.[17] found in their study of the British engineering industry that there was a major difference between American and British practise, such that

> none of the case study plants operated a procedure for internal promotion in which seniority was the only guiding principle, and there was no evidence that managements were under pressure from unions or workers to recognise the very informal procedures used to determine such promotion. This contrasts with much American experience, where promotion has become an important issue in labour-management relations, and the criteria used in selecting candidates for promotion have become a matter for collective bargaining.

Nonetheless the investigators conclude that plants did make use of their ILMs to meet those requirements for labour which could not be met satisfactorily by means of direct recruitment; and other sectors of industry may well have ILMs which are rather more structured than those found in engineering. However, evidence of greater use of entry tests, employee referral rather than application at the gate, and the greater importance of seniority in determining pay in the United States relative to the United Kingdom[18] suggests that ILMs are less significant in the latter case.

Not only is the prevalence of the ILM of crucial importance to the question of equal opportunity, but so is the extent to which discrimination manifests itself as a consequence of the operation of the ILM. This involves two main aspects: (1) the extent to which enterprises with well developed ILMs fail to hire workers of equal ability as a consequence of cheap screening devices or "excessive" use of credentials and (2) the extent to which workers in certain disadvantaged groups fail to advance through the organisational hierarchy.

Barriers to Entry into the ILM

In the extreme case of an ILM in which workers are recruited at the lowest job level and all higher graded jobs are filled by means of internal promotion, lifetime productivity becomes even more of a consideration than productivity in initial job grade. Therefore, assuming that it is not practicable to hold certain workers at the initial job grade, the costs of defective hiring procedures are exacerbated.[19] While we might expect hiring practises to be more elaborate in the context of the ILM, employers may still be forced to utilise 'rule of thumb' techniques, particularly where assessment of productivity is difficult or impossible prior to entry into the ILM, and these techniques may work to the disadvantage of minority groups. Aspects of hiring procedures which are relevant in this context will now be examined.

Screening Devices

An employer is said to be using a 'cheap screen' when he automatically distinguishes between individuals who do and who do not display a particular, readily ascertainable characteristic (such as race or sex), with the implication that unfavourable treatment will be given on the basis of this characteristic without consideration of other characteristics and attributes. Screening devices do not, therefore, sort perfectly, but this must be assessed against the cost of fine sorting. An alternative way of evaluating prospective employees is to use a self-selection device. This is defined by Salop and Salop[20] as a pricing scheme which causes job applicants to reveal their characteristics by their market behaviour. Thus, wage structures favouring educational qualifications will exclude the less educated from being hired for jobs.[21] While these forms of behaviour may be based on prejudice or misconception, there will also, however, be an economic rationale. Stiglitz[22] has demonstrated that under certain plausible assumptions—differences in productivity between groups, individual productivity differences unascertainable prior to performance of the job, high fixed costs of replacement and equal pay—discrimination in hiring practises based on group attributes is an efficient means of allocating labour. Adopting a similar approach, Spence[23] has noted that while some individual characteristics observable to the employer prior to hiring are subject to manipulation by the individual, others are not. Thus, while education and training can be acquired, race and sex are unalterable. We may refer to alterable characteristics as 'signals' and unalterable ones as 'indices'.[24] Spence suggests that a situation in which employers draw inferences about productivity from indices because the latter are correlated with productive capacity within the population be referred to as 'statistical discrimination', but as Aigner and Cain[25] point out, race and sex discrimination are a consequence of group discrimination, rather than of discrimination among individuals, which is inevitable even where there is no 'discriminatory' intent. Discrimination may be present in relation to signals, since these too are frequently only proxies for underlying attributes; indeed, this is covered by the indirect discrimination provisions of the British Sex Discrimination Act and Race Relations Act. Thus, if it is more difficult for a member of a minority group to enter certain education courses than for the majority, a given level of education implies more talent in the case of the minority, and this casts doubt on the principle of equal treatment for people with the same test scores, signals, or indices. Equal treatment in terms of actual productivity may imply unequal treatment at the level of signals and justify 'reverse discrimination'.

Credentialism

To some extent education may also be used as a screen in the same way as race or sex when judging applicants, and it is possible that employers may demand educational requirements which are higher than required and often unrelated to actual job performance—the problem of 'credentialism'.[26] One American study has found that in service and to some extent in white-collar occupational categories 'dead end' jobs (as defined by employers) appeared to have higher entry requirements than those from which promotion was possible. Even allowing for a desire by employers to 'cream the market', this would seem to point to requirements which for some reason or other were set too high.[27] One explanation is that higher educational requirements serve as an effective screening device for reducing the number of applicants to a manageable size for personnel decision-making, though this in itself hardly seems adequate to explain the phenomenon. Whatever the explanation, this constitutes a barrier for people with less than the specified level of education, who are excluded from employment not because they cannot perform the work but simply because they fall outside the employer's hiring requirements.[28] Against the above finding must, however, be set the results of Layard and Psacharopoulos,[29] which suggest that the rate of return on incompleted courses is as high as on completed courses, that standardised educational earnings differentials rise with age, and that there is no evidence that employers attempt to undercut their competitors by employing less-educated labour.

Employment Tests

Employment tests, which lead to hiring and promotion only for those who achieve a pre-determined minimum score, are rarely validated in terms of job performance. Further, a test could have disparate impacts on various groups of applicants, as evidenced by disproportionate rejection rates among race and sex groups. For example, on the average, one group might score lower than another group on a particular test. If a single cut-off score is used, the result could be a higher rejection rate for one group than for the other. Recent research evidence on tests points to two conclusions. McCormick and Ilgen point out that, first, differential validity (i.e. higher rejection rate for one group than the other) is much less common than was originally assumed, and second, when differential validity does exist, the direction of the differences is such that the selection system is detrimental to the majority group almost as often as it is to minority groups. [30]

Employment Interviews

Employment interviews are the most widely used method of selecting employees, despite research that indicates that, being highly subjective, they have limited reliability and validity. [31] Because of its basic subjective nature, the interview process is vulnerable to the personal biases, prejudices, and stereotypes of interviewers. Interviewers may, therefore, form poorer evaluations of minority-group members than of non-minority candidates, even when the candidates are substantially similar with regard to their job qualifications.

There are two possible mechanisms that contribute to differential evaluations: stereotyping and differential behaviour during the interview. For instance, the specific nature of stereotypes that interviewers hold concerning different minority groups may well influence their evaluations of these candidates during the interview process. To the extent that the stereotypes are basically negative, [32] deviate from the perception of what is needed for the job, [33] or translate into different expectations and standards of evaluation for minority-group members, [34] stereotypes may well have the effect of lowering the evaluations of interviewers, even when the candidates are equally qualified for the job. [35]

Another explanation for different evaluations of minority and women candidates is that they behave in a manner that seems different and unfamiliar to interviewers. [36] Studies on the discriminatory effects of the interview have generally employed one of the three kinds of research strategies:

(1) In a resume study subjects are asked to review a series of job resumes to determine the suitability of each candidate for employment and/or the starting wage they might offer. Each resume usually contains information about the subject's educational background and past experience, with a glossy photograph attached. The race and sex of the job candidates can be varied by changing the photographs and the names which are printed on each resume. Thus, half of the interviewers may be asked to make evaluations concerning, for example, five males and five females. The other half of the interviewers may be asked to evaluate five males and five females, with the only change being that the names and photographs have been switched. No change whatsoever has occurred with regard to the qualifications of the candidates; the only changes are in sex and race. The interviewers are unaware that the resumes they are evaluating may differ from those being evaluated by other interviewers. In addition, some studies have added several other variables, such as attractiveness of applicant or type of job, to determine whether these characteristics might interact with minority status and influence the evaluations. Since in these studies a face-to-face interview is not included, it is implied that any discriminatory effect found is assumed to be applicable to actual interview circumstances. [37]

(2) In an in-basket study participants are asked to assume the role of a personnel director or manager working through an in-basket load requiring action on a number of problems. These problems are written in two or more versions, varying the sex and for race of one or more of the characters in the problem.

(3) Typically, the subjects in videotape studies or field experiments interview (or observe) only one job candidate and evaluate the suitability of the candidate for hiring. Efforts are made to control the content of the interview to ensure that the same questions are asked and similar responses delivered by the interviewers. [38]

Table 3.1, adapted from Arvey, summarises the results of 18 studies relating to race and sex bias in the interview. As

TABLE 3.1

Summary of Studies Investigating Discriminatory Effects in the Interview

Study	Applicant Status		Other Variable(s) Investigated	Major Criterion Utilized	Comments
	Sex	Race			
Resume Studies					
Fidell (1970)	+				Applicants considered for academic position
Wexley and Nemeroff (1974)		0	Perceived similarity of applicants to interviewer	Hire recommendation	
Rosen and Jerdee (1974a)	+		Job demands	Hirability	Sex and job demands interaction
Dipboye, Fromkin, and Wiback (1975)	+		Qualifications and attractiveness of candidates	Hirability and starting salary	Qualified and attractive candidates more likely hired, regardless of sex
Cohen and Bunder (1975)	+		Type of job	Hirability	Sex interacted with type of job to influence decisions
Haefner (1977)	+	+	Competence	Hirability	Sex interacted with competence; race interacted with sex and age; age interacted with competence

Study	Effect	Independent variables	Dependent variable	Findings
Dipboye, Arvey, and Terpstra (1977)	+	Qualifications, attractiveness of applicants, sex and attractiveness of interviewer	Hirability and starting salary	Applicant sex and attractiveness interact to influence ratings
Cash, Gillen, and Burns (1977)	+	Type of job and applicant attractiveness	Hiring potential recommendation	Sex, attractiveness, and type of job interactions observed
Rose and Andiappan (1978)	+	Predominate sex of potential subordinates	Probability of success	Applicant sex and sex of potential subordinates interaction
Muchinsky and Harris (1977)	+	Rater sex, job type, qualifications	Recommendation to hire	Interaction between sex and qualifications
Heneman (1977)	+	Qualifications	Recommendation to hire	Interaction between sex and qualifications
Renwick and Tosi (1978)	0	Marital status, undergraduate degree, type of job	Job suitability	Little evidence for differential evaluations found
Zikmund, Hitt, and Pickens (1978)	+	Scholastic performance	Number of replies to job inquiry	
In-Basket Studies				
Rosen and Jerdee (1974b)	+		Promotion	

(continued)

Table 3.1 (continued)

Study	Applicant Status		Other Variable(s) Investigated	Major Criterion Utilized	Comments
	Sex	Race			
Terborg and Ilgen (1975)	0			Decision to hire, starting salary	No difference between male and female applicants in decision to hire, but females given lower salary
Rosen and Jerdee (1976)		+		Suitability of the job	Older individuals
Videotape or field studies					
Rand and Wexley (1975)	0		Prejudice and affiliation of interviewers	Job suitability	
Dipboye and Wiley (1977)	+		Aggressiveness of candidate		Female candidates rated higher

[a]+ = differential evaluation investigated and found to be significant.
[b]0 = differential evaluation investigated and found not to be significant.

Source: Richard D. Arvey, Fairness in Selecting Employees, ©1979, Addison-Wesley Publishing Company, Inc., Chapter 6, pp. 170-173, 'Summary of Studies Investigating Discriminatory Effects in the Interview'. Reprinted with permission.

can be seen, the resume approach has been used in the most studies, followed by the in-basket and videotape approaches in that order.

The studies in Table 3.1, no matter which of the three research designs they employed, indicate that females are generally given lower evaluations than men who have identical qualifications. One study, however, by Renwick and Tosi, did not find any direct evidence of differential evaluations due to applicant sex.[39]

Type of job appears to be a factor that interviewers take into consideration in evaluating candidates. Several studies found that interviewers gave lower evaluations to females being considered for traditionally male-oriented jobs, while significantly more females than males were recommended for traditionally female-oriented jobs.

Attractiveness of the applicants was another variable investigated. Physical attractiveness was found to be important for both males and females, but its importance depended on the type of job (masculine or feminine) being considered.

The third variable investigated was applicant qualifications or competence. Although the studies show mixed results, it appears that interviewers base their evaluations primarily on the qualifications of candidates and secondarily on other factors such as sex or race.

The last variable investigated was the predominant sex of the subordinates the candidates would supervise. As Rose and Andiappan suggest, interviewers' evaluations are strongly influenced by whether or not the applicant's and subordinate's sexes match, rather than by the applicant's sex alone.[40]

There is not much evidence that interviewers give lower evaluations to black job applicants when the qualifications of white and black applicants are identical. Arvey points out that this may be due to the fact that studies were conducted during the past five years and interviewers may have been sensitive to the legislation prohibiting discrimination.[41]

Narrow Channels of Recruitment

Some firms tend to establish rather narrow and stable channels of recruitment, including referral of friends and relatives by present employees.[42] Reliance on a narrow set of recruitment channels has advantages both to the employer and to the potential employee. It results in applicants' having characteristics resembling those of the incumbent workforce and possessing certain predictable traits, each of which is important in the context of the ILM. For the applicant, relatives and friends can provide a clear picture of prospective employment, thereby reducing the costs of trial and error and job search. These benefits encourage the continuance of any set of recruitment channels once they are established, and discriminatory recruitment practises may continue to yield employment patterns that exclude coloured workers and women from certain high-level jobs, even long after discriminatory intent has been removed.

Misconceptions

Where behaviour is based on misconceptions, such as a mistaken belief that members of a minority group are less productive than members of the employed group, the absence of the minority from employment means that there is no disconfirming experience. As Spence[43] notes, once the pattern of exclusion is broken, employers' market experience changes and we might expect a fairly rapid "tipping" phenomenon as employment moves to a new equilibrium. A minimum quota may be a useful policy device in this context. However, if the barrier is based on prejudice, such a change may not take place. Where failure to hire is based on misconceptions, or more specifically a failure to update stereotypes on the basis of labour-market changes such as the changed participation rates of married women, legislation which over-rides employer hiring standards (e.g. quotas or affirmative action) need not distort the allocation of labour and might even improve it. Such behaviour, however, suggests that sub-optimal hiring policies are being pursued, which we would expect to be eliminated in the long run.[44] Having dealt with questions of initial entry into the ILM, it is now necessary to turn to questions relating to advancement in the hierarchy of the ILM.

Barriers to Advancement within the ILM

At the post-entry level the ILM is concerned with the numerous transactions that occur inside an organisation which affect employees in such matters as promotion, demotion, or transfer. Discrimination may occur with respect to each of these factors, including the level at which an individual is hired, the rate of wage increase, and the rate at which he or she moves up through the organisational hierarchy. Discrimination may also be related to conscious and unconscious personnel policies related to personal characteristics of employees such as race, sex, marital status, education, and experience. Indeed, a major source of disadvantage among minority workers is the lack of human capital possessed by these groups. Thus, it is not only the structure of the economic environment in which individuals and minority groups work but also, on the supply side, the characteristics of individuals which keep them in low-income, low-level jobs. Discussion of the human-capital approach is, however, postponed until the third part of this chapter.

In the context of advancement within the ILM and equal-opportunity legislation, it is also important to bear in mind that marital status may influence the level of occupation and earnings in a number of ways. First, it is possible that employers may regard marital status as a proxy for commitment to work. If it is judged that family responsibilities make married men more stable employees than single men, then married men will predominate in the better paid jobs. On the other hand, the Malkiels[45] and Gordon and Morton[46] suggest that employers may prefer single to married females because they expect higher absence and turnover rates in the latter case, with the general assumption that a geographical job change by her husband will cause a married woman to quit her job.[47] Ferber and Lowry[48] take the view that in the absence of labour-market discrimination one would expect single women to earn more than single men on the grounds that 'strong, independent career oriented' women will choose to remain single and 'less aggressive, perhaps unsuccessful' men fail to marry. On the other hand, Gwartney and Stroup[49] present evidence to suggest that the employment preferences of men and women are most similar for single employees and dissimilar for those married with spouse present. Yet they acknowledge the difficulty of isolating supply-side from demand-side functions in a situation where neither employee preference nor employer bias can be directly observed. A further difficulty, noted by Rosen,[50] is the fact that 'never married' is before-the-fact rationalisation. If females expect to become married at some uncertain future date, this will affect the rate at which they invest in human capital and will make it difficult to infer what precise part of the residual in adjusted male/female earnings equations is the result of discrimination. At the minimum, however, it seems legitimate to expect, even in the absence of discrimination, that married women will fare worse than single women and either single or married men in terms of level of earnings and occupational advancement.[51]

Two other aspects of the ILM may influence the degree of inequality of opportunity. First, Cassell et al.[52] suggest that there may be a relationship between the method of payment and the degree of discrimination, or more precisely that the "objectivity" of payment-by-results may diminish discrimination.

Secondly, Smith[53] finds that sex is an important source of differences in government differentials over the private sector. That is, women appear to enjoy a premium in wages as a result of government employment, and this premium increases with the level of government (i.e., women do relatively better in federal government than in local government). The public sector may, therefore, be less discriminatory than the private sector.

To summarise the above discussion of the concept of the ILM, there are clearly a large number of ways in which earnings and occupational level may differ among various groups in the labour market, some of which may reflect efficiency criteria and some of which may reflect forms of discrimination. As Doeringer and Piore[54] note, since the ILM is at least in part the product of the employer's attempt to minimise the fixed costs of recruitment, hiring, and training, it is not at all certain that the removal of 'statistical' discrimination will raise economic efficiency.

THE INFLUENCE OF DUAL LABOUR MARKETS ON EMPLOYMENT OPPORTUNITIES FOR MINORITY GROUPS

The concept of the dual labor market (DLM) is not only an extreme form of labour market segmentation but also a logical progression from the analysis of the internal labour market, since it broadens the coverage of the ILM (in the form of primary markets) to a consideration of the external labour market and attempts to deal more specifically with mobility, or the lack of it, between the two sectors. An important feature of the hypothesis of the DLM is the suggestion that the character of such markets is best explained by institutional and sociological factors rather than by narrow economic variables in the neo-classical sense. Thus, according to Doeringer and Piore,[55] in contrast to the assumption of human capital theory, much on-the-job training is not so much the outcome of economic decisions as of a process of socialisation (i.e. acceptance of and conformity to group norms) and so is related to worker motivation. In particular, social acceptability is a key factor in obtaining primary-sector skills, which means that promotion may be influenced by factors such as shared social beliefs, race, and sex.

Simply put, DLM theory states that the labour market can be divided into two quite distinct sectors. First, the primary labour market is characterised by high wages and fringe benefits, skilled jobs with opportunities for further training and promotion, employment stability, and high levels of unionisation. By contrast the secondary labour market offers low wages and few fringe

benefits, lack of skill and an absence of opportunities for promotion, employment instability, and lack of unionisation. A
high concentration of white adult males is to be found in the
primary market, while there is a disproportionate number of
females,[56] young workers, immigrants, coloured employees,
and other minorities in the secondary sector. As Andresani[57]
points out, this does not mean that all coloured employees and
women, for instance, are confined to the secondary sector, that
there is no upward mobility for such workers, or that human
capital has no value to them. Rather, he holds that:

> What upward mobility occurs and what value there is
> from investments in the schooling and training of dis-
> advantaged workers derives solely within the primary
> labour market sector, and that blacks and women are
> disproportionately relegated to the secondary sector
> at the very outset of their labour market career inde-
> pendently of their abilities and skills. Abilities and
> skills in other words are thought to be of no value
> within the secondary sector and of no value in escap-
> ing from secondary jobs.

The meaningfulness of the distinction is dependent on the
existence of mobility barriers between the two markets such that
certain workers become "trapped" in the secondary market. In
the case of race, such barriers will include not only overt discrimination by employers and unions but also the culture of the
ghetto itself (Flanagan).[58] 'Statistical discrimination' will occur
where certain workers are trapped merely because their super-
ficial characteristics resemble those of secondary workers.
    Later investigators have felt the need for a more precise
definition of the primary and secondary sectors. As Osterman[59]
notes, 'simply segmenting the labour force into two parts . . .
leaves a primary sector of enormous variety and poor definition.'
Indeed, it appears that the differences among groups within
the primary sector are in some ways no less important than the
distinction between the primary and secondary sectors. Thus,
Piore[60] suggests that at the minimum one should distinguish
between an upper and a lower tier of the primary sector. The
former group consists largely of managerial and professional
groups with a considerable degree of job discretion, general
training, and often substantial job mobility. The latter group
comprises both white-collar and blue-collar employees engaged
in routine tasks, with specific skills and consequently low mobility, and it is this group on which the emphasis is normally placed
in DLM analysis.

Secondary markets may be expected where it is costly to create a well developed ILM, it is difficult to reduce turnover or the benefits of so doing are relatively unimportant, and unions are weak. Alternatively, certain groups of employees may not value job security very highly (e.g. moonlighters or married women who are in the labour market only temporarily). In the latter case it may be suggested that in some cases workers in the secondary market are relatively well paid, such as those engaged on civil engineering or construction contracts, though the temporary nature of such employment implies that differences in lifetime earnings will be rather less. The particular case quoted also suggests that it is wrong to infer that secondary markets are the sole preserve of small firms. Large firms may well segment their operations in such a way that the effects of instability of demand in the product market are felt by a clearly differentiated group of their employees.

We need to explain why, if (as the DLM theorists contend) secondary workers are basically sound employees, new firms do not enter the market to utilise their skills. Explanations could be found in lack of information, discrimination, or feedback effects resulting in poor work habits. The last of these possibilities suggests that the motivation of workers may be a key factor and one with which human-capital models find it difficult to cope. The job satisfaction and performance of disadvantaged workers will be influenced by a number of factors in the social system, including the organisation providing the job, community organisations, informal peer groups, and family circumstances. Behavioural scientists generally agree that behaviour is a product of expectancies about behaviour-reward contingencies and the attractiveness of the rewards. Thus, high attendance (i.e. low rates of job turnover, absenteeism, and tardiness) would occur when workers believe that remaining on the job leads to desired rewards whereas leaving the job does not. It is not unreasonable to suggest that desired rewards will be forthcoming more frequently in the primary market and less often in the secondary market.

One consequence of such differences is that a process of self-selection by the disadvantaged may operate to create marked occupational segregation, insofar as members of such groups do not apply for particular jobs or to particular firms (Chiplin and Sloane).[61] An individual worker may not apply for a particular job either because he or she has a high propensity to quit and the wage structure favours those with low quit rates or because he or she has a lower level of productivity than the minimum required for entrance to or advancement within that job. Equally, however, the individual may have misconceptions about his or her own characteristics with respect to these variables. It is difficult to isolate this process of self-selection from demand-side job barriers reflected in employer hiring patterns, since these practises influence self-selection and may result in self-confirming behaviour.

As Cain[62] has noted in relation to segmented labour market theories in general, there is no single clearly developed model of the DLM which can be subjected to rigid empirical testing. Some investigators have attempted to detect the existence of DLMs using a single measure. Thus, Bosanquet and Doeringer[63] suggest that a test for the presence of a DLM is differential rates of increase of earnings with age in age-earnings profiles of particular groups of employees, though one problem that emerges is the fact that labour statistics do not divide workers into classifications which accord precisely with those of the DLM theory. However, the results of age-earnings profiles would hardly seem by themselves to be an adequate test of DLM theory, since such results are capable of a number of interpretations. An alternative approach is to examine job tenure and turnover. Thus, Edwards et al.[64] find that there are significant differences in the job tenure rates of the groups this study assumes to be heavily represented in the primary sector (i.e. white males) and those in the secondary market (i.e. blacks, youths, and all females over 25). Here again, however, demographically defined groups are used as proxies for market determined categories, and the results can be interpreted in a number of ways. The same criticism applies to a third possible measure—unemployment rates for different segments of the labour force. To some extent Gordon's (1971) factor analysis of multiple occupational and industrial characteristics[65] overcomes the problem of a single measuring rod. He examines weeks worked per year, whether or not the worker was looking for work during the year, and personal characteristics such as marital status, head of household, and years in the labour force. Primary white and black males both exhibit greater average job tenure in their first and present jobs than secondary white and black males, but the average duration of tenure seems remarkably stable even in the secondary sector—8.90 years for secondary whites and 5.95 years for secondary blacks in their present jobs.[66]

Some rather more detailed examinations of the DLM hypothesis than the above have, however, been undertaken. Osterman,[67] using data from the 1967 U.S. Survey of Economic Opportunity, assigns each male worker to one of the three segments in the Piore model, which provides 4130 observations in the lower

primary tier and only 242 in the upper primary tier and 234 in
the secondary tier.[68] Semi-log regressions were run to establish
whether there were fundamental differences in the earnings functions among the three segments of the labour force and, if so,
whether these were in line with the predictions of the DLM
theory.[69] Strong support is claimed for the theory, substantial
differences being shown in the earnings function among the
three segments. The race variable is insignificant in both the
upper primary and the secondary sector, which suggests that
racial discrimination is confined to the lower primary sector.[70]
One problem with this particular study, acknowledged by the
author, is the fact that workers were assigned to each segment
of the labour market on the basis of subjective judgments. This
increases the importance of further research currently underway
to develop more refined classification procedures. But more
serious is the criticism of Cain[71] and Kruse[72] that the procedure
adopted leads to the truncation of the dependent variable (log
earnings), thereby biasing downwards the estimated absolute
values of the coefficients on age and schooling in the secondary
sector. A similar criticism can be levelled at Rumberger and
Carnoy,[73] who attempt to examine mobility between the occupational and industrial segments of the U.S. economy from 1965
to 1970 and differences in the returns to education, training,
and experience within segments for whites and blacks, using
the 1970 Census of U.S. population. They find evidence of
upward mobility for both whites and blacks, though less so for
the latter, and evidence that human-capital variables (e.g.
education and experience) are essentially unrewarded in the
secondary sector. On this basis they conclude that some of
the notions of the segmented labour market theorists hold but
others do not. In a rather different type of analysis, Andresani[74]
set out to examine three empirical issues—the incidence of mobility
between the two sectors, the importance of skills in obtaining
access to the primary sector, and differences in the importance
of skills within each sector—using a cohort of males aged 14-20
in 1966 from the U.S. National Longitudinal Survey of Work
Experience and examining them over a period of three years.
He found that, first, although 43 percent of whites and 64 percent of black youths started their careers in the secondary
labour market, only 17 percent and 36 percent, respectively,
remained there at the end of the period.[75] Second, among both
blacks and whites investments in human capital increase the
likelihood that the individual will be in a primary rather than
a secondary job. Third, the returns on investment in human
capital appear to be just as high in the secondary as in the

primary sector for both groups. Thus, the secondary sector hardly appears to be 'a prison from which there is no escape'. This finding is in line with that of Flanagan,[76] who found that some of the barriers emphasised by the dual theorists did not appear to operate as predicted. Thus, using a housing segregation model, it was found that for given characteristics ghetto residence did not depress market productivity. Flanagan's study is paralleled by Rosenberg's approach.[77] He traces the career patterns of male workers living in low-income areas in four U.S. cities and classifies jobs into the primary and secondary sectors on the basis of four dimensions—vocational preparation, educational development, job discretion, and wage levels. The regression results suggest that explanations based on differential human-capital characteristics of individual workers are helpful in explaining initial career position but less so in explaining upward occupational mobility. However, the DLM model fares no better in the latter respect. What is interesting is that blacks in low-income areas fare about the same as blacks in the surrounding areas, with the consequence that the relatively disadvantaged among the whites have better occupational prospects than average blacks. There have also been two attempts to test for labor market segmentation in Britain. First, Psacharopoulos[78] has used data on men in Britain's 1972 General Household Survey (GHS) to test for the existence of a DLM, using a 'general desirability occupational ranking scale' devised by Hope and Goldthorpe. He finds that occupational level rises sharply with age (at least until the age of 27) to the detriment of other explanations and that there is considerable inter-generational mobility in the sense that many individuals whose fathers were in the secondary sector rise into the primary sector. Second, Mayhew and Rosewell,[79] using data on over 10,000 men from the Oxford Social Mobility survey, assigned employees to one of Osterman's three segments on the basis of judgment of the individual's occupation and status; they also experimented with the Hope-Goldthorpe scale. They found substantial mobility among the three segments and, further, that human capital variables were important determinants not only of the segment in which their subjects started their careers but also of upward mobility between segments. All in all, the empirical evidence on the DLM is hardly conclusive; rather, what firm evidence there is tends to cast doubt on the dichotomous model. Yet there is no doubt that the hypothesis has had a certain appeal in terms of policy formulation, at least as far as the United States is concerned.

THE HUMAN CAPITAL APPROACH TO EMPLOYMENT
OPPORTUNITIES

Unlike the screening hypothesis, the human capital approach
to which reference has already been made puts the emphasis on
returns to investment in training in the context of individual
utility maximisation. It is generally assumed that the individual
is free (and sufficiently well informed) to invest in the acquisition
of skills where the rate of return is greatest. As Rosen[80] has
suggested, 'The theory of human capital is at heart a theory of
"permanent" earnings'. The fact that attention is focussed on
lifetime rather than current earnings means that it is particularly
appropriate for the analysis of ILMs.

The basic human-capital model developed by Jacob Mincer[81]
takes the form:

$$\log E = a + bS + cX + dX^2 + U$$

where

E = earnings
S = years of schooling
X = years of experience
U = error term

Since earnings are the result of the interaction of supply and
demand for labour, this is a reduced-form equation. The amount
of on-the-job training and other types of investment in human
capital will tend to decrease with age or experience, since de-
preciation and obsolescence reduce the investment's value over
time, and it is this fact which makes age-earnings profiles con-
cave from below. It is generally assumed that the logarithm of
earnings is linearly related to years of schooling and quadratically
related to years of work experience. Education and training
are then at the heart of the human-capital approach, the former
normally being undertaken prior to entry into the labour force
and imparting general skills on which a return is recouped over
the whole working lifetime and the latter being undertaken during
the years of work. Years of schooling are normally used to
measure the extent of an individual's education but are, in practise, a crude proxy, hardly allowing adequately for qualitative
differences, and could possibly bias the results to indicate racial
and sex discrimination. To the extent that productivity is improved simply by doing a job, earnings will be related to experience.[82] Where there is a well developed ILM, length of service

with the enterprise will be more highly correlated with earnings than outside experience. Age is often used as a proxy for experience where data limitations prevent more appropriate measurement. More precisely, experience is often calculated as age minus years of education minus five or six years. In the case of females, who often have breaks in length of service as a consequence of child-rearing, this must give misleading results. Consequently, separate earnings equations should be estimated for males and females.

Using his basic equation, Mincer[83] was able to explain a third of the variance in earnings for white non-farm men in 1959 based on the U.S. Census, and over a half with certain additional assumptions. Using the same model, Psacharopoulos and Layard,[84] from a sample of 6873 adult males in the 1972 GHS in Britain, were able to explain a third of the earnings inequality. Mincer and Polachek,[85] using data from the 1967 U.S. National Longitudinal Survey of Work Experience, also found that the earnings function could explain 25-30 percent of the relative divergence in wage rates of white married women and 40 percent in the case of white single women. Comparing the results with those for comparable males, differences in work experience appear to account for roughly half the gap in male/female wage rates. However, for reasons outlined in the Introduction, studies of individual establishments seem more appropriate for the analysis of discrimination. Even here, however, commitment to work may differ among groups according to sex or marital status, which would make any precise measurement of discrimination difficult, if not impossible. The human-capital-based establishment studies have, in the main, analysed white-collar employees, where measurement of productivity is more difficult. Results have also been influenced by the number of independent variables and the functional form used by investigators.[86]

Also, some investigators (e.g. Cassell et al.)[87] include race and sex as dummy variables in single-equation models. But the fact that separate equations for men and women generally show significant differences in the values of the coefficients of the independent variables—true also where marital status is identified[88]--indicates that the procedure of Cassell et al. is, at the minimum, dubious. For instance, in an analysis of three British ILMs, Sloane and Siebert[89] found that the education variable was in most cases highly significant but that this did not apply to married women in two cases.

In general studies at the establishment or unit-of-employment level by the Malkiels,[90] Cassell et al.,[91] Gordon and Morton,[92] Ferber,[93] Smith,[94] Osterman,[95] Rosenbaum,[96] Chiplin and

Sloane,[97] and Siebert and Sloane[98] have been able to explain between 50 percent and 90 percent of the variance in earnings for the various sex and marital-status employment groups. Education and experience are highly significant in most but not all equations, while age is sometimes significant. This is in line with other studies, including Rees and Schultz's major analysis[99] of the Chicago labour market, where seniority was the most important determinant of individual earnings and age was in most cases not significant, though it was more strongly associated with earnings in high-wage occupations. The explanatory power of the human-capital model seems remarkably high in some equations, given the relatively small number of independent variables in the model. The Malkiels[100] were also able to use an expanded model employing publications as a proxy for productivity (as well as possession of Ph.D., critical area of study, absense rate, and marital status). The additional productivity variables did increase the power to predict salary levels, explaining more than 75 percent of the variance in male and over 80 percent in female salaries (as opposed to 71 percent and 68 percent, respectively). In some equations the Malkiels include organisational job level, which causes the earnings gap to disappear, but women with particular levels of training and experience are found to be in lower job levels than males with similar levels. Likewise in the Chiplin and Sloane[101] and Rosenbaum[102] studies, there was some evidence of discrimination in terms of access to the higher job level. It is important, therefore, to conduct analyses in terms of occupations as well as pay. Cassell et al.,[103] following Birnbaum,[104] consider as well the impact of initial grade on current grade and wage and find that for current wage, regression's explanatory power is raised from 33-57 percent to 50-62 percent and for current grade from 29-63 percent to 64-86 percent when initial grade is included. Further, all race coefficients become insignificant, which might indicate that discrimination occurs at the time of hire rather than in the course of employment.

In general, these results provide considerable support for the human-capital theory, since low earnings can be at least partly explained by low levels of human-capital investment. Further, in the context of the ILM, experience may reflect on-the-job training, and the flatter experience-earnings profiles[105] for women and coloured employees are suggestive of less on-the-job training and less rapid movement up the promotion ladder.[106] The finding of lower rates of return on education for females (though not consistently) and for coloured workers in some studies has been taken to imply the presence of discrimination, but there are problems of interpretation here. Different groups can have different levels of schooling for both supply and demand reasons; that is, because of the terms on which funds for education differ or the teste for education varies, for instance. A priori, we cannot be sure that a lower rate of return on education for minority groups is a result of discrimination.

POLICY IMPLICATIONS

There appear to be three broad types of manpower policy which might be utilised to assist minority workers. First, taking labour supply and demand as givens, one might attempt to make the labour market operate more efficiently by means of placement activities, worker counselling, and labour mobility or related measures, which would be appropriate regardless of the structure of labour markets. Second, one might attempt, consistent with the human-capital approach and the general findings reported in this chapter, to upgrade the labour supply of minority workers by means of greater investment in education and training.[107] U.S. findings that human capital raises earnings even in the secondary sector add strength to such a proposal. Third, following the labour-market segmentation approach, one might recommend solutions lying on the demand rather than the supply side, with a requirement that government employment and expenditure policy favour those in the secondary sector. This would include equal-opportunity and affirmative-action programmes.

NOTES

1. The two concepts are related because dualism implies that minority groups are denied access to ILMs as well as to primary markets; the distinction between the two is discussed more fully in this chapter.

2. There are a number of recent surveys of work in this area, including the following:

M. Blaug, 'The empirical status of human capital theory: A slightly jaundiced survey', Journal of Economic Literature, vol. 14, no. 3 (December 1976);

G. G. Cain, 'The challenge of segmented labour market theories to orthodox theory: A review', Journal of Economic Literature, vol. 14, no. 4 (September 1976);

M. Wachter, 'Primary and secondary labour markets: A critique of the dual approach', Brookings Papers on Economic Activity, vol. 3 (1974).

However, these have not attempted to link the structure of labour market concepts with the legislative framework relating to employment discrimination. For this integration, see H. C. Jain, Disadvantaged groups on the labour market and measures to assist them, Paris, France: OECD, 1979.

3. Thus, Wachter, in 'Primary and secondary labour markets', suggests that as far as the United States is concerned 'court rulings following the 1971 Griggs v. Duke Power Co. decision (401 US 424) have in effect adopted the dualist view of the workings of the labour market. The decision makes almost no effort to control for the lower labour market endowments of blacks. For example, with blue-collar occupations, courts commonly find labour market discrimination when the percentage of blacks in the firm is substantially lower than the percentage of blacks in the community. This may be good social policy—or at least it is aimed at achieving a desirable social end—but its economic underpinning is open to controversy.' Wachter feels that the dualist policy of moving secondary workers directly into primary jobs is more likely to result from individual legal bases concerning discrimination than from manpower programmes and related measures. However, his survey omits discussion of equal-opportunity laws, 'since the only disagreements about them concern implementation.' We argue here that the form of the legislation is itself an important issue.

4. P. B. Doeringer and M. J. Piore, Internal Labour Markets and Manpower Analysis. Lexington, Mass.: D. C. Heath, 1971.

5. As Cain ('Segmented labour market theories') notes, relative to Oi's work on labour as a quasi-fixed factor of production, given certain assumptions—a positive relationship between skill and specific training, greater complementarity to fixed capital the higher the skill level, fixed costs of recruitment and dismissal positively related to skill, and uncertainty as to the phases of the business cycle—firms will tend to lay off unskilled rather than skilled workers in a recession.

6. Existing schemes, however, generally specify that all employees with less than one year of service must be released before inverse seniority provisions come into play.

7. S. Friedman, D. C. Bumstead, and R. T. Lund, 'Inverse seniority as an aid to disadvantaged groups', Monthly Labour Review, vol. 99, no. 5 (May 1976).

8. C. Kerr, 'The balkanisation of Labour Markets', in E. Wight Bakke, ed., Labour Markets and Economic Opportunity. Cambridge, Mass.: The Technology Press, MIT, 1954.

9. A. J. Alexander, 'Income experience and internal labour markets', Quarterly Journal of Economics, vol. 88, no. 1 (February 1974).

10. K. Taira, 'Internal Labour Markets, Human Resources Utilisation and Economic Growth'. Paper presented at Research Conference on Urban Labour Markets, International Institute for Labour Studies, Geneva, September 9-13, 1976.

11. This interpretation of the ILM contrasts with that of the DLM theorists, who claim, according to Wachter ('Primary and secondary labor markets') that 'although efficiency factors are relevant to managerial decision-making in the ILM, they are not dominant. More specifically, they claim that productivity at a high wage adheres to the job rather than to the worker; that the wage structure is dominated not by efficiency considerations but rather by custom and habit; and that good jobs go to people who are already with the firm, by means of promotion that largely reflect institutional arrangements. Consequently the distribution of jobs and income in the primary sector is not dictated by ability and human capital.'

12. R. C. Edwards, M. Reich, and D. M. Gordon, eds., Labour Market Segmentation. Lexington, Mass.: D. C. Heath, 1975.

13. It is appropriate to assume, in general, that workers in the ELM are unionised to a lesser degree than workers in the ILM, if at all.

14. B. Chiplin and P. J. Sloane, Sex Discrimination in the Labour Market. London: Macmillan, 1976.

B. Chiplin and P. J. Sloane, 'Male/female earnings differences: A further analysis', British Journal of Industrial Relations, vol. 14, no. 1 (March 1976).

F. D. Blau, 'Sex segregation of workers by enterprise in clerical occupations', in Edwards, et al., Labor Market Segmentation.

15. Doeringer and Piore, Internal Labour Markets and Manpower Analysis. Lexington, Mass.: Lexington Books, 1971.

16. N. Bosanquet and P. Doeringer, 'Is there a dual labour market in Great Britain?', Economic Journal, vol. 83, no. 330 (June 1973).

17. D. I. Mackay et al., Labour Markets Under Different Employment Conditions. London: Allen and Unwin, 1971.

18. For detailed information on this question, compare Mackay et al., Labour Markets under Different Employment Conditions, for the United Kingdom; and A. Rees and G. P. Schultz, Workers and Wages in an Urban Labour Market, Chicago: University of Chicago Press, 1970, for the United States.

19. As long as the employer can rectify errors ex post facto, there is little necessity to establish entry barriers. However, it is likely that unionisation and protective legislation have made dismissals increasingly difficult and costly. For an analysis of the extent to which companies discriminate in their recruitment on the basis of race, see N. J. Newman, 'Discrimination in recruitment: An empirical analysis', Industrial and Labor Relations Review, vol. 32, no. 1 (October 1978).

20. Salop and Salop, 'Self-selection and turnover in the labour market', Quarterly Journal of Economics, vol. 90, no. 4 (November 1976).

21. J. Salop and S. Salop, ibid., suggest that a major problem for employers is to identify workers with a high propensity to quit and that this can be achieved by a wage structure favouring length of service. This will tend to make income distribution more unequal (e.g. favouring men relative to women).

22. J. E. Stiglitz, 'Approaches to the economics of discrimination', American Economic Review, Papers and Proceedings, vol. 63, no. 2 (May 1973).

23. A. M. Spence, Market Signaling: Informational Transfer in Hiring and Related Screening Processes. Cambridge, Mass.: Harvard University Press, 1974.

24. Spence, ibid., notes that 'it is possible (and may be desirable) to make observable, unalterable characteristics like sex and race unobservable. To do so would probably involve an institutional or social decision. Colleges, for example, are forbidden in many states to seek to acquire information about an applicant's race, colour, religion, or national origin. There are obvious difficulties in designing effective disguises. But suppressing the observability of a characteristic does not make it adjustable.'

25. D. J. Aigner and G. G. Cain, 'Statistical theories of discrimination in labour markets', Industrial and Labor Relations Review, vol. 30, no. 2 (January 1977).

26. This is not to say that education does not provide any useful information, since in that event we would expect it to be discarded as a screen.

27. G. S. Hamilton and J. D. Roessner, 'How employers screen disadvantaged job applicants', Monthly Labor Review, vol. 95, no. 9 (September 1972).

28. H. C. Jain, 'Is education related to job performance?', in H. C. Jain, ed., Contemporary Issues in Canadian Personnel Administration. Scarborough, Ontario: Prentice-Hall, 1974, pp. 106-109.

29. R. Layard and G. Psacharopoulos, 'The screening hypothesis and the returns to education', Journal of Political Economy, vol. 82, no. 5 (1974).

30. The uniform guidelines on employee selection in the United States require employers to validate any of their selection techniques that have disparate impact on different groups. 'Adoption by four agencies of uniform guidelines on employee selection procedures (1978)', Federal Register, vol. 43 (1978), pp. 38, 295–308, 309. For the two conclusions on tests, see N. J. McCormick and D. Ilgen, Industrial Psychology, seventh edition, Englewood Cliffs, N.J.: Prentice-Hall, 1980, p. 219.

For studies on differential validity or unfair test discrimination, see the following sources: R. D. Arvey, Fairness in Selecting Employees. Reading, Mass.: Addison-Wesley, 1979. F. L. Schmidt, 'Are employment tests appropriate for minority group members?', Civil Service Journal, vol. 18 (December 1977), pp. 10–11. R. L. Linn, 'Single-group validity, differential validity, and differential prediction', Journal of Applied Psychology, vol. 63 (1978), pp. 507–512. F. L. Schmidt and J. E. Hunter, 'The future of criterion-related validity studies in employment discrimination cases', The Personnel Administrator, vol. 22 (1977) pp. 39–42.

31. E. C. Mayfield, 'The selection interview: A reevaluation of published research', Personnel Psychology, vol. 17 (1964) pp. 239–260;

L. Ulrich and D. Trumbo, 'The selection interview since 1949', Psychological Bulletin, vol. 63 (1965) pp. 100–116;

O. R. Wright, 'Summary of research on the selection interview', Personnel Psychology, vol. 22 (1969) pp. 391–413.

32. In a study by Terborg and Ilgen, for example, the researchers found that attitudes about women correlated significantly with a subject's decision to hire a female engineer. Thus, individuals with essentially negative attitudes about women were less likely to give favourable evaluations than were those with more positive attitudes. See J. R. Terborg and D. R. Ilgen, 'A theoretical approach to sex discrimination in traditionally masculine organizations', Organizational Behavior and Human Performance, vol. 13 (1975) pp. 352–376.

33. See, for instance, the studies by Schein. In one study ('The relationship between sex role stereotypes and requisite management characteristics', Journal of Applied Psychology, vol. 58 (1973) pp. 95–100) the researcher asked 300 male managers to indicate which of 92 adjectives best described (1) women in general, (2) men in general, or (3) successful middle managers. Each manager described only one of these

subgroups. Schein found that the relationship between the average description of middle managers and the average description of men was much higher than the relationship between the description of managers and of women. These results were also replicated in a survey of a group of 167 female managers who described the various subgroups: Schein, 'Relationships between sex role stereotypes and requisite management characteristics among female managers', Journal of Applied Psychology, vol. 60 (1975) pp. 340-344.

As Arvey points out, 'These findings suggest that even before an interview or any formal selection process has begun, the perceived similarity between the characteristics of successful managers and of men in general increases the probability of a male's rather than a female's being given a higher evaluation'. See R. D. Arvey, 'Unfair discrimination in the employment interview: Legal and psychological aspects', Psychological Bulletin, vol. 86, no. 4 (1979) p. 744.

34. A study by Cecil, Paul, and Olins reveals that standards used to evaluate females are more clerical and cosmetic in nature, whereas the standards for males are along aggressive and persuasive dimensions. E. A. Cecil, R. J. Paul, and R. A. Olins, 'Perceived importance of selected variables used to evaluate male and female job applicants', Personnel Psychology, vol. 26 (1973) pp. 397-404.

35. R. D. Arvey, 'Unfair discrimination'.

36. E. T. Hall, The Hidden Dimension. New York: Doubleday, 1966.

37. This entire section on employment interviews and evidence is based heavily on R. D. Arvey, 'Unfair discrimination', pp. 155-185, and Fairness in Selecting Employees, Reading, Mass.: Addison-Wesley, 1979.

38. Ibid., p. 169.

39. P. A. Renwick and H. Tosi, 'The effects of sex, marital status, and educational background on selection decisions', Academy of Management Journal, vol. 21 (1978) pp. 93-103.

40. G. L. Rose and P. Andiappan, 'Sex effects on managerial hiring decisions', Academy of Management Journal, vol. 21, (1978) pp. 104-112.

41. R. D. Arvey, Fairness in Selecting Employees, p. 177.

42. For the United Kingdom see Department of Employment, 'Employers, recruitment and the employment service', Department of Employment Gazette, vol. 86, no. 12 (December 1973).

Note that where, for instance, coloured workers are geographically separated from white employers extra search and information costs will be incurred. Aigner and Cain, 'Statistical theories of discrimination in labour markets'.

43. Spence, Market Signaling.

44. As Aigner and Cain note in 'Statistical theories of discrimination in labour markets', 'A theory of discrimination based on employers' mistakes is even harder to accept than the explanation based on employers' "tastes for discrimination", because the tastes are at least presumed to provide a source of "psychic gain" (utility) to the discriminator'.

45. B. G. Malkiel and J. A. Malkiel, 'Male and female pay differentials in professional employment', American Economic Review, vol. 63, no. 4 (September 1973).

46. M. Gordon and T. E. Morton, 'The staff salary structure of a large urban university', The Journal of Human Resources, vol. 11, no. 3 (1976).

47. They also point out, particularly in relation to marital status, that a bias may emerge because certain independent variables measure different things in men and in women. Thus, using the equation for men together with the means of the women's characteristic variables in order to measure discrimination is tantamount to saying that in the absence of discrimination married women would earn more than single women. This suggests that it is necessary to run separate regressions not only according to sex but also according to marital status or, as in the study by Smith, 'Government wage differentials by sex', The Journal of Human Resources, vol. 11, no. 2 (Spring 1976), to introduce interaction terms between marital status and experience.

48. M. A. Ferber and H. M. Lowry, 'The sex differential in earnings: A reappraisal', Industrial and Labor Relations Review, vol. 29, no. 3 (1976).

49. J. Gwartney and R. Stroup, 'Measurement of employment discrimination according to sex', Southern Economic Journal, vol. 39, no. 4 (April 1973).

50. S. Rosen, 'Human capital: A survey of empirical research'. Discussion paper 76-2, Department of Economics, University of Rochester, January 1976.

51. The importance of marital status has been confirmed in a number of recent studies. See, for instance, the following articles:

Ethel B. Jones and James E. Long, 'Part-week work and human capital investments by married women', The Journal of Human Resources, vol. XIV, no. 4 (Winter 1979).

Martha S. Hill, 'The wage effects of marital status and children', The Journal of Human Resources, vol. XIV, no. 4 (Winter 1979).

G. J. Duncan and S. Hoffman, 'On-the job training and earnings differences by race and sex', Review of Economics and Statistics, vol. LXI, no. 4 (November 1979).

52. F. H. Cassell, S. M. Director, and S. I. Doctors, 'Discrimination within internal labour markets', Industrial Relations, vol. 14, no. 3 (October 1975).

53. Ibid.

54. Ibid.

55. P. B. Doeringer and M. J. Piore, 'Unemployment and the dual labour market', Public Interest, vol. 38 (Winter 1975).

56. Thus, D. M. Gordon in Theories of Poverty and Under-employment: Orthodox, Radical and Dual Wage Perspectives, Lexington, Mass.: D. C. Heath, 1972 notes that 'women are much less able than previously "disadvantaged" workers to identify with "advantaged" workers and to follow their model in the transition to stable work. Further, the social definition of family and sex roles continues to undercut employment stability among women. And, as the percentage of women in the labour force continues to increase, some employers seem more and more likely to move many jobs into the secondary market in response to the (expected) behavioural characteristics of the secondary women employees.'

57. P. J. Andresani, 'Discrimination, segmentation and upward mobility: A longitudinal approach to the dual labour market theory'. Philadelphia: Temple University, 1976. Mimeographed.

58. R. J. Flanagan, 'Segmented market theories and racial discrimination', Industrial Relations, vol. 12, no. 3 (October 1973).

H. C. Jain, Disadvantaged Groups on the Labour Market and Measures to Assist Them. Paris, France: OECD, 1979.

59. P. Osterman, 'An empirical study of labour market segmentation', Industrial and Labor Relations Review, vol. 28, no. 4 (July 1975).

60. M. J. Piore, 'Jobs and training', in S. H. Beer and R. E. Berringer, eds., The State and the Poor. Cambridge: Winthrop Publishers, 1970.

61. Chiplin and Sloane, Sex Discrimination in the Labour Market.

62. Ibid.

63. Ibid.

64. Edwards et al., Labor Market Segmentation.

65. David M. Gordon, 'Class productivity and the ghetto: A study of labour market stratification'. Ph.D. dissertation, Harvard University, 1971. Reported in Edwards et al., Labor Market Segmentation.

66. Wachter ('Primary and secondary labor markets') notes that neither the distribution of industries nor the distribution of

workers by earnings shows any evidence of bipolarity. While
it is preferable to consider several variables rather than one,
even here the results are mixed, and the null hypothesis is
that there is a continuum of jobs.

67. Wachter, 'Primary and secondary labor markets'.

68. The danger of this procedure is that to segment workers
into three separate groups is to deny the possibility of movement
between groups. Yet upward mobility is precisely the way in
which most of the gains due to education are secured.

69. The independent variables in the model are age, years
of schooling, race, weeks unemployed in the previous year,
hours worked in the previous week, and dummy variables for
the industry in which the individual worked.

70. Osterman ('An empirical study') claims that the results
show that policies designed to increase the human capital of
secondary workers are not likely to improve their earnings.
This claim is surprising in view of the fact that when separate
equations were run for whites and for blacks the education variable was significant for blacks in the secondary sector.

71. Ibid.

72. W. J. Kruse, 'An empirical study of labour market
segmentation: A comment', Industrial and Labor Relations Review,
vol. 30, no. 2 (January 1977).

See also the criticisms and attempts to replicate Osterman's
results using a different data set:

P. C. Langley, 'An empirical study of labour market segmentation: Comment', Industrial and Labor Relations Review,
vol. 32, no. 1 (October 1978).

73. R. W. Rumberger and M. Carnoy, 'Segmentation in
the U.S. labour market: The effects on the mobility and earnings
of whites and blacks', Cambridge Journal of Economics, vol. 4
(1980). The authors are aware of the problem of truncation bias
but claim, rather unconvincingly, that it could apply equally
to the high-income and the low-income group.

74. Ibid.

75. D. E. Leigh, 'Occupational advancement in the late
1960s: An indirect test of the dual labour market hypothesis',
Journal of Human Resources, vol. 11, no. 2 (Spring 1976), also
found that inter-firm and inter-industry mobility was similar
for blacks and whites in similar age groups. Leigh states that,
in general, his findings 'cast doubt on the literal interpretation
of the dual hypothesis as a guide for explaining labour market
processes—at least during periods of full employment'.

76. Ibid.

77. S. Rosenberg, 'Male occupational standing and the dual labour market', Industrial Relations, vol. 19, no. 1 (Winter 1980).

78. G. Psacharopoulos, 'Labour market duality and income distribution: The case of the United Kingdom', in A. Shorrocks and W. Krelle, eds., The Economics of Income Distribution. Amsterdam: North-Holland Publishers, 1978.

79. K. Mayhew and B. Rosewell, 'Labour market segmentation in Britain', Oxford Bulletin of Economics and Statistics, vol. 41, no. 2 (May 1979).

80. Ibid.

81. J. Mincer, Schooling, Experience and Earnings. National Bureau of Economic Research, New York: Columbia University Press, 1974.

82. However, as Blaug ('The empirical status') notes, this model does not take into account 'the role of costless learning by doing as a simple function of time, not to mention the organisational imperatives of the ILM'.

83. J. Mincer, 'Progress in human capital analyses of the distribution of earnings', in A. B. Atkinson, ed., The Personal Distribution of Incomes. London: Allen and Unwin, 1976.

84. G. Psacharopoulos and R. Layard, 'Human capital and earnings: British evidence and a critique', Review of Economic Studies, June 1979.

85. J. Mincer and S. Polachek, 'Earnings of women', Journal of Political Economy, vol. 82, no. 2, Part II (March/April 1974).

86. This problem is particularly well illustrated in the analysis of Ferber and Lowry ('The sex differential'). In order to investigate the extent to which sex segregation of jobs influences women's earnings, they set up regression models as follows:

$$Ym_i = b_0 + b_1 Em_i + b_2 M_i$$

$$Yf_i = c_0 + c_1 Ef_i + c_2 M_i$$

where

Y_i = median earnings in occupation i (Ym for men and Yf for women)

E_i = median years of schooling

M_i = proportion of male employees in occupation i.

The results reveal that schooling is a better investment for men than for women and that earnings in general rise with the proportion of male employees, while the addition of an interaction term raises the amount of explainable variance from 76 percent to 84 percent in the case of males and from 50 percent to 84 percent in the case of females. The authors conclude that 'the lower earnings in occupations with a higher proportion of women cannot be ascribed solely to the lower productivity of women, unless, of course, one is prepared to believe that women's productivity is somehow adversely affected by the mere presence of men and that men become less productive when they work with women.' Given, however, that their model does not take experience into account, this result is hardly surprising. If mean male experience exceeds that of females and is a significant determinant of earnings, a direct relationship might be expected between proportion of males in the labour force and earnings. But the implications to be drawn are quite different from those stated by the authors. For more detailed criticisms of this study, see David Snyder and Paula M. Hudis, 'The sex differential in earnings: A further reappraisal: Comment'. Industrial and Labour Relations Review, vol. 32, no. 3 (April 1979).

87. Ferber and Lowry, 'The sex differential'.

88. Thus, Gordon and Morton ('Staff salary structure') found that unmarried males earned 2.7 percent ($t = -2.25$) less than married males, whereas there was no such effect for women.

89. P. J. Sloane and W. S. Siebert, 'Hiring Practices and the Employment of Women'. Paper prepared for the Manpower Services Commission, Paisley College of Technology, 1977.

90. Ibid.

91. Ibid.

92. Ibid.

93. M. A. Ferber, 'Sex and race differences in non-academic wages in a university', The Journal of Human Resources, vol. 11, no. 3 (1976).

94. Ibid.

95. P. Osterman, 'Sex discrimination in professional employment: A case study', Industrial and Labour Relations Review, vol. 32, no. 41 (July 1979).

96. James E. Rosenbaum, 'Hierarchical and individual effects on earnings', Industrial Relations, vol. 19, no. 1 (Winter 1980).

97. B. Chiplin and P. J. Sloane, 'Personal characteristics and sex differentials in professional employment', Economic Journal, vol. 86, no. 344 (December 1976).

98. W. S. Siebert and P. J. Sloane, 'The measurement of sex and marital status discrimination at the workplace', Economica, vol. 48 (1981).

99. Ibid.

100. Ibid.
101. Ibid.
102. Ibid.
103. Ibid.
104. H. Birnbaum, 'The economic effect of career origins', in Edwards et al., Labor Market Segmentation.
105. See the following articles:

Allen G. King, 'Is occupational segregation the cause of the flatter experience/earnings profiles of women?', The Journal of Human Resources, vol. XII, no. 4 (Fall 1977).

G. J. Duncan and S. Hoffman, 'On-the-job training and earnings differences by race and sex', Review of Economics and Statistics, vol. LXI, no. 4 (November 1979).

Mary Corcoran and G. J. Duncan, 'Work history, labour force attachment, and earnings differences between races and sexes', The Journal of Human Resources, vol. XIV, no. 1 (Winter 1979).

106. Flanagan ('Segmented market theories') notes that when employers are uncertain of the employment stability of job applicants, it may be possible for them to protect themselves against capital loss by shifting a larger proportion of the training costs (and returns) onto the trainee. However, equal-opportunity legislation prohibits the implied lower wage per amount of training needed. For what may be required is a lower wage for females and coloured employees during training and a higher wage than white males thereafter. It is doubtful, however, if employers would be allowed by majority workers or their representatives to pay higher wages to minority workers in this way on completion of training.

107. A note of caution may be required here, however, since it is possible that labour market efficiency requires equilibrium of supply and demand in all sectors, including the unskilled, and that over- as well as under-investment may be possible even in this area.

4

RACE, SEX, AND MINORITY-GROUP DISCRIMINATION LEGISLATION IN NORTH AMERICA AND BRITAIN

INTRODUCTION

Despite the considerable problems of identification outlined in the previous chapter, [1] reports of widespread discrimination in the workplace against minority groups, notably in relation to sex and race, are prevalent in both North America and Britain. Thus, in Canada, the Royal Commission on the Status of Women (1970) and several studies on racial discrimination[2] have directed our attention to the incidence of employment discrimination against minority groups. Similarly, Equal Opportunities Commission (EOC) and Commission on Racial Equality (CRE) Reports, as well as Political and Economic Planning (PEP) Studies in Great Britain[3] and Congressional hearings in the United States have also suggested a prevalence of such discrimination. In this chapter we concentrate mainly but not exclusively on race and sex discrimination in Canada, the United States, and Britain in order to reveal the extent of coverage of the legislation in these countries. There is more detailed and longstanding evidence on the working of equal-opportunity legislation relating to race and sex in North America than in other countries, and developments in Britain tend to mirror those in the United States and Canada.[4] Discrimination may also manifest itself in relation to age (against young or elderly employees), marital status, religion, physical or mental incapacity, appearance, and other characteristics. The question of which minority groups are to be protected by legislation is itself of some significance, since any gain made by one group may impose corresponding losses on another.[5] Thus, the failure of such legislation to be comprehensive, notwithstanding the fact that it is logically impossible for all groups in the labour market to suffer from discrimination (unless a decline in labour's share in the national income is so construed), is in itself discriminatory with respect to the excluded groups.

What, then, will determine which groups are covered? Much may depend upon the cohesiveness of the group and its ability to act as an effective pressure group in articulating its demands. Also, a general acceptance that discrimination is not only widespread but significant in its effect will doubtless assist in acceptance of the case. But there is also reason to believe that the size of the group relative to the total population will be of some significance in this respect. First, politicians will be eager to gain the votes of minority groups (and particularly of women, who comprise roughly half of the population). Even if some voters disapprove of minority rights legislation, such negative reactions may not be sufficient to lose the votes of this group, while the importance of such policies to minority groups may ensure their vote for the party which advocates them, regardless of other policies.[6] Second, as Becker[7] has suggested, the extent of discrimination may increase as the size of the minority group increases and it becomes more of a perceived threat to the majority group in terms of both job competition and a downward influence on the wage rates of particular occupations. Therefore it is important to consider the number of women and coloured workers the legislation in the three countries is designed to assist. Women constitute an important segment of the labour force in all three countries. Thus, in 1971 women comprised 32.8 percent of all workers (employed and unemployed) in Canada, 38.2 percent in the United States, and 37.8 percent in the United Kingdom. In quantitative terms, there were 2.8 million women out of a total of 8.6 million workers in Canada, 32 million out of a total of 84.1 million in the United States, and 8.5 million out of a total of 22.7 million in the United Kingdom. The bargaining power of women in the labour force is, however, diminished by the fact that many of them work on only a part-time basis and the extent of unionisation for them is much lower than in the case of men, as outlined in Chapter 5. In the United States[8] there were 5.5 million black and other males and 4.4 million black and other females (compared to 48.6 white males and 30 million white females) in the civilian labour force in 1973.[9] In the case of Britain, Smith concludes that the 1971 Census estimate of 1.3 million non-white people in Britain originating from New-Commonwealth Countries (but not necessarily born there) is reasonably accurate. This would amoun to 2.5 percent of the total population, but by 1974 the figure had risen to 2.9 percent. In line with the above, Richmond[10] estimates that there were approximately 930,000 coloured immigrants (first-generation) in the United Kingdom and 404,000 in Canada in 1974. This represents approximately 1.8 percent of the total population in both cases. He points out that the fact that coloured immigrants have been established for some time in both countries means that natural increase is an important source of growth; thus the total estimated coloured population of Great Britain in 1971 was 1,385,600, of whom just over 63 percent were foreign born[11] and just under 37 percent U.K.-born.[12] Comparable 1971 figures for Canada (excluding native and Eskimo) are 350,000, of whom 63 percent were immigrants. Moreover, the recent increase in black and Asian immigration, despite limitations that have been placed in Canada, will mean that natural increase will become increasingly important as a source of growth of the coloured population. It is interesting to speculate whether discrimination will be lower in the case of second-generation than in the case of first-generation immigrants. Adaptation to the cultural values of the host country and diminished language problems should certainly improve the employment prospects of the former group.[13]

In examining the use of law as a means of reducing discrimination, it should be borne in mind that there are a number of possible alternative approaches, including economic policies which rely on a system of taxes and/or subsidies and various social measures. There is also the question of which forms of employment behaviour should be made unlawful.[14] Thus, if it is a cost-minimising practise to employ one group rather than another, i.e. if there is no prejudice in the form of aversion to a group as such, should this selectivity be permitted or prohibited? How far, for instance, should language problems be regarded as a legitimate reason for not employing immigrants in certain jobs?[15] Is the same legal apparatus appropriate for all forms of discrimination or should there, for instance, be separate approaches to race and sex discrimination? These are some of the issues it is necessary to focus upon in assessing the role of law in alleviating discrimination in employment.

THE ROLE OF LEGISLATION

In their first annual report (April 1967), the Race Relations Board in Britain summarised the role of legislation as follows:

(1) A law is an unequivocal declaration of public policy.
(2) A law gives support to those who do not wish to discriminate but who feel compelled to do so by social pressure.

(3) A law gives protection and redress to minority groups.
(4) A law thus provides for the peaceful and orderly adjustment of grievances and the release of tensions.
(5) A law reduces prejudices by discouraging the behaviour in which prejudice finds expression.

The first two and the last of these objectives are mainly concerned with the effect of legislation on people in a position to discriminate, including both employers and co-workers. To the extent that behaviour is based on traditional prejudices, legislation and education might be regarded as complementary, but it is difficult to know on which of these the main emphasis should be placed. The third and fourth objectives are concerned with redressing the grievances of minority groups in the event of only partial success in relation to the other objectives.

While these objectives are useful as benchmarks, it is important to realise that such legislation is limited in its scope and even in the absence of such limitations is unlikely by itself to eliminate discrimination. As Lester and Bindman[16] have suggested, legislation is aimed at the majority of the community who are ordinarily law abiding and does not restrain the determined law-breaker. Also, law will be relevant only if the economic and social environment enables people to develop their abilities and compete for opportunities on more or less equal terms. In the absence of equal access to education and training, this might not be possible. Finally, it is not enough to enact such legislation. It must be effectively implemented.

EQUAL-EMPLOYMENT LEGISLATION

The scope of the legislation in the three countries is summarised in Table 4.1. In the United States the equal-employment opportunity legislation has five separate components: (1) Title VII of the Civil Rights Act of 1964, as amended in 1972; (2) Presidential Executive Orders 11246, 11375, 11141, and 11758; (3) the Equal Pay Act of 1963 and its extended coverage of executive, professional, and administrative employees in 1972; (4) the Age Discrimination in Employment Act of 1967; and (5) the Rehabilitation Act Amendments (Sections 500 and 503) of 1974.

In Canada the federal and provincial human rights legislation prohibits discrimination in employment. In addition, each jurisdiction in Canada has enacted laws (either as part of the human rights statutes or separately) which require equal pay

TABLE 4.1

Prohibited Grounds for Discrimination in Employment
in the United States, Canada, and Britain

United States	Canada[a]	Britain[b]
Race	Race	Race
Religion	Religion	Colour
Colour	Colour	National origin
National origin	Nationality	Nationality
Age[c]	Ancestry	Ethnic origin
Sex	Place of origin	Sex
Mental and physical handicaps[d]	Age	Marital status
	Sex	
	Marital status	
	Political opinion or belief[e]	
	Physical handicap[f]	
	Sexual orientation[g]	
	Conviction for which pardon has been obtained[h]	

[a]In Canada, British Columbia enumerates grounds, but those listed in the column are not meant to be limiting.

[b]Discrimination on the basis of sex and marriage are proscribed under the Sex Discrimination Act.

[c]Under the Age Discrimination in Employment Act of 1964 (46-65 years) and Executive Orders.

[d]Under the Rehabilitation Act Amendments of 1974, as well as under Presidential Executive Order 11758.

[e]In the human rights codes of Manitoba, British Columbia, Newfoundland, and Quebec.

[f]Applicable in Nova Scotia, New Brunswick, and Prince Edward Island and under federal jurisdiction.

[g]Discrimination against homosexuals is prohibited in employment, housing, and access to public facilities in the province of Quebec as of December 1977.

[h]Prohibited grounds under federal jurisdiction, effective as of March 1, 1978.

Source: Compiled by the authors.

for equal work without discrimination on the basis of sex. As
of March 1978 the federal legislation requires equal pay for work
of equal value (consistent with International Labour Organisation
[ILO] convention No. 100).

In Britain equal-pay and equal-opportunity laws with respect
to women (and married persons) became fully operational at the
end of 1975. The first of these makes it unlawful to discriminate
in terms of wages and conditions, while the second makes it unlawful for an employer to discriminate on account of sex or marriage in relation both to potential benefits (e.g. opportunities
for recruitment, training, and promotion) and to actions which
may be detrimental to employees (e.g. short-time working or
dismissals). Similarly, the Race Relations Act was first applied
to employment in 1968[17] and was considerably extended in coverage under the Race Relations Act of 1976 to bring it more into
line with the sex discrimination legislation.

PROHIBITED GROUNDS AND COVERAGE
UNDER THE LAWS

In the United States race, colour, sex, religion, national
origin, and age are the main prohibited grounds for discrimination
in employment. Title VII of the Civil Rights Act applies to employers, unions, employment agencies (public and private),
and joint labour/management committees controlling apprenticeship or other training programmes. Discriminating on the basis
of race, colour, religion, sex, or national origin with regard to
any employment condition, including hiring, firing, promotion,
transfer, compensation, and admission to training or apprenticeship programmes is prohibited. This is the most significant law
affecting both private and public sector employers and institutions of higher learning with 15 or more employees. The presidential Executive Orders apply to federal government contractors
and subcontractors, including construction contractors. In
addition to the prohibited bases of discrimination enumerated
above, age (no specified ages) as well as physical and mental
handicaps are also considered illegal grounds for discrimination
under the Executive Orders. Under the Age Discrimination in
Employment Act employers and unions with 20 or more workers,
employment agencies, and all levels of governmental agencies
are prohibited from discriminating against employees between
40 and 65 years old.

In Canada[18] the prohibited grounds for discrimination in
employment include race, religion, colour, nationality, ancestry,

place of origin, age, sex, sexual orientation, marital status, and conviction for which pardon has been granted. Laws in several provinces and the Canadian Human Rights Act have also prohibited physical handicap as a basis for discrimination in employment. Generally the relevant statutes apply to employers, employment agencies, and trade unions and, in some jurisdictions, to self-governing professions. Discrimination is prohibited with respect to advertising and terms and conditions of employment, including promotion, transfer, and training.

In Great Britain the prohibited grounds are race, sex, marriage, colour, nationality, ethnic origin, and national origin. The statutes (i.e. the Sex Discrimination Act (SDA) and Race Relations Act (RRA)) prohibit discrimination against contract workers and against partners in a firm of six or more (partners), and apply to trade unions, employers' organisations, qualified bodies, vocational training bodies, employment agencies, and the Manpower Services Commission and its two agencies—the Training Services Agency and the Employment Services Agency. Discrimination is prohibited with respect to recruitment and in access to training and promotion.[19] The few exceptions include cases where 'genuine occupational qualifications' apply. In the case of women these include jobs as models, actors, toilet attendants, hospital and prison staff, and personal welfare counsellors and jobs to be performed abroad in a country where law or custom requires discrimination. In the case of race the exceptions are rather narrower.

INTERPRETATION OF ANTI-DISCRIMINATION LAWS

Definition

To understand the practical implications of equal-opportunity legislation, it is necessary to understand how 'discrimination' is defined in law. In the United States the concept has been redefined on three occasions since the Second World War.[20] Initially, discrimination was defined as 'prejudicial treatment', that is, harmful acts motivated by personal antipathy towards the group of which the target person was a member. However, since it is difficult to prove intent to harm, discrimination came to be defined in the courts as 'unequal treatment'. Under this second definition, the law was interpreted to mean that the same standards (job requirements and conditions) should be applied to all employees and applicants. In other words, the employer was allowed to impose any requirement provided that it was

imposed on all groups equally. Yet many of the most common
requirements, such as education and testing, had unequal effects
on various groups, even though they were imposed on all groups
alike. Thus, there was a tendency for minorities to remain at
the bottom of seniority lists and to suffer more than proportionate
unemployment. In recognition of such concerns, the U.S. Supreme
Court articulated the third definition of employment discrimination
in Griggs v. Duke Power Co. in 1971, when the concept of indirect discrimination was first propounded. The Court struck
down employment tests and educational requirements that screened
out a greater percentage of blacks than whites on the grounds
that such practices had the consequence of excluding blacks
disproportionately, and because they bore no relationship to
the jobs in question.[21] Thus, the motivations of the employer
who discriminated do not matter. What is important is the effect
of an act or a policy rather than reasons underlying it. The
fact that a person 'did not mean to discriminate' or was motivated
by good intent is not an excuse under the law. Both the SDA
(1975) and the RRA (1976) in Britain have borrowed and adopted
this definition of indirect discrimination from the United States.
Similarly, the Human Rights Act in the federal jurisdiction in
Canada includes a provision on indirect discrimination.

Enforcement

Under the SDA and the RRA in Britain, aggrieved individuals must bring proceedings in industrial tribunals, with the
possibility of assistance from one of the relevant commissions—
the Equal Opportunities Commission (EOC) in the case of complaints regarding sex and marriage and the Commission for Racial
Equality (CRE) in the case of charges based on race, colour,
nationality, and ethnic or national origin—and also the possibility
of action by a Conciliation Officer of the Advisory Conciliation
and Arbitration Service (ACAS). In addition to the stress put
on conciliation,[22] a novel procedure allows the prospective complainant to require the respondent to answer a number of basic
questions on prescribed forms which may be used for the purpose
of both asking and replying to such questions; any reply or lack
thereof is admissible in evidence before an industrial tribunal.
Freed from the obligation to process each complaint, which
the Race Relations Board was obliged to do under the 1968 RRA,
the EOC and the CRE are now given strategic functions which
empower them to investigate a company's or an industry's employment practices, to issue non-discrimination notices enforceable

through the civil courts, to follow up in case of persistent discrimination, and to demand that relevant information be produced. Also, enforcement proceedings concerning discriminatory advertisements can be initiated only by the two Commissions. These strategic functions are the most important part of their role as direct enforcement agencies under the two Acts.[23] In respect to strategic investigation the British legislation is based on the U.S. experience. In the United States there are several precedents for strategic investigations and findings of discriminatory practices leading to settlements on a corporationwide basis. The Equal Employment Opportunity Commission (EEOC) has, for example, secured massive conciliation agreements with the larger, more visible firms such as American Telephone and Telegraph and industry agreements such as that with the steel industry.[24] Under Title VII of the Civil Rights Act in the United States, an aggrieved individual has the option of taking individual action through the courts or without the assistance of the EEOC or of filing a complaint with the state equivalent of the EEOC or the EEOC itself. In addition, the various federal agencies (under Executive Orders), including the EEOC, can initiate strategic investigations of employers.

In Canada, although Human Rights Commissions in some provinces may file a complaint or commence an investigation on their own initiative, court cases or massive conciliation agreements, typical in the United States, are rare.[25] However, recent legislation in Saskatchewan (the human rights code proclaimed in August 1979) provides for class-action suits; Canada's Human Rights Act is being interpreted in the same light. Moreover, two court cases have recently been initiated in Ontario. These developments have the potential of corporationwide investigations and conciliation agreements typical of the U.S. scene.

In one respect the British and Canadian enforcement procedures are similar. In both countries most complaints are settled at the conciliation stage. For example, in Ontario, since the inception of the Human Rights Code and the Commission in 1962, only 99 Boards of Inquiry were appointed out of 9775 formal cases as of the end of March 1977.[26] The British Race Relations Board's experience (under the 1968 RRA) was similar. For instance, the number of occasions on which the Board started county proceedings was few in proportion to the number of complaints. To take one year, 1973, by way of example, 885 complaints were received, 130 opinions of discrimination were formed, and settlements or assurances were secured in 102 cases.[27] In only seven of the remaining cases (involving four respondents) were county court proceedings brought.[28] Recent experience of race and sex discrimination cases in Britain is discussed later in this chapter.

While there are the above mentioned similarities in the manner of dealing with complaints by the two countries' commissions, there are vast differences in their respective powers of enforcement. In the federal and Ontario jurisdictions of Canada a human rights officer can enter the premises of anyone associated with the complaint without a warrant, except when the place is being used as a dwelling. An officer can order employment applications, payrolls, records, documents, writings, and papers relevant to the inquiry to be produced for investigation and may remove these for the purpose of making copies or extracts. Inquiries relevant to the complaint of any person can also be made separate or apart from another person. According to Hill,[29] the former chairman of the Ontario Human Rights Commission, 'Essentially the Ontario process requires a judicious blending of the "velvet glove" and "iron fist" approaches.' In actual practise, this means that the officer investigating a complaint 'concentrates rather less on the issues of legal guilt than on the issue of effectuating a satisfactory settlement', Hill continues. Thus, the human rights officer combines both functions, investigation and conciliation, with an emphasis on settlement. This is probably the reason that in Canada, where the Ontario legislation has been the prototype of statutes in most other jurisdictions, the strategic functions of massive conciliation agreements, class-action suits, and pattern or practice suits, which are typical of the United States, have not been in evidence, although recent class-action suits in the employment discrimination area in Ontario might change that situation.

In Britain, on the other hand, it is widely recognised that the Race Relations Board had been unable to exercise its conciliation machinery to obtain information on its own initiative. Its enforcement powers were circumscribed in a number of important respects, most notably in relation to securing the cooperation of those who were under investigation and obtaining documents, as well as to the circumstances under which the courts could be asked to intervene and the relief which might be obtained.[30] This is why the Board, in its entire existence, considered 7000 complaints but rejected most of them in the end.[31]

Learning from the U.S. experience, Britain incorporated strategic functions in its recent statutes, which give extensive enforcement functions to the two commissions. In the United States, prior to its receipt of enforcement powers in 1972, the EEOC had to settle charges of employment discrimination by conciliation and persuasion. During its first five years the EEOC received more than 52,000 charges, of which 34,145 were recommended for investigation. In 63 percent of these the EEOC found evidence of a discriminatory practise. In less than half of such cases, however, was it able to achieve a totally or even partially successful conciliation. In other words, the respondent refused to make a change in employment or referral policies to resolve alleged unlawful practises.[32]

Guidelines, Court Decisions, Consent Decrees, and Other Decisions

In the United States two principal agencies administer the equal-employment and affirmative-action programmes. The former programme, under Title VII of the Civil Rights Act of 1964, as amended in 1972, is enforced by the EEOC, while the latter, under various presidential Executive Orders, is carried out by the Office of Federal Contract Compliance Programs (OFCCP) of the U.S. Department of Labor. These agencies have issued detailed guidelines to employers interpreting the legislation. These guidelines include topics such as discrimination related to sex, religion, and national origin; selection procedures; pre-employment inquiries; overall affirmative-action programmes; and obligation of contractors.[33] The U.S. courts have interpreted the law in such a way that these guidelines, which favoured the increased representation of minority groups and women, have been upheld.[34] This has had a dramatic impact on hiring and promotion procedures and practises by employers, as well as on the rationalisation of the personnel and human resources function in organisations. For instance, in 1971 the U.S. Supreme Court upheld the EEOC guidelines on employee selection. In the Griggs v. Duke Power Company case, the Court declared that no test used for hiring or promotion is valid under the statute if it operates to exclude minorities and if it cannot be shown to be related to job performance. Thus, if a test results in a greater rejection rate for minorities than for the majority, a prima facie case is made for adverse impact. The adverse impact, in itself, is sufficient to demonstrate potential discrimination. Thus, if blacks and/or females score lower on the average than the majority, white males, on a test, there are usually differential rejection rates and, consequently, a potential for unfair discrimination. The adverse impact in itself is not sufficient, however, to outlaw tests. The second aspect of the Court's decision is that if such a test (one that operates to exclude minorities) cannot be shown to be related to job performance, the practise is prohibited. Thus, the employer must show that tests that lead to adverse effect are in fact related to successful performance on the job.[35]

This makes business necessity the prime criterion in hiring and promotion decisions. Contrary to the popular belief in the business community in the United States that all testing is illegal, which has led to industry's decreasing reliance on tests, [36] the Court made it clear that the process of testing was legal and encouraged it. For example Chief Justice Burger stated in the Duke Power Company case that 'nothing in the Act precludes the use of testing or measuring procedures. . . .' The U.S. Supreme Court reaffirmed its deferential treatment of the EEOC guidelines requiring validation standards for tests in the Albemarle Paper Co. v. Moody case in 1975. The uniform guidelines on employee selection procedures adopted by four agencies (EEOC, Department of Labor, Department of Justice, and Civil Service Commission) in 1978 put forward the concepts of adverse impact, bottom line, and alternative procedures.

Adverse Impact and the 'Four-Fifths Rule'

Adverse impact is determined by the four-fifths or 80-percent rule. Where the selection rate for any race, sex, or ethnic group is less than four-fifths of the rate for the group with the highest selection rate (e.g. white males) this is generally regarded as evidence of adverse impact by the government agencies, while a rate greater than four-fifths is generally not regarded as evidence of adverse impact. In the case of smaller differences among selection rates, evidence of adverse impact exists when such differences are significant in both statistical and practical terms or when the employer's actions have discouraged applicants disproportionately on grounds of race, sex, or national origin.

The Bottom-Line Concept

The previous EEOC guidelines (1966 and 1970) required employers to validate the individual components of the selection procedure. If there is no adverse impact as defined above, the uniform guidelines state that the government agencies will usually not examine the individual components of the selection process (i.e. tests, interviews, etc.). This is called the bottom-line concept. Exceptions to this rule are situations where the selection procedure is a significant factor in continuing patterns of assignments of incumbent employees caused by prior discriminatory practises or where the weight of court decisions or administrative interpretations has held that a specific component of the hiring process, such as height and weight in the case of police officers and fire fighters, for instance, is not job related.

Alternative Procedures

The uniform guidelines require that an employer search for alternative selection procedures in order to minimise the adverse impact of such procedures on minorities and women. Thus, where two or more selection procedures are available which are substantially equally valid (that is, job related), the employer is required to use the procedure which has been demonstrated to have the lesser adverse impact.

These guidelines are by no means unambiguous. For instance, as Abram points out, [37] even though employers will not be obligated to validate their selection procedures if they meet the four-fifths rule (i.e. check that they are not discriminatory), the current state of the law is such that employers cannot be sure that by complying they will be immune from all challenges; similarly, the bottom-line approach, like the four-fifths rule, may lull employers into a false sense of security. This is because employers who do not validate such procedures may be in serious difficulty if an individual plaintiff challenges the hiring process as discriminatory. Thus, bottom-line statistics will not protect employers from the need to show the relation to a job of a selection component when faced with a claim of exclusion from a job by a single applicant. Moreover, an employer who changes a selection procedure for the sole purpose of reducing the percentage of successful whites and/or males, without attempting to show that the new procedure is job related, may end up being charged with 'reverse discrimination'. Thus, an employer must adopt, as Abram has suggested, only those procedures which are job related and defensible. [38]

The various guidelines issued by the EEOC and other agencies prior to 1978 and since that time have affected all the primary personnel practises. Active recruitment of minorities and females is required. Advertisements must be adapted to legal requirements. In selection for hiring, testing seems to be the key concern. Interviews and application forms, as well as paper-and-pencil and skill tests, must be made reliable and valid. Job descriptions, job specifications, and performance appraisals must also be analysed for relevance. Of special concern are education and experience requirements set at too high a level. In the case of selection for transfer, training, promotion, layoff, recall, and termination, special efforts must be made to train and promote minorities and women. The EEOC and OFCCP take a special interest in upward mobility and seniority. Thus, performance appraisals as predictors of performance at higher levels are being closely scrutinised. In pay and benefits, equal pay for equal work is carefully observed, and benefits must be equal. Similarly, discriminatory working conditions are not allowable.

In Canada, most jurisdictions forbid employers from asking either in an application form or in an employment interview for information directly or indirectly concerning prohibited grounds of discrimination. Most human rights commissions issue a guide for employers indicating what constitutes legal and illegal pre-employment inquiries and pertaining to application forms. For instance, in Ontario the Human Rights Commission has issued a guide for employers and employees regarding employment application forms and interviews under the Ontario Human Rights Code. The Commission draws a distinction between pre-employment and post-employment inquiries. In some cases, a question which could be construed as a violation of the code if asked of an applicant who has not yet been hired may be appropriately asked after hiring as long as the information is necessary, for instance, for personnel record-keeping and is not used for discrimination in employment on the restricted grounds.

According to the guide, the following inquiries are prohibited at the pre-hiring stage: race or colour: race, colour, complexion, colour of eyes, and colour of hair; creed: religious denomination or customs and recommendation or reference from clergyman; nationality, ancestry, place of origin: birth-place, birth or baptismal certificate, place of birth of parents, grandparents, or spouse, and national origin. In addition, employers are prohibited from asking information about clubs and organisations which would indicate the applicant's race, creed, colour, nationality, ancestry, or place of origin; name and address of closest relative; willingness to work on any particular religious holiday; and military service (outside Canada), among other inquiries. Requests for information about race, creed, colour, age, sex, marital status, nationality, ancestry, or place of birth can be made, however, if they are bona fide occupational qualifications and requirements for the position or employment.

In Britain the Race Relations Board, under the RRA, of 1968, issued guidelines; but they were closer to the guidelines described above (for Ontario) than the EEOC guidelines, given that they may have no legal effect and may not be binding on the courts. These guidelines were issued to advise employers about the racial balance provisions under the 1968 RRA. This much criticised provision, which allowed employers to discriminate in favour of members of a racial, ethnic, or national group in order to preserve a reasonable balance of workers of different racial, ethnic, or national groups, was repealed under the Race Relations Act of 1976.

DECISIONS OF THE BOARDS OF INQUIRY IN CANADA BY PROHIBITED GROUNDS OF EMPLOYMENT DISCRIMINATION

In Canada cases have touched on a number of aspects of discrimination. Thus, considerations such as lack of living quarters, toilet, and washroom facilities for women (Jean Tharp v. Lornex Mining Corporation Ltd.); male-dominated work; marital status (Kerry Segrave v. Zellers Ltd.); work being too physically demanding (for a woman); and working alone in the evenings (for a woman) (Betty-Anne Shack v. London Driv-Ur-Self Ltd.) are no longer relevant for claiming exemption under Canadian human rights legislation.

The most significant and interesting of these cases is Kerry Segrave v. Zellers Ltd. (September 22, 1975). The complainant alleged that he was refused employment and training because of his sex and marital status by Zellers Ltd. The applicant arranged for an interview with Zellers in response to an advertisement in the Hamilton Spectator for personnel manager trainees and credit manager trainees. He was interviewed by a female management trainee who told him that only women held the position of personnel manager and that the salary would not be attractive for a male; her district manager had told her that '. . . we could get an executive at half price by getting rid of men.' She also told him that they did not hire men because women would not go to them with their problems. The applicant then expressed interest in the credit manager trainee position. He was given a preliminary interview for the position but was not processed further because of his 'undesirable' marital status. He had been divorced three months before, and Zellers took this as 'a sign of instability in his background which could cross over into his business life as well.' The Board of Inquiry ordered that Zellers direct its personnel managers that in all hiring practises men and women should be treated equally, and that all references to marital status in the selection steps be deleted. Zellers was ordered to be prepared to submit any current directives guiding the hiring of personnel to the Ontario Human Rights Commission. They were also ordered to have an approved personnel agency administer the employment tests to Mr. Segrave, who, if he passed the tests, was to be offered a job and compensated for his period of unemployment as well as for general damages.

GUIDES IN BRITAIN

Both the EOC and the CRE have issued guides on equal
opportunity in employment arguing in favour of positive policies.
The CRE's second guide, 'Monitoring an Equal Opportunities
Policy', was devoted to explaining how employees should be
classified in the records to establish whether, in comparison
with the workforce as a whole or in comparison with the relevant
labour market, any ethnic group is significantly under- or over-
represented in a particular area.

Recording ethnic origin is in line with the previous Race
Relations Board's view that such records are 'neutral'. The
CRE suggests classifying employees into persons born in or
whose recent forebears were born in various parts of the world—
Africa, Asia, the Caribbean, U.K. and Irish, Other European,
and Others. It is, however, difficult to distinguish colour where
the records do not record this directly. Thus, in the 1971 Census
of Population individuals were identified as 'born in a New-
Commonwealth Country' (grouped as Africa, America, Asia, or
Europe) or 'born in the U.K., one or more parents born in a
New-Commonwealth Country'. This definition, however, will
include people born into British families working abroad who
are not members of ethnic minorities. In the Civil Service, for
instance, the standard employee records do not record colour,
race, or ethnic origin. However, clues are provided by name,
birth-place, and nationality of the applicant, and in certain
cases countries of education and previous residence. For certain
people this will not allow one to determine colour. [39] Thus,
identification of ethnic minority groups is not an easy matter.

The CRE has prepared a general Code of Practice. After
consultation with various parties this was put to the Employment
Secretary in May 1980 for approval before being laid before
both Houses of Parliament. This Code will have the same status
as the ACAS Code. Breaches of it do not of themselves make
anyone liable in tribunal proceedings, but the Code may be
admitted in evidence and tribunals may take relevant parts of
it into account in making their decisions.

The Code recommends that employers adopt formal equal-
opportunity policies and that the policies be provided in written
form for every member of staff. In order to make the policy
effective overall responsibility should be given to a member of
senior management; trade union or employee representatives
should be involved in preparing the content and in its implementation; training and guidance should be given to all supervisory
staff; existing procedures and criteria should be regularly re-

viewed; and the ethnic composition of the workforce and of job applicants should be monitored on a regular basis.[40]

On recruitment, the Code states that reliance should not be placed solely on methods which effectively exclude applicants from racial minorities. Examples are word of mouth from a predominantly white workforce in a multi-racial area or unions' supplying applicants who are mainly or wholly white. Selection procedures should not require a higher standard of English or a higher level of education than is required for the safe and effective performance of the job. Selection tests should be validated to ensure they are related to the requirements of the job and administered in such a way as to avoid irrelevant culture bias.

Where employees have particular cultural and religious needs which conflict with existing work requirements, the Code suggests that employers change these requirements whenever it is practicable and reasonable to do so. Where minorities have difficulties with English, it is suggested that English-language training facilities be provided. There is no suggestion, however, as to what range of costs employers might reasonably be expected to incur in these cases.

As for monitoring, the Code recommends analyses of the ethnic composition of the workforce of each plant, department section, shift, and job category and changes in their distribution over time; selection decisions with reasons for recruitment, promotion, transfer, and training according to racial groups; and comparative use of grievance and disciplinary procedures according to such groups.[41] The Code concludes by noting that while positive measures are not legally required they are often essential to the development of genuine equal opportunity. It remains to be determined, however, how successful a voluntary code can be in influencing the behaviour of the parties in industrial relations. Certainly experiments of this type in the past in Britain have been singularly unsuccessful.

LEGAL CASES IN BRITAIN

The case law which has been built up as a result of the decisions of the industrial tribunals, Employment Appeal Tribunal (EAT) and the Court of Appeal now provides a number of guidelines for employers, employees, and trade unions. Equality of opportunity covers such questions as entry into the firm or organisation, promotion within it, level of pay within each occupation, and dismissal or acts to the detriment of employees; it is convenient to analyse each of these aspects in turn. It should be noted that as far as equal opportunity between the sexes is concerned the European Court of Justice has said that whenever there is an inconsistency between European Economic Community (EEC) law and the law of a member state, community law must over-ride domestic legislation; this fact is likely to have growing significance as the EEC attempts to expand its legal framework in the employment field. This puts British law in a rather different position from that of North America.

Entry into the Firm

In many cases it will be very difficult to prove that the reason a member of a minority group was not selected for a job was his or her membership in that group rather than his or her personal attributes relative to the job compared with those of the successful applicant. However, tribunals can infer the existence of discrimination where a minority applicant is informed that there is no vacancy, while other evidence indicates the reverse. Thus, in Wright and Scott v. Littlewoods Organisation Ltd., two coloured applicants who applied in person were told there were no vacancies. However, when they later telephoned they were told the vacancies still existed. On presenting themselves a second time they were told again there were no vacancies. They then asked a white English friend to apply, and he was offered the job. The tribunal found that there was clearly discrimination in this case.

Questions at an interview concerning, say, sex, marital status, family circumstances, or ability to mix with members of the other sex or other racial groups might be held to imply discriminatory behaviour. However, in Saunders v. Richmond-upon-Thames Borough Council, the EAT did not consider it unlawful to ask a female applicant for a golf professional vacancy such questions as whether men would respond as well to a female as to a male golf professional or whether she would be able to control disputes over starting times. In the absence of evidence of discriminatory behaviour of the form outlined above, tribunals may be inclined to examine statistical evidence. Tribunals have in fact been reluctant to infer discrimination from the absence of members of a minority group in the employment unit concerned. Thus, in Downer v. Liebig Meat Company (Canning) Ltd. the tribunal rejected the use of such statistical evidence as follows:

At first blush the statistics would appear to show an undue preponderance of white chargehands in propor-

tion to the total number of white members of the work
force, but this is partly due to historical reasons and
partly to the failure of black members to offer themselves for appointment. One can no more read from
the statistics that there has been a policy of racial
discrimination than one can infer from the fact that
of the High Court judiciary only two are female, while
10 percent of the members of the bar are of that sex,
that there is a policy of sex discrimination in the
office of the Lord Chancellor.

On the other hand, what about cases, where members of
minority groups are already employed? In some early race cases
tribunals tended to find the presence of other black employees
suggestive of an absence of discrimination. However, in Johnson
v. Timber Tailors (Midlands) Ltd., it was noted that giving
weight to the presence of minority workers already in employment
would enable an employer to take on a token number of minority
workers and then be at liberty to discriminate against minority
applicants. A further problem is to establish what the relevant
population of a minority group is with respect to recruitment to
a particular plant or occupation within it. While British courts
have generally not gone as far as the U.S. courts in defining
the percentage of a minority group in the total population of a
city, Standard Metropolitan Area, State, or region, in Price v.
Civil Service Commission and Civil Service National Whitley
Council (Staff Side) the EAT considered in relation to the concept
of indirect discrimination that the appropriate pool was all qualified men and women rather than the entire population.
Cases so far make it clear that employers cannot use as a
defence the possible or actual prejudices or reactions of their
workforce or customers to the employment of minority workers.
In Mills v. Brook Street Bureau Ltd. and Another it was a condition of employment that staff not discriminate on account of
race, sex, or religious beliefs (the last of these not being included
in the British legislation). The employer being an employment
hiring agency, there was also a procedure for reporting cases
where outside employers appeared to infringe the RRA. That
might well have been regarded as a defence under Section 32(3)
of the RRA as taking 'such steps as were reasonably practicable
to prevent the employee from discriminating'. However, the
tribunal found that this defence failed because the policy did
not appear invariably to be strictly adhered to in practice. A
further question concerns whether the fact of bias being unconscious can be a defence under Section 32. In Bains v. Salop

County Council there was a disagreement on this question. A
majority of the tribunal felt that the RRA covered only deliberate
acts, since it would not be possible for an employer to take
reasonable steps to avoid discrimination if he were unaware of
its very existence. However, this seems at odds with EAT
decisions on the SDA which stress effect rather than intent.

Indirect discrimination may occur through the imposition
of arbitrary age limits, excessive qualifications, dress requirements, or language tests. One of the most important cases,
Price v. Civil Service Commission, suggests that age limits should
not be unduly restrictive. The case was brought over the imposition of an age barrier of 28 for direct entry into the executive
officer grade of the Civil Service, which in practice made it harder
for women than for men to fulfil the entrance requirements.
While it was accepted that it was desirable to ensure that a proportion of direct entrants to the grade in question was drawn
from the lower age groups in order to maintain a balanced career
structure, it was held that there were alternative ways of achieving this that the defendants had not considered and that were
non-discriminatory. In Bohon-Mitchell v. The Common Professional Examination Board, a case was brought against the Council
of Legal Education, which required overseas graduates without
a law degree to complete two years' study rather than one, as
in the case of similar graduates from British or Irish universities,
in order to become a barrister. The tribunal found in favour
of the American complainant on the grounds that the Council's
requirement meant that a considerably smaller proportion of
overseas graduates could comply than was the case with home
graduates, while the defendants had failed to prove that the
requirement was justified for reasons other than nationality or
national origins. A third example of indirect discrimination
occurred in Hussain v. Saints Complete House Furnishers. The
company concerned had imposed a ban on recruitment from a
certain district in the city centre of Liverpool because in their
experience people from that district were troublesome. In fact
most of the black population of the city lived in that area, and
in the inner city as a whole 10 percent of the population was
coloured as opposed to 2 percent for the whole conurbation.
That there was no intention to discriminate was found to be
irrelevant here. Generally, it is still not clear to what extent
the impact on the various groups must differ in order to be
significant under the legislation, unlike the case in the United
States, where the rule of thumb has been that a 20-percent
difference in the proportion of those able to comply is sufficient
to amount to discrimination.

In certain circumstances a requirement may be held to be justifiable. Thus, in Bains v. Somerset County Council, the tribunal found that a College's age requirement was justifiable on the grounds that it was based on the need to keep down the wage bill and to obtain lecturers who would be motivated to work hard in order to improve their position. This was regarded as more than a matter of convenience. Similarly, EAT upheld a tribunal decision in Singh v. Rowntree MacIntosh that a 'no beards' rule in a food factory did not amount to indirect discrimination against Sikhs, on the grounds that this 'hygiene rule' was a matter of commercial necessity rather than mere convenience. That this will not always suffice is illustrated in a sex discrimination case, Steel v. Union of Post Office Workers and the Post Office, where it was suggested that it was right to distinguish between a requirement which was necessary and one which was merely convenient (in this case, promotion being dependent on seniority in terms of 'permanent' status). For this purpose it was relevant to consider whether the employer could find some other (non-discriminatory) way of achieving its objective.

Training and Promotion

It is permissible, under both the SDA and RRA, where during the previous 12 months there have been no (or comparatively few) members of a minority group doing a particular type of work, to give special encouragement or mount a special training scheme for members of that group. That this is exceptional in practise is indicated by the fact that in a survey of 500 companies the EOC found only seven employers who had made use of such positive discrimination and that this was mainly in managerial occupations.[42] How far this represents an unwillingness on the part of members of minority groups to offer themselves for training is unknown.

It is common to find the majority of members of a minority group confined to the lower levels of the job hierarchy. Thus, one study of men and women in 26 organisations found that women were often blocked from better paid jobs because of lifting requirements, inability to do shift or overtime work, or the use of traditional promotion paths from male preserves.[43] It is, however, extremely difficult to prove that a failure to promote is a consequence of discrimination, and in no case has a tribunal found in favour of an applicant on such grounds under the RRA. Defences may be that the individual concerned is lacking in

leadership qualities or technical knowledge. As an example, in
Walters v. Louis Newmark Ltd., the tribunal were unwilling to
draw an inference of discrimination from the fact that the coloured
applicant had been employed for 25 years without being offered
promotion, though there had been eight appropriate vacancies
over this period. This was because there was evidence of long-
serving Europeans' being similarly overlooked for promotion.

Promotion prospects may also be adversely affected by the
effects of earlier discriminatory practices. Thus, in Steel v.
Post Office, a policy of promotion by seniority was found to have
adversely affected women, who until 1975 had been barred from
acquiring 'permanent' status with consequent seniority rights.
It may not be sufficient, therefore, for an employer to abolish
a previously discriminatory policy if the effects of that policy
continue to be felt by members of the workforce.

DETRIMENTAL ACTS, REDUNDANCY, AND DISMISSAL

Both the SDA and the RRA require equality of treatment
with respect to acts which are to the detriment of workers, such
as redundancy or dismissal. Women and immigrants may be faced
with a particular disadvantage through the operation of 'last-in,
first-out' procedures for determining which workers will be laid
off first when there is a temporary or permanent decline in demand. Since women tend on average to have less seniority than
men, they will tend to be disproportionately affected by such
procedures. In Noble and Others v. David Gold and Son (Hold-
ings) Ltd., the EAT found that it was discriminatory to select
women warehouse workers to be laid off to eliminate redundancy
rather than men, even though the men did heavy work and the
women were concentrated in light work, where the diminution
in the level of work had occurred. However, this decision was
overturned in the Court of Appeal, which placed a narrow interpretation on the appropriate unit of selection, saying that in this
case men and women could be regarded as being in separate
establishments. Dismissal is covered by separate legislation,
which requires a qualifying period that may disallow a claim by
a member of a minority group. In one such case, Haroun v.
Johnson (Troy Auto Spares), the complaint was dismissed on
grounds of lack of capability by a new manager with whom there
was mutual antipathy. The tribunal found that part of the reason
for the antipathy was the applicant's colour. On three occasions
he had complained to the manager about graffiti in the toilets,
but nothing had been done. The tribunal awarded £75 for injury
to feelings.

The question of a failure to provide the same benefits to one sex as to the other arose in Automotive Products Ltd. v. Peake. The EAT considered that the fact that women were allowed to leave work five minutes before the men for reasons of good administration and safety amounted to discrimination against men. The Court of Appeal, however, refused to accept that the five-minute rule was either less or more favourable treatment (referring in passing to questions of chivalry) because the matter was not sufficiently substantial. In another Court of Appeal case, Jeremiah v. Ministry of Defence, Lord Denning referred to the above case and stated that he now felt that the earlier decision was correct only on the de minimis (trifles) principle and not on the question of chivalry and administrative practise. In the later case the Court of Appeal upheld the decision of the EAT that additional payment for obnoxious work did not prevent the discrimination from being a detriment. It would appear therefore that it is a dangerous procedure to limit unpleasant jobs to men, even if extra recompense is given to those who perform them.

The EAT has recently decided that it is not indirect sex discrimination to dismiss a woman because she is pregnant (Terley v. Allders Dept. Stores Ltd.).[44] The majority ruled that there is no male equivalent to a pregnant woman, while the dissenting view was that pregnancy was a medical condition and a male might require time off during the course of the year for such a reason. In turn, this raises the question of whether it might be lawful to reject an applicant for a job on the basis that she may in due course have a child. Over a quarter of the cases brought so far under the SDA have concerned the question of dismissal, and this is clearly an important area of the legislation.

It would appear that direct racial and sex discrimination is always hard to prove. However, both Section 65 of the RRA and Section 74 of the SDA enable an aggrieved person to request an employer to set out on the appropriate form relevant information and the reasons for the treatment against which there is a complaint. Though there is no legal obligation on the employer to respond to such a request, failure to do so or evasive responses may be construed by the courts as an indication of unlawful actions. Thus, in Eaton v. Nuttall, the EAT suggested that an employer was under an obligation to provide a tribunal with relevant and comprehensive information (including, in this particular case, adequate details of job evaluation and payment systems). Relevant data might include the ethnic or sex breakdown of the workforce and the number of minority workers in posts reached by promotion. In Rasul v. Commission for Racial Equality, the complainant, who was one of two coloured persons interviewed out of a short list of nine drawn from 154 candidates, alleged that he had better qualifications and more seniority and experience than the successful candidate. He requested discovery of all the applicants' references and curricula vitae and an ethnic breakdown of all applicants and current CRE staff. The EAT held that the only relevant evidence was that relating to the nine short-list candidates and ordered discovery of applications, references, and curricula vitae of these individuals, together with all the documents relating to them available to the Commission at the time of interview. Further, in Jalota v. Imperial Metal Industry (Kynoch) Ltd., the EAT refused the complainant's request for discovery of the ethnic composition of staff and payroll jobs on grounds which included the statement that the number of coloured employees was not relevant to the question of whether the respondents were discriminating against the complainant. Further, it was suggested that in order to comply with this request the respondents would have to classify all their employees and define who was coloured, which was regarded as being difficult, divisive, and undesirable. This, however, seems to conflict with the guidelines laid down by the CRE, as outlined earlier in this study.

In the main, tribunals have been reluctant to draw an inference of discrimination in the absence of direct evidence of prejudice. However, under the law applicants need only prove their case on the balance of probabilities, and this ought not to be an especially heavy burden. An inference of discrimination might, therefore, be drawn from facts such as that no attempt was made to enquire into an individual's background or experience, to take references, or to ask probing questions in an interview.

DEVELOPING EQUAL-OPPORTUNITY POLICIES

The EOC has reported that there is widespread ignorance among employers of the details of the equal-opportunity legislation. In its survey of 500 leading employers it found that only 25 percent of the respondents had written equal-opportunity policies, only 14 percent had established executive responsibility for implementation, and only 12 percent had introduced particular policies for women. As for race, one investigation[45] found that two-thirds of 60 organisations contacted either did not have an equal-opportunity policy or were unwilling to discuss the matter;

a second[46] found that of 283 employers at plant level only 14 claimed to have such a policy in relation to recruitment and only 8 percent had taken steps to implement such a policy.

The EOC has suggested[47] that apart from questions of law and justice it is economically rational for employers to develop the potential of all employees to the full. While this may be true with respect to racial factors, ignoring language problems, in the case of women the suggestion should be qualified. Given higher rates of turnover and absence and the possibilities of different levels of performance in particular jobs, it will rarely be most profitable for the employer to ensure that women are equally distributed with men in all occupational groups. A more direct reason for developing an equal opportunities policy is the requirement for information if an employer is involved in proceedings before an industrial tribunal. It has been suggested[48] that the prior introduction of such a policy may be an adequate defence for an employer in showing that he has taken reasonable steps to prevent individual employees from committing an unlawful act, though it is clear that such a policy must be fully implemented in practise.

As might be apparent from the legal cases as well as the EOC survey of leading employers, the British equal-opportunity legislation seems to have had only a minor impact on the behaviour of the parties and on the welfare of minority groups. This conclusion is reinforced by the following analysis of the outcome of applications to industrial tribunals under the SDA and the RRA.

RACE AND SEX DISCRIMINATION COMPLAINTS TO
INDUSTRIAL TRIBUNALS IN BRITAIN

The results of race and sex discrimination complaints have been summarised by Britain's Department of Employment for sex cases[49] over the period from the implementation of the legislation on January 1, 1976 to December 31, 1979, and for race cases[50] over the period from implementation on June 13, 1977, to June 30, 1979.

The most noteworthy feature of the sex discrimination legislation is the decline in its use. Sex discrimination claims fell from 243 in 1976 to 229 in 1977, and 171 in 1978, rising marginally to 178 in 1979. For race, in contrast, the number of cases rose from 146 in 1977-1978 to 364 in 1978-1979, a much higher incidence given the fact that racial minorities comprise only a small percentage of the labour force compared to a figure of approximately 40 percent for women. However, it should also be borne in mind

that in the first 12 months after the race legislation was passed
the number of complaints of unfair dismissal under the Trade
Unions and Labour Relations Act was 70 times greater. Questions
relating to sex discrimination and race relations have formed
less than 5 percent of the work of the ACAS, which plays a key
role in the context of the legislation. Thus, ACAS carried out
three surveys and projects on these subjects in 1977, 20 in 1978,
and 13 in 1979. It also made 312 advisory visits relating to these
issues in 1979, 230 in 1978, and 441 in 1979, representing at the
most 3.5 percent of its total engagements.[51] Until further research is undertaken it is a matter of conjecture to what extent
the low utilisation of the legislation is a consequence of lack of
knowledge of their rights by individual employees, a reaction
to the depressed state of the labour market and fear of retaliation
by the employer, or the knowledge that prospects of a successful
outcome for the applicant are rather low relative to other forms
of employee protection legislation. The relatively higher incidence
of use of the race legislation could represent a greater willingness
on the part of males to pursue their rights (there being a clear
majority of male applicants under the race legislation) or a result
of the more positive approach adopted by the CRE than by the
EOC. An instance of the latter relates to the possibilities of
formal investigations of individual employment units and the
issuance of non-discrimination notices on recalcitrant employers.
Although the EOC announced in 1978 that it had developed its
strategies considerably in this area, so far it has undertaken
only five such investigations in the employment area, on which
reports still have to be made. While the CRE too has yet to
report on any of its formal investigations, 17 out of 31 investigations so far commenced have been in the employment field, being
concentrated in labour markets where a high proportion of ethnic
minorities are found. While it is still early to assess the long-
run effects of legislation in Britain the signs are that its impact
is likely to be small. There are no published data on the black/
white earnings differential, but the New Earnings Survey does
provide data on the male/female earnings differential and shows
that after an initial tendency for the differential to narrow it
has begun to widen again.[52] Indeed, there is reason to believe
that the initial narrowing may have been due more to the flat-
rate provisions of various incomes policies than to the equal-
opportunity legislation.[53]

OUTLINE OF CASES UNDER THE EQUAL-OPPORTUNITY
LEGISLATION

Both the Sex Discrimination Act of 1975 and the Race Relations Act of 1976 distinguish between direct and indirect discrimination, but there have been relatively few cases of the latter.
83.7 percent of all cases under the SDA have concerned direct
discrimination on the grounds of sex; the corresponding figure
under the RRA is 75.7 percent. Of the latter cases, however,
10.6 percent have involved allegations of segregation. Less
than 5 percent of cases under the SDA have involved married
people. What is striking is the number of applications brought
by men under the SDA—no less than 25 percent; under the RRA
22.4 percent of applicants have been female.

Age profiles of applicants are similar for both men and
women under the two forms of legislation, with relatively few
young or elderly applicants. Regionally, between 25 percent
and 40 percent of all cases arise in the South-East region,
including London. As far as race is concerned, the figures
reflect the settlement pattern of the main ethnic groups, with
very few applications in the North, Wales, and Scotland, where
their members are few. The occupational analyses show that
clerical and related occupations make up the largest single group
of applicants in relation to sex discrimination cases—20.7 percent
of the total. As for race, the clerical group is less significant
than managerial and professional groups, perhaps reflecting
the fact that racial discrimination is more pronounced in the
highest ranges of the occupational strata.

Applications can also be analysed by type of complaint.
Only 1 percent of sex discrimination cases involved respondents
other than employers, while the corresponding figure for race
cases is 5.7 percent. Thus, few cases involve, for instance,
trade unions, perhaps reflecting the unfavourable employment
situation over the period. Acts to the detriment of employees,
notably dismissals, form a substantial proportion of applications—
37.5 percent of all sex discrimination and 46.5 percent of race
discrimination cases. Opportunities for occupational advancement
are less significant than initial offers of employment in the case
of race applications—16 percent as opposed to nearly 32 percent—
but are more or less of equal importance in the case of sex
discrimination—34 percent and 27.6 percent, respectively.

In roughly 80 percent of applications information is available
on size of firm, and it might be supposed that ignorance of the
legislation would be more marked in small firms. 26.3 percent

of applicants under the SDA were employed in firms with less
than 100 workers, compared with 17.7 percent under the RRA.
There may well be a tendency for women to be more than proportionately concentrated in small firms, compared with racial minorities. Thus, 44.5 percent of applicants under the RRA were
employed in firms with 1000 or more workers, compared with
32.4 percent under the SDA. Size may also be related, however,
to the industrial distribution of employment. In sex discrimination cases the service sector is of great importance. Surprisingly,
perhaps, the latter is also true of race cases, with the financial,
professional, and miscellaneous services sector accounting for
no less than 25 percent of applications. While the data do not
allow us to compare the public and private sectors, public administration and defence account for over 10 percent of all race
and sex discrimination cases.

Before a case comes before an industrial tribunal, attempts
are made to settle the problem by means of conciliation under
the auspices of ACAS. In some cases private settlements may
be reached or applicants may be persuaded that their complaints
are out of the scope of the legislation. In fact, the majority of
applications are cleared without the necessity for a tribunal
hearing—60.6 percent of sex discrimination and 50.2 percent of
race discrimination applications. Only in a minority of cases
have tribunals upheld a complaint and made an order declaring
rights, awarded compensation, or recommended a particular
course of action (21.9 percent of sex discrimination and 24.8
percent of race discrimination cases).

CONSENT DECREES AND COURT CASES
IN THE UNITED STATES

The EEOC has concentrated in recent years on securing
massive conciliation agreements with the larger, more visible
firms, such as the American Telephone and Telegraph Company
(AT & T), and industry agreements, such as that with the steel
industry. In addition, pattern or practice court suits involving
job inequality throughout an entire employment system, as well
as class-action suits affecting an entire class of employees, are
on the upswing. Thus, the emphasis, in terms of enforcement
efforts, has been on systemwide (companywide or industrywide)
job discrimination; this means concentration on large, visible
employers. Smaller firms remain virtually untouched except for
the complaint process. In an attempt to reduce its vast complaint
backlog, the EEOC has also attempted to have complainants recon-
ciled with their organisations.

A consent decree is an out-of-court settlement which is granted judicial approval and protection by the courts. The AT & T settlement represents the largest settlement ever made in the United States and was negotiated and signed by the company, the OFCCP, and the EEOC. It covers all of the AT & T's 24 operating companies and 700 establishments within the Bell system. It is a landmark case, since it demonstrates what an affirmative-action programme via court settlement actually means in terms of statistical goals and timetables for a large private employer with 771,000 employees (including 401,000 women). Prior to the settlement the vast majority of employees at AT & T worked in sex segregated job classifications. For example, in the Bell system, males constituted 98.6 percent of all AT & T craft workers on December 31, 1971, while 96.6 percent of all office and clerical employees were women. The 1973 settlement, concluded after two years of public hearings and negotiations, included an undertaking by the company to make a one-time back payment of $38 million immediately to 13,000 women and 2000 men who claimed to be victims of discrimination and $23 million of immediate pay increases to 36,000 employees because of allegations of prior discrimination in job placement. In addition, the AT & T agreed to future wage increases amounting to $200 million for the six-year decree, which ended in 1979. Specific remedial steps for upgrading all qualified college-trained women were also included. The unions attacked the AT & T's 1973 consent decree on the grounds that the decree's 'affirmative action override'[54] conflicted with provisions in their collective agreements with the company concerning competitive seniority in transfer and promotion. The union had also argued that the decree is inconsistent with Title VII and the Due Process Clause of the Fifth Amendment. The Supreme Court refused to review the legality of the consent decree.

The AT & T has been able to meet most of its numerical targets by aggressive recruitment, training, and development of women and minorities and holding managers accountable 'for meeting EEO [equal employment opportunity] goals and for giving equal weight to EEO as to other business objectives'.[55]

A further major consent decree case occurred in the steel industry. Nine of the largest steel companies and the United Steelworkers of America entered into two major out-of-court settlements, with the EEOC, OFCCP, and the Department of Justice in April 1974. The first decree covers employment practises regarding production and maintenance personnel,[56] while the second covers employment practises in management positions. The decrees provide five mechanisms to remedy the effects of past discrimination:

(1) use of continuous service in plant (rather than in a particular department) as a measure of seniority
(2) transfer rights, providing members of aggrieved classes an opportunity to transfer to a different unit or department
(3) pay rate retention, permitting transferred employees to retain their former rate of pay (if it is more favourable) when they transfer, until the pay rate in the new unit equals the rate in the old unit
(4) hiring and promotion goals
(5) a backpay fund of approximately $31 million

These measures compensated some 40,000 minority-group members and women who were alleged to have been discriminated against on the basis of race, sex, or national origin. Other consent decrees have been signed by a large number of organisations, including Uniroyal, Standard Oil of California, Bank of America, United Air Lines, and others.

'Class-action' suits or charges can be filed on behalf of a large number of persons, in addition to the individual actually filing the charge. The right to file a class-action suit has been helpful in enlarging the scope of both investigations and remedies to cover all people 'similarly situated' who have suffered as a result of the same practises. Such actions are possible under all of the laws and regulations prohibiting discrimination. One notable example was the class-action suit filed on behalf of discriminatees by an employee of the Bowman Transportation Company. In this case, the essential fact that the company had discriminated against black workers in hiring, transfer, and discharge was not in dispute. To circumvent the Civil Rights Act, the company introduced a 'buddy system' whereby no new driver would be hired without the sponsorship of a driver who would train him. Blacks were not sponsored, and blacks hired for other jobs were not transferred to over-the-road positions. A collective-bargaining agreement with the union perpetuated the discriminatory practises. In this case, the Supreme Court of the United States declared that the remedy for the in-hire discrimination was the employment of the discriminatees with full seniority, back to the date of their application for work. This is but one example of a number of cases brought by an individual employee and decided in favour of the affected class of employees in a particular company or industry. The basis for retro-active seniority is that merely to order an employer to recruit a job applicant who has been unlawfully refused employment, as a new employee, rather than requiring seniority retro-active to the date at which the applicant was first refused employment falls short of a 'make whole' remedy. It has also been ruled, however, that Title VII of the Civil Rights Act should be construed to permit the assertion of plantwide (as opposed to departmental) seniority only with respect to new job openings, and that white male incumbents should not be bumped out of their jobs even by blacks or women with greater plantwide seniority.

Thus, in enforcing the anti-discrimination legislation in the United States, the courts have provided for drastic remedies, including back pay, hiring quotas, reinstatement of employees, abolition of testing programmes, 'affirmative action override' of seniority provisions in collectively negotiated agreements (as in the AT & T case),[57] creation of special recruitment or training programmes, and others.

AFFIRMATIVE ACTION AND REVERSE DISCRIMINATION

Actions by the courts in the United States have led some critics to charge that affirmative-action programmes either have led to or have the potential of leading to reverse discrimination against the majority. There has been some confusion as to the meaning of concepts such as affirmative action and reverse discrimination, and it is necessary to analyse these concepts in the context of anti-discrimination laws in the United States, Canada, and Britain.

In the United States, Executive Orders require affirmative action on the part of federal contractors and federally assisted contractors. This requirement, under Executive Order 11246, covers employers with contracts for more than $10,000;[58] it involves taking affirmative action, or positive steps to hire, train, and promote qualified or qualifiable minorities and women. Affirmative action means the setting of goals and timetables for minority employment in job categories where minorities and women have been under-utilised. The numerical goals, according to the guidelines issued by the U.S. Department of Labor, should be significant, measurable, attainable, and planned for specific results. Failure to develop and implement an acceptable affirmative-action programme within a specified time may result in cancellation or termination of existing contracts. According to Weldon Rougeau, Director of the OFCCP, some 300,000 contractors, including most major corporations in the United States, are covered by the Executive Orders. These corporations employ an estimated 41 million workers. The combined staff and financial resources allotted to the OFCCP for the programmes include about 1500 positions and approximately $56 million.[59]

The concepts of the 'relevant labour market area' and 'under-utilisation' are obviously crucial to the implementation of affirmative-action programmes. Executive Revised Order No. 4, issued in December 1971, lists several criteria that contractors should consider in determining the appropriate utilisation rates of minority groups and women on the basis of the relevant labour market area. The Order suggests several features on which to base such a determination, including size of minority population or occupied and unemployed workforce within the labour area surrounding an establishment relative to total population or workforce; availability of minority candidates with the requisite skill within either the immediate labour market area or the area in which the contractor can reasonably recruit; availability of promotable minority employees within the contractor's organisation; anticipated expansion, contraction, and turnover in the labour force; presence or absence of training bodies capable of providing requisite skills for minorities; and degree of training the contractor is reasonably able to undertake as a means of making all job classifications available to minorities.

These criteria by no means provide unambiguous guidelines, and the courts have fallen back on a number of other criteria, including the percentage of blacks in the total population of a city, Standard Metropolitan Statistical Area, State, or region. This is because the available statistics, as supplied by either the Census or the Department of Labor, are extremely inadequate. For example, the Census data are out of date. Moreover, in the official surveys an 'unemployed worker' is defined as one who is 'able and willing to work'. What is needed, from an employer's point of view, is a redefinition of the 'unemployed worker' as one who is 'qualified and willing to work', at a specific kind of job at a particular rate of pay.

For certain professional groups, the relevant labour market may be the number qualified in the economy as a whole. Here goals are defined in accordance with the number or percentage of qualified women and minorities available, not with their general representation in the population. For example, women receive about 23 percent of the doctorates awarded in psychology in the United States, and research indicates that 91 percent of women with doctorates work. Furthermore, approximately 23 percent of the psychologists listed with the National Register of Scientific and Technical Personnel are female. Thus, if none or substantially less than 23 percent of a university's department of psychology were women, 'under-utilisation' would presumably exist. Such a presumption, based on crude statistical analysis, has been upheld in the courts. Indeed, statistics such as these have been used as <u>prima facie</u> evidence of discrimination during litigation. As Rosenblum notes, however, courts are becoming more sophisticated in the use of statistics.[60]

It is not surprising, therefore, that critics have charged that goals have turned into quotas, and industry has increasingly reacted to this charge. For instance, Sears, Roebuck and Co.'s Mandatory Achievement of Goals (MAG) Program states, 'The basic policy will be at the minimum to fill one out of every two openings with a minority man or woman of whatever races are present in your trading/hiring area. . . .'[61] Similarly, one Bell Telephone Company spokesman says, 'Every management meeting we run, the first thing we get hit with is: "We're running a quota system."'[62]

Other charges levelled against affirmative-action programmes in the United States include preferential treatment of minorities and women due to federal pressures to hire and promote not only the qualified but the qualifiable; the cost of mounting an affirmative-action programme, and trade unions' unhappiness over the court-ordered as well as the EEOC- and the OFCCP-negotiated affirmative-action over-rides of collectively bargained seniority rights.

The government agencies and others in favour of affirmative-action programmes have defended them on the grounds of 'institutional racism', since the requirement of a high school diploma or a minimum grade in a test is often unrelated to the job and disproportionately affects blacks and other minorities, and of past discrimination. They contend that, first, the aim of numerical goals is not punitive and employers are not required to fire anyone; second, goals do not constitute preference when undertaken to remedy past discriminatory practices; third, goals do not require employers to give preferences to minorities and women but instead require employers to cease giving preference to majority (white) males; and fourth, the obligation to meet the numerical goal is not absolute. The employer must be able to demonstrate, when unable to meet the goal, that good faith efforts to recruit minorities and women were made; that job criteria were job related; and that the criteria were applied equally to all workers.

Two recent cases have thrown some light on the issue of affirmative action and reverse discrimination. In 1978 the Supreme Court decided <u>Regents of University of California v. Alan Bakke</u>. That case dealt with a special admissions programme to the University of California at Davis Medical School, which set aside 16 of the 100 places in entering class for members of minority groups. Although the case dealt with Title VI (rather than Title VII) of the Civil Rights Act of 1964 and also involved constitutional questions, it does have implications for employment quotas. However, the court was split into two distinct coalitions, with Justice Powell making the fifth vote but not a real majority opinion. Therefore, the holding in the case is suggestive rather than decisive. Essentially, the 'majority' of the Justices decided that quotas were invalid and therefore Bakke should be admitted to the medical school. However, consideration of an applicant's race in admissions decisions was not always barred. The decision seems to indicate that affirmative-action programmes are permissible, especially if past racial discrimination was proved, but that a straight quota was opposed by a majority of the Justices.

In 1979 the Supreme Court heard a challenge to an affirmative action plan collectively bargained by a union and an employer, brought by a white worker. The company, Kaiser Aluminium and Chemical Corporation, historically had utilised a requirement that all craft workers hired in its plants must have previous craft experience. This requirement had a severe adverse impact on blacks in light of the history of exclusion of blacks from craft jobs. In several of the company's installations blacks had successfully sued and backpay remedies running as high as $250,000 had been imposed. In 1974 Kaiser, to avoid the risk of further liability, entered into a collective agreement with United Steelworkers of America that contained an affirmative-action plan designed to increase black participation in Kaiser's then almost exclusively white craft workforce.

The plan set hiring goals and established on-the-job training programmes to teach craft skills to unskilled workers. The plan mandated that 50 percent of those to be trained be black. Brian Weber had greater seniority than some of the blacks who were admitted to the programme. He brought a class-action suit against the company alleging that this racial preference violated certain provisions of Title VII. The Supreme Court upheld the voluntary private affirmative-action plan at Kaiser. The Court relied on the 'spirit of the law' and concluded that the primary concern of the Civil Rights Act of 1964, as amended, was to remedy the 'plight of the Negro in our economy' and that Congress did not 'intend to prohibit private and voluntary affirmative action efforts as one method of solving the problem'.[63]

As McFeeley has stated, several elements, such as traditional patterns of discrimination, no discharge of innocent third parties, no absolute bar to advancement by whites, and temporariness of the affirmative-action programme may be keys to the Court's acceptance of a voluntary affirmative-action plan to increase employment opportunities for minorities.[64]

BRITAIN AND CANADA

British legislation (both the SDA and RRA) as well as the Canadian human rights legislation in several jurisdictions permit positive discrimination in favour of women and coloured groups; in both cases positive discrimination is allowed but not required of employers. For instance, the British Acts contain provisions allowing employers and training organisations to provide special training facilities to members of such groups and to encourage them to take advantage of opportunities for doing particular work.

Unlike the United States, seven of the provinces in Canada— British Columbia, Manitoba, Nova Scotia, New Brunswick, Ontario, Saskatchewan, and Prince Edward Island—and the federal government make explicit provisions for the adoption of 'special' programmes or measures, i.e. affirmative-action programmes, and explicit provision that these are not to be considered to be in contravention of the relevant anti-discrimination statutes.[65] Professor Turnopolsky, after a careful review of the jurisprudence in Canada, has concluded that Section 15 of the Canadian Human Rights Act,[66] as well as legislation in the other seven jurisdictions in which similar specific provisions for affirmative action are made, 'can in no way be held to be unlawful. . . .'[67]

There is some evidence of the presence of voluntary affirmative-action programmes in the private and public sectors. Several large Canadian business organisations, such as the Royal Bank of Canada,[68] Canadian National, and Bell Canada,[69] have established affirmative-action programmes to promote and accelerate training and promotional opportunities for women. This is also the case within the public sector at the federal as well as the Ontario Government level.[70] A survey of 1804 firms with 100 or more employees in Ontario revealed that 372 firms (20.6 percent) claimed to have a formal affirmative-action programme, as defined by Ontario Women's Bureau criteria, while another 338 firms (18.7 percent) reported informal affirmative-action activities. The service industry, which employs 40.5 percent of Ontario's total female labour force, reported the highest number of formal affirmative-action programmes; largest firms—those employing 1000 or more—and U.S. subsidiaries (48.8 percent relative to 36.7 percent Canadian-owned firms) reported a greater incidence of affirmative-action programmes.[71] Despite these voluntary programmes, some critics have charged that the majority of Canadian organisations have taken little or no affirmative action. For instance, Moore and Laverty have criticised the human rights legislation in Canada for its insufficient strength in stimulating affirmative-action programmes.[72]

One way to increase the incidence of affirmative-action programmes is through contract compliance. Several large resource developers, including Amok and Eldorado Nuclear in Saskatchewan, and Syncrude in Alberta, have established affirmative-action programmes to recruit, employ, and train native people.[73] Amok, in particular, has been required by the surface-lease agreement entered into in 1978 between the company and the government of Saskatchewan to undertake a comprehensive programme for native people. The agreement spells out in detail the intent, goals, timetables, and mechanisms Amok must make available to Northern residents in employment, contracting, and purchasing practices; the agreement also specifies the Cabinet Minister's powers to enforce the agreement, which include termination of the lease. This type of agreement is also conceivable under the Pipeline Agency Act; the federal government has recently approved the building of the Alaska gas pipeline by the Foothills Company. This, in resource based industries, especially in multi-million dollar projects such as the James Bay project in Quebec, where native employment programmes have been successful, affirmative action is increasingly becoming part of contract compliance.

In order to assess, in part, attitudes concerning contract compliance, the Canadian Employment and Immigration Department commissioned a survey of government contractors, manufacturers, and union leaders; a total of 576 personal interviews were conducted in November and December 1979. The survey revealed that 41 percent of the contractors and 38 percent of the manufacturers interviewed supported the idea that the government should give preference in contracting decisions to firms with programmes for the disadvantaged. Also, 32 percent of contractors and 39 percent of manufacturers indicated their approval of legislation requiring goals and timetables. Union officials indicated a consistently higher positive response on these questions. Significantly, when asked whether their company would comply with the law or would not seek government business, 82 percent of the contractors and 63 percent of the manufacturers predicted that their company would comply; there was, not surprisingly, a direct correlation between the degree of importance a company placed on government contracts and its willingness to comply.[74]

To summarise, while in the British and the Canadian legislation there is some provision for affirmative action or positive discrimination with the intent of increasing the supply of qualified coloured and women workers to compete effectively against the white male workers and of redressing past discrimination in this manner, the U.S. Executive Orders require employers to submit numerical goals to eliminate past discrimination by active recruitment and staffing as well as via internal transfer, training, promotion, etc., of minority and women workers. The current controversy in the United States over the use of quotas as opposed to the more flexible numerical goal does have certain lessons for British and Canadian policy-makers.

CONCLUSIONS

Legal remedies are necessary but not sufficient tools to eliminate institutional discrimination in employment. This is because the evolution of law and legal principles is a slow process; the case-by-case approach adopted thus far in Canada and Britain and in seniority cases in the United States illustrates this point. Moreover, legal approaches are also limited because they operate only on the demand side of the labour market and do little to influence labour supply. Thus, simply lowering racial and sexual barriers to employment and advancement cannot ensure an adequate supply of people qualified to take advantage of these new opportunities.

An important issue in the use of law in this area is whether the same laws and enforcement agencies can deal with different forms of discrimination. In North America the tendency to uniformity of approach has perhaps been greater than in Britain. Title VII of the Civil Rights Act covers various types of discrimination, including those relating to race, sex, and age. However, there are also separate Age, Equal Pay, and Rehabilitation Acts in the United States. Similarly, in Canada the human rights legislation and the provincial Human Rights Commissions concern themselves with several forms of discrimination, though there is separate legislation relating to pay. In Great Britain, by contrast, although separate Acts and separate enforcement agencies (CRE and EOC) relate to race and to sex, the legislation is virtually identical in the two cases and the policy has been to harmonise the two areas without actually merging them. In relation to sex and race in particular, some fundamental differences present themselves.[75] Men and women are equal in numbers, combine in families, and are geographically spread equally; while the races are frequently unequal in numbers and geographically isolated. Women's participation in the labour force and their inducement to acquire human capital is lower than those of men, while these features are much more similar in the case of different races. Differences on the supply side of the market suggest, therefore, that without fundamental social changes, including changes in family relationships, the potential of legislation in removing labour market inequality is much less in the case of sex than in that of race. Whether these differences imply that the form of legislation must be different if it is to operate in its most efficient manner remains, however, to be determined.

There is a major enforcement problem as far as the use of law as an anti-discriminatory weapon is concerned. In the United States the emphasis has been placed on systemwide enforcement through such devices as pattern or practise and class-action court suits, while in Canada human rights officers have the right of entry into an establishment without warrant and can demand relevant documents. In Britain, by contrast, the emphasis is placed on individual complaint.

As outlined above, the criteria used in the United States to determine the presence or absence of discrimination have included the percentage of blacks in the total population of a city, Standard Metropolitan Statistical Area, State, or region. Problems arise, however, from the possibility of employers' locating in predominantly white areas to facilitate discrimination or from the effect of past discrimination if the employer's own records of area of recruitment are the basis of evaluation. In view of these difficulties, it may be preferable to base evidence on the success rate of coloured relative to white applicants or female relative to male applicants with given characteristics in relation to both hiring and promotion. This, in fact, is what the uniform guidelines on selection procedures in the United States now advocate, as discussed above. In both Britain and Canada, action depends largely on individual complaints of acts of discrimination even where enforcement agencies such as the EOC, the CRE, and the Human Rights Commissions provide backing. There is reason to believe that the use of formal systemwide or corporationwide investigations in both Britain and Canada has been limited. This might change, however, as class-action suits provided for in the Saskatchewan legislation and implied in Canada's Human Rights Act become frequent, and as court cases attempt to establish a common-law cause of action for damages to victims of a discriminatory act.[76] For the present, in an unfavourable economic climate it appears that equality of opportunity has been given low priority by employers.

NOTES

1. It should be recalled, however, that economic and legal definitions of discrimination are not equivalent.

2. B. Ubale, Equal Opportunity and Public Policy. Toronto: Indian Immigrant Aid Services October 30, 1977. The following sources are also pertinent:

G. S. Saunders, 'The labour market adaptation of third world immigrants', paper delivered at a conference on multiculturalism and third world immigrants in Canada, University of Alberta, September 5, 1975;

Life Together: A Report on Human Rights in Ontario. Toronto: Ontario Human Rights Commission, July 1977;

'Study shows job, real estate agencies are willing to screen out non-whites', The Globe and Mail (January 11, 1977), p. 4;

Equality of Opportunity: The Emerging Challenge in Employment. Ottawa: Conference Board of Canada, March 1978;

Annual Report, Canadian Human Rights Commission, 1979. Ottawa: Minister of Supply and Services Canada, 1980; and

Harish C. Jain and Diane Carroll, eds., Race and Sex Equality in the Workplace: Proceedings. Ottawa: Minister of Supply and Services Canada, 1980.

3. W. W. Daniel, Racial Discrimination in England. Harmondsworth: Penguin, 1968;

N. McIntosh and D. J. Smith, The Extent of Racial Discrimination. London: P.E.P. Broadsheet No. 547, 1974; and

D. J. Smith, Racial Disadvantage in Britain. Harmondsworth: Penguin, 1977.

4. H. Street, G. Howe, and G. Bindman, Street Report on Anti-Discrimination Legislation. London: P.E.P., 1967.

5. See, for instance, P. Doeringer and M. J. Piore, Internal Labor Markets and Manpower Analysis. Lexington, Mass.: D. C. Heath 1971.

6. G. Tullock, The Vote Motive, Hobart Paperback no. 9, London: The Institute of Economic Affairs, 1976, refers to this form of political behaviour as 'implicit log-rolling'.

7. G. S. Becker, The Economics of Discrimination, 2nd edition. Chicago and London, University of Chicago Press, 1971.

8. In April 1972 the black population numbered approximately 23.4 million and comprised 11.3 percent of the total U.S. population.

9. Manpower Report of the President. Washington, D.C.: U.S. Government Printing Office, April 1974, Table A-3, p. 256.

10. A. H. Richmond, 'Black and Asian immigrants in Britain and Canada: Some comparisons', New Community (Winter/Spring 1975-76).

11. The White Paper on racial discrimination issued in September 1975 states, 'Ten years ago, less than a quarter of the coloured population had been born here: more than three

out of every four coloured persons then were immigrants to this country, a substantial number of them fairly recent arrivals. About two out of every five of the coloured people in this country now were born here and the time is not far off when the majority of the coloured population will be British born.' (paragraph 4). The paper goes on to suggest that there were 1.5 million coloured people in Great Britain at that time (paragraph 12). Racial Discrimination, Cmnd. 6234. London: HMSO, September 1975.

12. It is estimated that of the coloured people born overseas 604,000 were in employment in the United Kingdom and another 250,000 employed were born in the United Kingdom. Trade Unions and Race Relations, TUC Circular No. 152, on Industrial Language Training, 1976/77.

13. We should not neglect the possibility of discrimination against non-coloured immigrant workers. In 1971 there were, for instance, 963,045 Irish born people resident in Great Britain, and it is estimated that immigrants, including workers born in the Irish Republic, account for about 6 percent of all those economically active in the United Kingdom. See Unit for Manpower Studies, The Role of Immigrants in the Labour Force. Department of Employment, 1977.

14. One lawyer has suggested that 'a mass of rules defining a mass of loopholes is the worst possible basis on which to educate the reluctant members of society into acceptance of general statements of approved standards of conduct'. R. W. Rideout, 'More loopholes than law: The sex discrimination act', Bankers Magazine (October 1976).

15. Smith (Racial Disadvantage) found that 27 percent of all Asians in a national survey covering England and Wales spoke English only slightly, and 15 percent not at all. While there are some jobs in which this might not be an insurmountable problem, the restriction of such workers to a narrower range of occupations must operate to their disadvantage.

16. Anthony Lester and Geoffrey Bingham, Race and Law. Harmondsworth: Penguin, 1972, pp. 85-86.

17. The 1968 Race Relations Act was limited to discrimination on grounds of race, colour, or ethnic or national origin in certain places of public resort.

18. In Canada, unlike Britain and the United States, the federal labour laws cover employment in designated industries or undertakings and thus affect only a small portion (5-10 percent) of the labour force. The provincial governments have full jurisdiction in matters of employment in undertakings employing more than 90 percent of Canada's labour force.

19. Separate provisions relate to Northern Ireland. In addition, there is a Fair Employment (Northern Ireland) Act of 1976 which makes unlawful religious and political discrimination in employment. Its jurisdiction applied initially only to firms employing more than 25 workers, but the Act now applies to all employees in Northern Ireland. In an analysis of the 1971 Census of Population, the Fair Employment Agency found that Roman Catholics were under-represented in the main areas of employment and in higher paying jobs. Thus, in shipbuilding and machine engineering the total of Catholics was 4.8 percent, while Protestants totalled 89.5 percent. In construction Catholics make up 55 percent of the manual labour force but held only 18 percent of managerial jobs. (See Fair Employment Agency, An Industrial and Occupational Profile of the Two Sectors of the Population in Northern Ireland, Belfast, January 1978). It is not clear why protection against religious discrimination has not been extended to the rest of the United Kingdom in view of allegations of its presence elsewhere (including the West of Scotland).

20. See A. W. Blumrosen, 'Strangers in paradise: Griggs and Duke Power Co. and the concept of employment discrimination', Michigan Law Review, vol. 71 (1972) pp. 59–110.

21. H. C. Jain and J. Ledvinka, 'Economic inequality and the concept of employment discrimination', Labor Law Journal, vol. 26 (1975), pp. 579–584.

22. The procedure is that a copy of any complaint filed with an industrial tribunal must be sent to the Advisory Conciliation and Arbitration Service. An officer of that service can seek to promote a settlement prior to processing of the complaint by an industrial tribunal. Moreover, conciliation can also be attempted on behalf of a prospective complainant, that is, before a formal complaint is filed.

23. Thus, W. B. Creighton, in 'Enforcing the sex discrimination act', The Industrial Law Journal, March 1976, finds, 'However effective enforcement by individual complaint might be, it can have only a marginal effect upon the broader problems of sex based discrimination in employment and in society as a whole. This being so, it is all the more necessary that there should be some agency which can adopt a more broad based approach to the problem and which can, ultimately, take effective remedial action in order to enforce its findings.'

24. H. C. Jain, 'Affirmative action in practice: A prototype for Canadian action', Human Relations, vol. 15 (1975), pp. 16–20.

H. C. Jain and B. O. Pettman, 'The impact of anti-discrimination legislation on the utilisation of minority groups: The American experience', International Journal of Social Economics, vol. 3 (1976), pp. 109-134.

Also see H. C. Jain, 'Discrimination in employment: Legal approaches are limited', Labour Gazette, vol. 78 (1978), pp. 284-288.

25. One of the exceptions is the Human Rights Commission of British Columbia. In 1973 the Commission, upon receipt of 342 complaints from female hospital workers, was able to arrange a settlement between the Minister of Health and the Hospital Employees Union, which covered 8,000 employees throughout the Province. The agreement provided that over the lifetime of the collective agreement all forms of discrimination against female employees in pay, training, and promotional opportunities would be abolished. In addition, equal pay was given not only to those who could prove that they were doing substantially the same work as men but also to those earning less than the male base rate. Gail C. A. Cook, ed., Opportunity for Choice: A Goal for Women in Canada. Ottawa: Statistics Canada, 1977, p. 176.

26. See Daniel G. Hill, 'The role of a Human Rights Commission: The Ontario experience', University of Toronto Law Journal, vol. 19 (1969), and Annual Reports, Ontario Human Rights Commission, 1970-1974.

27. The annual number of complaints fluctuated in the region of 1000 in each year from 1968 through 1973. In the fiscal year 1970-1971, opinions of unlawful discrimination were formed in only 9.1 percent of employment cases; in the previous year, the figure was 6.4 percent (Lester and Bindman, op. cit.). There have been approximately 7000 complaints in the whole life of the Board (1966-1976).

28. G. Bindman, 'Law and racial discrimination: The new procedures', New Community, Autumn 1975.

29. Ibid.

30. 1975 White Paper, U.K. Government (paragraphs 28-47).

31. For instance, the Race Relations Board was unable to compel the attendance of witnesses or the production of documents or other information for the purposes of an investigation. In the absence of such power, the Board had to rely on information provided by an individual complainant or other witnesses and the voluntary cooperation of those against whom complaints had been made. Except by bringing legal proceedings if conciliation failed, the Board had no power to require unlawful discrimination

to be brought to an end, and discriminators had no obligation to satisfy the Board that they had altered their conduct to comply with the law.

32. See H. C. Jain and B. O. Pettman, 'The impact of anti-discrimination legislation on the utilisation of minority groups: The American experience', International Journal of Social Economics, vol. 3 (1976), pp. 109-134.

33. These guidelines include:

Equal Employment Opportunity Commission, 'Affirmative action guidelines—Technical amendments to the procedural regulations', Federal Register, vol. 44 (January 19, 1979), pp. 4422-4430;

Revised Standards for Selection of Subjects for Systemic Discrimination, Proceedings. Washington, D.C.: EEOC, June 20, 1978, pp. 1-2;

'Adoption by four agencies of uniform guidelines on employee selection procedures (1978)', Federal Register, vol. 43 (August 25, 1978), pp. 38,290-38,309; and

'Adoption of questions and answers to clarify and provide a common interpretation of the uniform guidelines on employee selection procedures', Federal Register, vol. 44 (March 2, 1979), pp. 11,996-12,009.

34. Chief Justice Burger of the U.S. Supreme Court, in the Griggs v. Duke Power Co. case, declared that the EEOC Guidelines should be given 'great deference' in interpreting Title VII. The EEOC originally issued Guidelines on Employment Testing Procedures on August 24, 1966. By the time the Griggs case reached the Supreme Court, EEOC's position had been further elaborated in a new set of Guidelines on Employee Selection Procedures, 29 CFR Sec. 1607, 35 F.R. 12333 (August 1, 1970). Since that time an even more sophisticated set of guidelines with an extensive preamble describing their history has been issued by four U.S. agencies. See 'Uniform Guidelines on Employee Selection Procedures (1978)', vol. 43 (1978), pp. 38,295-38,309.

35. See S. Zedeck and Mary Tenopyr, 'Issues in selection, testing and the law', in Leonard Hausman et al., eds. Equal Rights and Industrial Relations. Madison, Wisconsin: Industrial Relations Research Association, 1977, pp. 167-195.

36. Wall Street Journal, September 3, 1975.

37. Thomas G. Abram, 'Overview of uniform selection guidelines: Pitfalls for the unwary employer', Proceedings of the IRRA 1979 Annual Spring Meeting, April 25-27, 1979. Madison, Wisconsin: Industrial Relations Research Association, 1979, pp. 494-502.

For a more positive view see Peter C. Robertson, 'The search for alternatives: The need for research under the uniform guidelines on employee selection procedures', ibid., pp. 483-489.

38. Thomas G. Abram, 'Overview of uniform selection guidelines', pp. 495-502.

39. See Civil Service Department, Application of Race Relations Policy in the Civil Service, HMSO (1978).

40. The EOC recommends much the same in the case of women.

41. The Civil Service Department report, op. cit., suggests the adoption of two complementary approaches. Monitoring of reaction focusses on particular cases where applicants or employees claim there has been a case of discrimination. Monitoring by comparison focusses on similarities and differences in outcomes for two or more sub-groups of the applicant or employee population at successive stages of the recruitment process.

42. See Equal Opportunities Commission, Equality between the Sexes in Industry: How Far Have We Come? (1978).

43. P. Glucklich, M. Povall, M. W. Snell, and A. Zell, 'Equal pay and opportunity', Department of Employment Gazette (July 1978).

44. However, this may be unfair dismissal under the Employment Protection Act.

45. Income Data Services, Race Relations at Work. Study No. 217 (May 1980).

46. Runnymede Trust, Discriminating Fairly: A Guide to Fair Selection (1980).

47. See Equal Opportunities Commission, Guidance on Equal Opportunities Policies and Practices in Employment (1978).

48. Institute of Personnel Management Joint Standing Committee on Discrimination, Towards Fairer Selection: A Code for Non-Discrimination. IPM (1978).

49. See Department of Employment Gazette articles on 'Equal pay and sex discrimination'. (April 1977, April 1978, April 1979, and April 1980).

50. See Department of Employment Gazette articles on 'Racial discrimination at work'. (October 1978 and December 1979).

51. See ACAS Annual Reports 1978 and 1979, HMSO.

52. For all full-time women workers, excluding those whose pay was affected by absence, weekly earnings rose from 54 percent of male in 1976 to 65 percent in 1977 but fell back to 62 percent by 1979. For hourly earnings excluding overtime. the corresponding figures were 63 percent in 1970, 74 percent in 1977, and 71 percent in 1979.

53. For a fuller discussion, see P. J. Sloane, ed., Women and Low Pay. London: Macmillan, 1980.

54. This allows the company to over-ride greater seniority and greater qualifications to promote a basically qualified person in order to meet annual targets on the way to attaining a long-range goal.

55. World of Work Report (May 1977).

56. See Gopal Pati and Darold Barnum, 'Human resource programming: The experience of steel's consent decree: I', Human Resource Planning, vol. 2 (1979) pp. 175-185.

57. However, in another case, McAleer v. AT & T, a qualified but less senior female employee was promoted over a male. The U.S. District Court for the District of Columbia held that McAleer should be paid damages by the company but that he should not get his promotion because that would interfere with AT & T's fulfilment of its obligation under the consent decree to advance minorities and women. This apparently contradictory finding is now moot, since the case was settled out of court, but the issues raised by the decision remain. See Theodore Purcell, 'Management and affirmative action in the late seventies', in L. Hausman et al., eds., Equal Rights and Industrial Relations, p. 96.

58. Weldon J. Rougeau, 'Enforcing a clear national mandate', The Journal of Intergroup Relations, vol. 8 (1979), pp. 4-7.

59. Ibid., p. 4.

60. Marc Rosenblum, 'Availability and labour market determination', Human Resource Planning, vol. 2 (1979), pp. 5-13.

61. Purcell, 'Management and affirmative action in the late seventies', p. 79.

62. Ibid., p. 79.

63. See Weber v. Kaiser Aluminium and Chemical Company (1979).

Also see Peter C. Robertson's address in Harish C. Jain and Diane Carroll, eds., Conference on Race and Sex Equality in the Work Place, Proceedings. Ottawa: Minister of Supply and Services, 1980, pp. 151-171.

64. Neil D. McFeeley, 'Weber versus affirmative action?', Personnel, vol. 57 (1980), pp. 38-51.

65. Peter C. Robertson, 'Some Thoughts about Affirmative Action in Canada in the 1980's'. Paper prepared for the Canadian Employment and Immigration Commission, February 15, 1980.

66. Section 15 of the Act states that it shall not be a discriminatory practise to implement a 'special programme' to reduce

the disadvantages suffered by groups of a particular race, sex, or national origin.

67. See Walter Tarnopolsky, 'Discrimination and affirmative action', in Harish C. Jain and Diane Carroll, eds., Race and Sex Equality in the Workplace, Proceedings of a Conference, Ottawa: Minister of Supply and Services, 1980, pp. 72-98.

68. Peter H. Tucker, 'Equal opportunity—Royal bank', in Jain and Carroll, eds., Race and Sex Equality in the Workplace, pp. 99-102.

69. Harish C. Jain, 'Discrimination in employment: Legal approaches are limited', Labour Gazette, vol. 78 (1978) pp. 284-288.

70. For the federal affirmative-action programme, see Equal Opportunities for Women in the Public Service of Canada. Ottawa: Public Service Commission of Canada.

Also see Guy D'Avignon, et al., Report of the Special Committee on the Review of Personnel Management and the Merit Principle. Ottawa: Minister of Supply and Services Canada, September 1979.

For Ontario, see Report 1978-79, The Status of Women Crown Employees, Toronto: Ontario Ministry of Labour, November 1979.

71. Affirmative Action for Women in Ontario: Survey of the Incidence and Scope of Affirmative Action Activities for Women in Ontario: A Summary. Toronto: Ontario Ministry of Labour Research Branch and Women's Bureau, March 14, 1980.

72. Joy Moore and Frank Laverty, 'Affirmative action: A sadly passive event', Business Quarterly, vol. 41 (1976), pp. 22-26.

73. J. Slavik and Associates, Native Employment Programmes of Amok Ltd., Syncrude Canada Ltd. Eldorado Nuclear Ltd., Ottawa: Canadian Employment Immigration Commission, November 1979.

74. The Affirmative Action Study. Ottawa: Canadian Employment and Immigration Department, Ottawa, December 1979.

Also see Elizabeth McAllister, 'Contract Complaince: A Progressive Instrument for the 1980's', paper delivered at the Conference on Women and Employment in the 1980's (April 2, 1980).

75. For instance, B. Chiplin and P. J. Sloane, Sex Discrimination, and R. M. White, 'Does race equal sex?', New Community, vol. V, no. 4 (Spring/Summer 1977). The latter suggests that 'whereas to remove racial discrimination in Britain is merely to incorporate more people into an otherwise largely unaltered cultural and political order, to remove sexual discrimi-

nation is a much larger and fundamental enterprise, for it requires the reordering of more areas of life and the alteration of more beliefs and attitudes than it is easy to imagine.'

76. See, for instance, Bhadauria v. Board of Governors of Seneca College of Applied Arts and Technology (1979). In this case, the plaintiff alleged refusal of employment causing damage because of ethnic origin. This case establishes a common law cause of action for damages to a victim of discrimination. The Court of Appeal allowed the plaintiff to take her case to the Supreme Court of Canada. See Ontario Reports, Second Series, vol. 27 (1979).

5

PAY DISCRIMINATION:
EVIDENCE, POLICIES, AND ISSUES

Naresh C. Agarwal [1]

Labour market discrimination can take two conceptually different forms: employment discrimination and pay discrimination. Employment discrimination can be broadly defined as unequal job levels for men and women (or for whites and non-whites) with similar qualifications. Likewise, pay discrimination can be defined as unequal pay levels for members of these employee groups holding equal jobs.[2] It is the latter form of discrimination that the present chapter deals with. Specifically, it is designed with the following objectives:

(1) to review the evidence on the extent of pay discrimination in Canada, the United States, and Britain
(2) to analyse the major approaches that can be employed to develop equitable, non-discriminatory pay systems in organisations
(3) to describe and review the public policy dealing with equal pay in the three countries under study

EXTENT OF PAY DISCRIMINATION

The issue of pay equality between men and women has been discussed in academic journals since the turn of the century.[3, 4] In fact, one of the classic cases on equal pay is contained in that literature:

John Jones earned good wages from a firm of outfitters by braiding military tunics. He fell ill and was allowed

118

by the firm to continue his work in his own home.
He taught his wife his trade, and as his illness became gradually more severe she did more and more
of the work until presently she did it all. But as
long as he lived it was taken to the firm as his work
and paid for accordingly.

When, however, it became quite clear, John
Jones being dead and buried, that it could not be
his work, Mrs. John Jones was obliged to own that
it was hers, and the price paid for it by the firm
was immediately reduced to two-thirds of the amount
paid when it was supposed to be her husband's.[5]

While the issue of pay discrimination has attracted attention
for a long period of time, it is only recently that empirical studies
directed at measuring its actual extent have been undertaken.
Two overall methodologies can be employed to measure pay discrimination against one class of workers relative to some other,
e.g. women relative to men or non-whites relative to whites.[6]
The first method may be called the sampling approach; it is conceptually more appropriate but operationally less feasible. It
involves a comparison of earnings between men (or whites) and
women (or non-whites) holding identical jobs within the same
establishment and having equal qualifications, performance, and
hours worked. Needless to say, such homogeneous samples within the labour force are extremely difficult to find. The second
general method of measuring pay discrimination may be called
the adjustment approach. It starts out by computing female-to-
male (or non-white-to-white) gross earnings ratios from the
raw data. These ratios are then adjusted for differences in
work-productivity-related factors[7] between the two groups.
The adjustments can be made by examining males and females
(or whites and non-whites) with similar characteristics[8] or by
using the somewhat more complicated procedure of regression
analysis.[9] The extent of pay discrimination is then inferred
from the adjusted earnings ratios, or more specifically from the
'residual' earnings differentials.

A number of empirical studies utilising some form of the
adjustment approach have provided estimates of pay discrimination
in Canada, the United States, and Britain. For each country
separately, a detailed summary of such studies[10] is provided in
Tables 5.1 to 5.5. The summary includes information on gross
earnings differentials, net earnings differentials ('residuals'),
work-productivity factors for which adjustments were made, and
data base. For Canada the tables relate to male/female earnings

TABLE 5.1

Estimates of Earnings Differentials by Sex in Canada

| Author[a] | Earnings Differentials[b] | | Adjustment Factors | Data Base |
	Gross	Net		
Ostry	.45	.20	Occupational distribution, hours worked, age, education	Civilian workers, 1961
Robson and Lapointe	.20	.10	Rank, field, degree, age, university size	University teachers, 1965–1966
Holmes	.59	.44	Occupation, part-time/full-time, class of worker, residence, region, age, immigration status	Civilian workers, 1967
Gunderson	.18	.07	Incentive system, labour productivity	Ontario workers in narrowly defined occupations within the same establishment, 1969

Gunderson	.40	.18	Education, experience, training, marital status, language, residence, province, hours worked, occupation, industry	Civilian workers working 35+ hours per week and 49+ weeks per year, 1970

aThe entries are arranged according to the year to which the data base relates, the oldest being the first.

bThe earnings differential is equal to 1 − F/M, where F and M represent females' and males' earnings in some form (form varies from study to study).

Sources:

S. Ostry, The Female Worker in Canada. Ottawa: Information Canada, 1968.

R. Robson and M. Lapointe, A Comparison of Men's and Women's Salaries and Employment Fringe Benefits in the Academic Profession. Ottawa: Royal Commission on the Status of Women in Canada, 1971.

R. A. Holmes, 'Male-female earnings differentials in Canada', Journal of Human Resources, vol. XI, no. 1 (1976) pp. 109–117.

M. Gunderson, 'Male-female wage differentials and the impact of equal pay legislation', Review of Economics and Statistics, vol. 57 (November 1975) pp. 462–470.

M. Gunderson, 'Decomposition of male-female earnings differentials: Canada, 1970', Canadian Journal of Economics, vol. 12 (August 1972) pp. 479–485.

The results of this study are broadly similar to those of R. E. Robb, 'Earnings differentials between males and females in Ontario, 1971', Canadian Journal of Economics, vol. 11 (May 1978) pp. 350–359. The Robb study, however, does not present information on females' and males' earnings in the form needed for inclusion in this table.

TABLE 5.2

Estimates of Earnings Differentials by Sex in the United States

Author[a]	Earnings Differential[b]		Adjustment Factors	Data Base
	Gross	Net		
Sanborn	.42	.12	Detailed occupation, hours, age, education, color, and urban-ness within detailed occupations. Rough estimates of effects of turnover, absenteeism, and experience	Experienced civilian labor force, 1950
Fuchs	.40	.34	Color, schooling, age, city size, marital status, class of worker, length of trip to work	Nonfarm employed persons, 1960
Sawhill	.54	.44	Race, region, age, education, hours worked per week, weeks worked per year	Civilian labour force, 1966
Oaxaca	.35	.29	Experience, health, migration, hours, marital status, city size, region	Urban white workers, 1967
Suter and Miller	.57	.31	Education, occupation, work experience in 1966, lifetime career experience	Male wage and salary workers, 1967, plus special longitudinal subsample of women aged 30–44
Cohen	.45	.31	Hours, fringe benefits, absenteeism, seniority, education, unionisation	Nonprofessional workers aged 20–64 with a steady job working 35+ hours per week, 1969
Gunderson	.39	.21	Age, schooling, propensity to work full time, job status, sex composition of employment, occupation	Workers, 1970

122

Study			Description	
Wolff	.53	.31	Workers, 1970	Mean earnings differential within occupation Mean occupational distribution differential
Malkiel and Malkiel	.53 .35	.43 .09	Professional workers in a single firm, 1971	Schooling, experience, degree held, publications, marital status, field of study, absenteeism

aThe entries are arranged according to the year to which the data base relates, the oldest being the first.

bThe earnings differential is equal to 1 – F/M, where F and M represent females' and males' earnings in some form (form varies from study to study).

Sources:

H. Sanborn, 'Pay differences between men and women', Industrial and Labor Relations Review, vol. 17 (July 1964) pp. 534-550.

V. Fuchs, 'Differences in hourly earnings between men and women', Monthly Labor Review, vol. 94 (May 1971) pp. 9-15.

I. Sawhill, 'The economics of discrimination against women: Some new findings', Journal of Human Resources, vol. 8 (Summer 1973) pp. 383-95. The above table has been partially adapted from this study.

R. Oaxaca, 'Sex discrimination in wages', in O Ashenfelter and A. Rees, eds. Discrimination in Labor Markets. Princeton: Princeton University Press, 1973.

L. E. Suter and H. P. Miller, 'Components of income differences between men and career women'. Paper presented at the American Sociological Association Meetings, September 1971.

M. S. Cohen, 'Sex differences in compensation', Journal of Human Resources, vol. 6 (Fall 1971) pp. 434-447.

M. Gunderson, 'The influence of the status and sex compensation of occupations on the male-female earnings gap', Industrial and Labor Relations Review, vol. 31 (January 1978) pp. 217-226.

E. N. Wolff, 'Occupational earnings behavior and the inequality of earnings by sex and race in the United States', Review of Income and Wealth, series 22 (1976) pp. 152-166.

B. G. Malkiel and J. A. Malkiel, 'Male-female pay differentials in professional employment', American Economics Review, vol. 63 (September 1973) pp. 693-705.

TABLE 5.3

Estimates of Earnings Differentials by Race in the United States

Author[a]	Earnings Differentials[b]		Adjustment Factors	Data Base
	Gross	Net		
Gwartney	.42	.14	Age, quality of education, scholastic achievement, state distribution, city size	Urban male workers aged 25 years or more, 1960
Blinder	.34	.15	Schooling, age, city size, marital status, class of work, length of trip to work	Male workers aged over 25 years, 1967
Kiker and Liles	.11	.09	Age, marital status, family size, years of schooling, scholastic achievement test score, geographical region, city size, occupational classification	First term army (male) separatees, 1970
Wolff	.28	.20	Mean earnings differences within occupation	Workers, 1970
	.28	.17	Mean occupational distribution	

[a]The entries are arranged according to the year to which the data base relates, the oldest being the first.
[b]The earnings differential is equal to 1 - NW/W, where NW and W represent non-white and white earnings in some form (form varies from study to study).

Sources:

J. Gwartney, 'Discrimination and income differentials', American Economic Review, vol. 60 (June 1970) pp. 396-408.

A. S. Blinder, 'Wage discrimination: Reduced form and structural estimates', Journal of Human Resources, vol. 8 (Fall 1973) pp. 436-455.

B. F. Kiker and W. P. Liles, 'Earnings, employment and racial discrimination: Additional evidence', American Economic Review, vol. 64 (June 1974) pp. 492-501.

E. N. Wolff, 'Occupational earnings behaviour and the inequality of earnings by sex and race in the United States', Review of Income and Wealth, series 22 (1976) pp. 152-166.

TABLE 5.4

Estimates of Earnings Differentials by Sex in Britain

Author[a]	Earnings Differentials[b]		Adjustment Factors	Data Base
	Gross	Net		
Chiplin and Sloane	.14	.13	Experience, marital status, mobility, job level	Group of professional workers in a single organisation, 1974/1975
Greenhalgh	.24	.05	Education, experience, location, ages of children, colour, health, job mobility, occupation, industry	Married men/single women · Single men/single women — General Household Survey data tapes, 1975
	.10	.01		
Siebert and Sloane	.35	.001	Education service, occupation	Married men and women · Single men and women — Light Engineering Co., 1976
	.13	.03		
	.55	.08	Education experience, qualifications, job level	Married men and women · Single men and women — Public Services Dept., 1976
	.03	nil		
Siebert and Young	.28	.16	Education, professional qualifications, years of experience, years out of labour market, spells of unemployment, town size, library size	Married men and women · Single men and women — Questionnaire survey of U.K. professional librarians, 1976/1977
	-.007	-.03		

[a]The entries are arranged according to the year to which the data base relates, the oldest being the first.

[b]The earnings differential is equal to 1 - F/M, where F and M represent female and male earnings in some form (form varies from study to study). Net differential estimated using male coefficients.

Sources:

B. Chiplin and P. J. Sloane, 'Personal characteristics and sex differentials in professional employment', Economic Journal, vol. 86 (December 1976).

Christine Greenhalgh, 'Male–Female Wage Differentials in Great Britain: Evidence from the GHS, 1971 and 1975'. Unpublished manuscript, University of Southampton, March 1979.

W. S. Siebert and P. J. Sloane, 'Measuring sex and marital status discrimination at the workplace', Economica, vol. 48 (1981) (in amended form).

W. S. Siebert and A. Young, 'Sex Differentials in Professional Earnings: The Case of Librarians', Social Science Research Council Final Report (HR4416/2), 1978.

125

TABLE 5.5

Estimates of Earnings Differentials by Race in Britain

Author[a]	Earnings Differentials[b]		Adjustment Factors	Data Base
	Gross	Net		
Chiswick	.24	.25	Education, experience, weeks worked, urban residence, marital status, colour, years since migration	Foreign-born white and coloured men, General House-hold Survey data tapes, 1972.
McNabb and Psacharopoulos	.15	.12	Education, experience, weeks worked, marital status, whether British-born, urban residence, health, apprentice-ship training, union membership.	General Household Survey data tapes, 1972.

[a]The entries are arranged according to the year to which the data base relates, the oldest being the first.

[b]The earnings differential is equal to 1 – F/M, where F and M represent female and male earnings in some form (form varies from study to study). Net differential estimated using male coefficients.

Sources:

B. Chiswick, 'The earnings of white and coloured male immigrants in Britain', Economica, vol. 47 (1980).

R. McNabb and G. Psacharopoulos, 'Racial Earnings Differentials in the United Kingdom', Centre for Labour Economics, London School of Economics Discussion Paper No. 76, June 1980.

differentials; for the United States and Britain the tables relate to both male/female and white/non-white earnings differentials. Notwithstanding the fact that data base and adjustment factors differ from one study to another, the following general conclusions can be drawn from Tables 5.1 through 5.5.

First, the range of estimated female/male net earnings differentials is quite similar between Canada and the United States—7 percent to 44 percent and 9 percent to 44 percent, respectively. The range of the estimated non-white/white net earnings differentials in the United States is 9 percent to 20 percent. When averages are computed from these data, it could be said that the discriminatory contents of earnings differentials between males and females are about 20 percent and 28 percent in Canada and the United States, respectively, and about 15 percent between whites and non-whites in the United States. The data for Britain in Table 5.4 indicate that female/male net earnings differentials are rather smaller than in North America, but in part this may reflect the fact that in three of the four studies separate regressions were run for the various marital-status groups. Given household division of labour, it can be argued that the most relevant measure of sex discrimination can be obtained by a comparison of single men and women and that in other cases marital status/motivational considerations may be concealed. The British estimates of the net racial differential are comparable to those found in the U.S. studies.

Second, female/male net earnings differentials are relatively higher when measured in cross-sectional samples without adjusting for occupational distribution differences between the two groups (e.g. Fuchs' and Sawhill's studies, Table 5.2). The differentials are much smaller when such an adjustment is made [e.g. Ostry's study and Gunderson's Ontario Study, Table 5.1, and Sanborn's and Gunderson's studies, Table 5.3]. This is also true for Britain, though comparisons excluding occupation are not reported in Table 5.4.

Third, net earnings differentials between men and women employed in the same occupation within the same firm are minimal. The studies by Gunderson (Table 5.1), Malkiel and Malkiel (Table 5.2), and Chiplin and Sloane (Table 5.4) all employ such intra-occupation, intrafirm samples, and in each of those cases the net earnings differentials are under 10 percent. This suggests that pay discrimination within the same occupation within the same firm is small—but note that it still exists.

The net earnings differentials, however, should be viewed only as tentative indices of the extent of pay discrimination against women and non-whites. One might argue that the studies generally excluded direct measures of male/female (white/non-white) differences in performance, turnover, and absenteeism—that if adequate data were available and were included in estimation procedures, the female/male (non-white/white) earnings ratios would be raised even further. Thus, according to this reasoning, the actual extent of pay discrimination may be lower than indicated by the empirical studies. On the other hand, one might question the very validity of the "adjustment approach" in estimating pay discrimination. Based on equity theory developed by behavioral scientists,[11] one might reason that employees must perceive a parity between the inputs they provide to the organisation and the rewards they receive in return. In case of perceived under-payment, the employees may simply respond by lowering their inputs to attain parity. If so, lower productivity and high turnover among women (and non-whites), even if they do exist, might in fact be a consequence of discriminatory pay practises. Along the same line, Oaxaca[12] argues that adjusting for personal characteristics such as education, training, and skills neglects the feedback effects of labour market discrimination. Women and non-white workers might have less incentive to invest in acquiring such human capital attributes if they expect post-entry discrimination in labour markets. Bergmann[13] too argues that men and women have unequal access to occupations as a result of sex-stereotyping of occupations, unequal opportunities for education, and discriminatory practises of employers and unions. This results in "overcrowding" of women into certain occupations, in turn exerting a downward pressure on wages. According to Bergmann, then, to adjust for occupational factors in male/female (white/non-white) earnings differentials is to mask the effects of employment discrimination. But 'on the other hand, to exclude the job in which a person is employed from any model of wage differentials is to argue that differences in jobs are not related to wage differences!'[14]

Thus, there appears to be a controversy over the accuracy of the estimates of pay discrimination. Even so, it is clear that even the most conservative estimates do indicate considerable pay discrimination against females and non-whites. Clearly, elimination of pay discrimination would be an important goal in a society committed to social and economic equality for all its members. Aside from ethical grounds, we need to address this problem out of pure economic necessity. The changing composition of the labour force in Canada, the United States, and Britain implies that women and other minorities would increasingly constitute a critical source of labour supply. It is therefore imperative that equitable, non-discriminatory pay systems exist to

attract, retain, and motivate such employees. The following
section describes strategies to develop such pay systems.

DEVELOPMENT OF EQUITABLE PAY SYSTEMS

Two major approaches can be employed to developing equitable pay systems in organisations. These may be called the
external and internal labour market approaches. Historically,
the external labour market approach can be traced back to Adam
Smith, who published his Wealth of Nations in 1776. Smith advo-
cated that the market forces of demand and supply were preferable to custom and regulation in determining wages. Implicit in
this position was the notion that the market-determined wages
also constituted the true and just price of labour. This notion
was later on developed more fully by the marginalists. Assuming
competitive markets and long-run general equilibrium, they argued
that the market forces would establish a wage rate that was equal
to labour's contribution to output as measured by its marginal
productivity. If the wage rate were below the marginal productivity of labour, employers would find it profitable to hire additional workers. This would result in excess demand for labour,
increased competition among employers to find workers, and,
eventually, higher wages. Wage rates above the marginal
productivity of labour would produce exactly the opposite effect—
excess supply of labour, increased competition among workers
to find jobs, and, eventually, lower wages. Thus, competitive
market forces in the long run would ensure equality between
the wage rate and the marginal productivity of labour. In this
framework, as far as the individual firm is concerned, wage rate
is externally determined and treated as a given. The firm merely
adjusts its employment level to ensure equality between the given
wage rate and the marginal productivity of labour.[15]
The doctrine that the market forces could be depended on
to determine wage rates that were also fair and equitable continued
to dominate until the early part of the present century. Since
then, however, the existence of powerful unions and industrial
groups, inadequate labour mobility and information, differentiated
technologies, and the various types of government legislation
have all tended to produce labour markets which differ significantly from the competitive model. At the conceptual level, this
divergence has been recognized in the development of the internal
labour market concept.[16] An internal labour market lies within
the firm. It can be defined as an administrative unit comprising
a set of rules and policies to determine wages (and allocate labour).

While such rules may be influenced by external labour market factors,[17] they are in large part designed by the firm to suit its own specific situation. Thus, in a very real sense, it is the firm which has to develop its own pay system.

By definition, an equitable pay system is one in which jobs are paid for in proportion to their relative value. Given that the firm wishes to establish such a system, it necessitates the use of a process which not only measures the values of jobs individually but also permits comparisons among such values. Job evaluation is in fact such a process. It is 'an attempt to determine and compare the demands which the normal performance of particular jobs makes on normal workers without taking account of the individual abilities or performance of the workers concerned. . . . Job evaluation rates the job, not the man.'[18] Thus, job evaluation is a systematic procedure to determine job values within a firm. By providing a consistent measure of job worth, it determines the relative positions of jobs in the organisational hierarchy and thus forms a reliable base on which money rates can be established.

The development of a job evaluation system involves a series of steps. The first step consists of collecting detailed information about jobs. Job information is obtained through job analysis which notes and records 'what job holders do; how they get it done; the proximate and ultimate objectives of their work; the demands that the job makes of the job holder; relationship among jobs; and the environmental conditions.'[19]

The second step in the job evaluation process is to determine the compensable factors on which the determination of relative job values is to be based. The compensable factors are the job-related contributions recognised and rewarded by the organisation. Traditionally, the most commonly used factors have been responsibility, knowledge, education, experience, skill, job complexity, and adaptability. All of these characteristics are undoubtedly closely inter-related. Jobs which are rated high on responsibility will also be generally rated high on education, experience, skill, and complexity. The only set of factors which may be independent of the above factors are working conditions, work hazards, and physical demands. One study[20] listed 88 factors for factory jobs and 74 for white-collar jobs which were used in job evaluation processes in one organisation. There is ample research evidence to show that broadly similar results are obtained whether two or three factors or a multitude of factors are used.[21]

For compensable factors to form a suitable basis for job comparisons, they should have certain characteristics. First, the factors chosen should be measurable. Second, they should be present in different amounts in various jobs. If there is no variability on a given factor, it will be of little use in determining relative job values. Third, if more than one factor is selected, they should not overlap in meaning or content. To the extent they do, a given job-related contribution will be counted more than once. Fourth, the factors chosen should apply to all jobs under evaluation. More specifically, the factors must cover the entire range of job contributions. For this reason, a common practise among organisations making such comparisons is to use different job evaluation schemes for different employee groups, such as manual, clerical/administrative, technical, professional, and managerial.

The final step in job evaluation consists of establishing a hierarchy of jobs by comparing them on the compensable factors selected as described above. For example, if skill was one of the factors selected, jobs would be compared to determine the amount of skill required for each. By aggregating such comparisons on all the compensable factors, a hierarchy of jobs can be determined in which the relative position of the job depends on a composite of the degree to which it contains all the factors.

It should be emphasised that while pay inequities are highly probable in the absence of a job evaluation scheme, its presence does not necessarily guarantee pay equity. Whether or not a job evaluation scheme produces an equitable pay structure depends entirely on how the scheme is developed and administered. The first step in job evaluation, as stated above, is to collect detailed information about jobs. This information is used to write job descriptions, which subsequently become the basis for assessing and comparing job values. Needless to say, inaccurate job descriptions would eventually result in inequitable pay structure. Information about jobs can be collected through interviews, observation, combined interviews and observation, questionnaires, supervisory conferences, and check-lists. The frequency of use of these methods is in the order given. Combined interviews and observation would seem most preferable, but less than 40 percent of organisations use it.[22] Although interviews are most commonly used, many organisations interview only the supervisors and not the job holders. Exclusive reliance on interviews of supervisors may result in biased job descriptions reflecting supervisors' perceptions of subordinate jobs. Such perceptions may be partly influenced by who the job incumbent is (e.g. a male or a female) rather than entirely by the job content. Thus, a better approach may be to interview both the supervisor and the job incumbent, and wherever possible to supplement this information with actual observation by the job analysers.

Again, pay inequities may arise due to poor selection of compensable factors. A committee consisting of only one group of employees (top management or lower-level supervisors) may not be an effective means of developing such a scheme. It is quite possible that a committee of male employees, for example, may inadvertently choose a scheme which under-values female contributions such as dexterity and over-values male contributions such as physical effort.

The above discussion points to the critical place that a well developed job evaluation scheme has in establishing pay equity in organisations.

EQUAL PAY LEGISLATION IN CANADA, THE UNITED STATES, AND BRITAIN

In 1951 the International Labour Organisation (ILO) adopted the Equal Remuneration Convention (No. 100), embodying the principle of equal remuneration for men and women workers for work of equal value. Article 3 of the Convention recommends the use of job evaluation methods (objective appraisal of jobs) as a key to measuring work value. The concept of work of equal value is 'so abstract and lacking in precision that it allows the bodies responsible for implementing its quasi-discretionary powers of appreciation, with the implied risk that arbitrary, ill-founded and consequently unpalatable decisions may be taken. Job evaluation may be the "essential tool" whereby effect may be given in practice to the principle of equality based on work of equal value.'[23]

Federal labour laws in Canada cover employment in designated industries or undertakings and affect only a small percentage (5-10 percent) of the labour force. The provincial governments have full jurisdiction in matters of employment in undertakings that employ a total of about 90 percent of Canada's labour force.[24] All jurisdictions in Canada have laws which require equal pay for equal work within the same establishment, without discrimination on the basis of sex. These provisions have been incorporated either in human rights legislation (in federal jurisdiction, Alberta, British Columbia, New Brunswick, Newfoundland, Northwest Territories, Prince Edward Island, and Quebec) or in labour standards legislation (in Manitoba, Nova Scotia, Ontario, Saskatchewan, and Yukon Territory).

At the federal level, the equal-pay legislation was first put into effect in 1956 and was amended in 1970. It required equal wages for men and women performing the same or similar

work under the same or similar working conditions on jobs requiring the same or similar levels of skill, effort, and responsibility. This legislation remained in effect until 1977, at which
time it was replaced by the Canadian Human Rights Act, embodying the equal-value principle. According to the new legislation,
men and women performing work of equal value (regardless of
whether the work is similar or dissimilar) must be paid equal
wages. The Act goes on to elaborate how the value of work may
be assessed. Section 11(2) of the Act specifies that in assessing
the value of work performed by employees employed in the same
establishment, the criterion to be applied is a composite of the
skill, effort, and responsibility required in the performance of
the work and the conditions under which the work is performed.

Compared to the federal jurisdiction, the provincial jurisdictions in Canada follow a narrow definition of equal work.
The legislation in various provincial jurisdictions defines equal
work as 'same work', 'similar work', or 'substantially the same
work'. In six of the 12 jurisdictions (Ontario, Nova Scotia,
New Brunswick, Newfoundland, Prince Edward Island, and
Saskatchewan), the legislation also specifies the factors on which
equality of work may be established. These factors are education,
skill, experience, effort, responsibility, and working conditions.

Finally, the legislation in a majority of jurisdictions[25] provides for a general exception permitting differentials between
male and female workers' pay based on any factor other than sex.
In other jurisdictions, specific exceptions are listed, including
seniority, work experience, and merit.

A number of court decisions have helped to provide a more
precise interpretation of equal-pay legislation in Canada.[26] In
the Greenacres Nursing Home case in 1970, the Ontario Court
of Appeal ruled that 'the same work' did not necessarily imply
'identical work', and also that job comparisons should be based
on work actually performed rather than on formal job descriptions
or terms of employment. In the Riverdale Hospital case in 1973,
the concept of equal work was broadened even further. In that
case the Ontario Court of Appeal ruled that different job titles
do not necessarily indicate different work; that slightly different
job assignments do not make the work unequal; and that within
an occupation, as long as some men do the same work as women,
equal pay is justifiable for the whole occupation. The last point
was further clarified in a case in which the Saskatchewan Court
of Appeal considered whether the fact that only five out of 46
male caretakers performed work similar to that of female cleaners
could be considered a sufficient number within the provincial
equal-pay legislation. It ruled that such a number could be

viewed as 'some' and that 'some' employees' being paid a rate
of pay higher than others doing similar work was sufficient to
warrant equal pay.

The courts have also dealt with what might properly constitute 'a factor other than sex' in justifying male/female pay
differentials. In two separate decisions at the federal level—
the CTV Television Network case in 1975 and the La Société
Radio-Canada case in 1977—the Court ruled that differences in
quality of employees' work as assessed by management are sufficient to justify unequal pay. The Court acknowledged that such
assessment might be subjective and thus might involve error of
judgment; however, it held that it was not within the competence
of the judiciary to review the management's judgment. The courts
have also ruled on whether the existence of two separate bargaining units could be considered 'a factor other than sex' that would
permit pay differentials between them. The Alberta Court of
Appeal in the Gares case in 1976 decided that it was not.

In the United States, equal-pay issues are dealt with under
two legislative acts: the Equal Pay Act of 1963, which was passed
as an amendment to the Fair Labor Standards Act of 1938, and
Title VII of the Civil Rights Act of 1964. The essential provisions
of the Equal Pay Act are that:

> No employer . . . shall discriminate . . . between
> employees on the basis of sex by paying wages to
> employees . . . at a rate less than the rate at which
> he pays wages to employees of the opposite sex . . .
> for equal work on jobs the performance of which re-
> quires equal skill, effort, and responsibility, and
> which are performed under similar working conditions,
> except where such payment is made pursuant to (i)
> a seniority system; (ii) a merit system; (iii) a system
> which measures earnings by quantity, quality, or
> production; or (iv) a differential based on any
> other factor other than sex. . . .

Thus, the Equal Pay Act prohibits pay differentials between
men and women performing equal work, unless those differences
derive from a seniority system, a merit system, an incentive
system, or any factor other than sex. When it was passed in
1963, the Equal Pay Act covered about 30 million non-supervisory
workers in manufacturing, transportation, public utilities, communications, insurance, finance, real estate, and wholesale trade.
Subsequent amendments in 1966 and 1974 extended the coverage
of the Act to schools, hospitals, nursing homes, laundries, the

retail trade, and public employment. The Education Amendments Act of 1972 extended equal-pay coverage to professional, administrative, and executive employees. As a result of these extensions, over 75 million workers (over 70 percent of the total labour force in the United States) were covered by the federal Equal Pay Act in 1979.[27]

The equal-pay legislation at the federal level covers workers engaged in inter-state commerce or in the production of goods for inter-state commerce, or in enterprises which have employees so engaged. In addition to federal legislation, 45 States, the District of Columbia, and Puerto Rico also have equal-pay laws. The actual effect of state legislation is to supplement the federal law by extending the equal-pay principle to areas not covered by federal legislation, because in case of conflict or overlap the federal law takes precedence.

As in Canada, in the United States too court decisions have played a critical role in providing a precise understanding of the Equal Pay Act.[28] In a landmark decision, in the Wheaton Glass Company case in 1970, the first equal-pay case to reach an appellate court, the U.S. Court of Appeals ruled that the 'equal work' standard does not imply identical work but rather 'substantially similar work'—small differences in job content do not make jobs unequal; that formal classification and job descriptions are completely irrelevant in establishing that jobs are unequal, unless they accurately reflect job content; and that where some, but not all, members of one sex perform significant extra duties on their jobs, these extra duties do not justify giving all members of that sex a higher wage. Only those employees who perform the extra duties are entitled to the higher rate of pay.

The Equal Pay Act specifies that work equality must be established on the basis of equality in effort, skill, responsibility, and working conditions. Here too the courts have tended to interpret these criteria in broad terms. In the American Can Company case in 1970, the U.S. Court of Appeals ruled that the men's handling and loading functions did not involve substantially additional effort, as this duty was performed for only 2-7 percent of their work time. For 93-98 percent of the time, the male machine operators performed duties identical to the female operators' duties. Similar decisions have been handed down with respect to equal skill (the Brookhaven General Hospital case in 1970 and the Prince William Hospital Corporation case in 1974) and equal responsibility (the American Bank of Commerce case in 1971 and the Sears, Roebuck & Company case in 1976).

The courts have ruled on the exception to equal-pay requirement, which allows employers to justify unequal pay based on any factor other than sex. In the First Victoria National Bank case in 1969, the employer justified wage differences between male and female bank tellers on the grounds that all male tellers were management trainees. The court refused to consider this alleged training programme as a factor other than sex on the grounds that the trainees had never been informed that they were in a training programme and that the training programme had no identifiable content and had been limited to men only.

Section 703(a) of the U.S. Civil Rights Act of 1964 also deals with equal pay. Specifically, it prohibits 'discrimination against any individual with respect to his compensation . . . because of such individual's sex'. This clear directive was confused, however, by Section 703(h), known as the Bennet Amendment, which states:

> It shall not be unlawful employment practice under this title for any employer to differentiate upon the basis of sex in determining the amount of wages or compensation paid or to be paid to employees of such employer if such differentiation is authorized by the provisions of section 6(d) of the Fair Labor Standards Act of 1938, as amended [i.e. the Equal Pay Act].

The confusion concerns the precise interpretation of the Bennet Amendment—specifically, whether or not the Amendment includes both features of the Equal Pay Act: the four exceptions permitting male/female wage differentials and the 'substantially similar work' standard. If the second feature is not included in the Civil Rights Act, then another equal-work standard may be used, such as equal value or comparable worth.

In Britain, equal pay is covered under two separate legislations: the Equal Pay Act (1970) and the Race Relations Act (1976). The former covers pay discrimination based on sex and the latter discrimination based on race. The Equal Pay Act requires pay equality between men and women performing the same or broadly similar work within the same establishment, or among all establishments of the same employer if a common pay system exists. The Act also applies even when the work performed is dissimilar, provided such work is rated equal in value under a job evaluation scheme that the employer uses. The Act does not require employers to install job evaluation schemes; but if a scheme is being used or is planned to be used, it must be free of bias in the eyes of the Act.

The Equal Pay Act does allow pay differentials between men and women doing the same or similar work or work of equal value, provided such differentials are based on 'material difference', e.g. seniority, level of output, or degree of merit.

Under the British legislation individuals who believe they may be suffering discrimination in the employment area, including pay, can take their cases to an Industrial Tribunal. Industrial Tribunals are not courts of law, but are tribunals made up of men and women nominated by employers' associations and trade unions and chaired by a legally qualified individual. When a case concerns the terms of a collective agreement, it does not go to an Industrial Tribunal but to the Central Arbitration Committee; such references can be made only by the Secretary of State of Employment or by one or both of the parties to the agreement. Cases heard at Industrial Tribunals are subject to appeal on points of law to the Employment Appeal Tribunal.[29]

It should be noted that while the Equal Pay Act was passed in 1970, it did not come into effect until the end of 1975. Thus, the Act has been in operation only for about four years. In the first three years of its operation (1976-1979), for which data are now available, a total of 3099 cases of discrimination were filed under the Equal Pay Act. Of these, about 53 percent were withdrawn, a small number of these because settlements were reached privately and the rest for reasons unknown. Of the 1230 cases which reached the Tribunals, only 341 were upheld.

While the number of major cases that have been decided on by the Industrial Tribunals, the Employment Appeal Tribunal, and the Court of Appeal have been limited, important principles have begun to evolve from such decisions. Thus, a case for equal pay would fail if there were no men doing like work. The Mrs. Waddington v. Leicester Council for Voluntary Service case in 1976 involved a situation in which the complainant was being paid less than the male employee she helped select and for whom she was responsible. The case failed because the Court of Appeal held that her work being wider and carrying more responsibility was not the same or broadly similar to that of the other employee in question. However, the law has been considerably widened in this area as a consequence of the Macarthy Ltd. v. Smith case in 1979. The European Court of Justice has confirmed that Article 119 of the Treaty of Rome, which has precedence over the British legislation, has no requirement that employment of men and women should be contemporaneous; this allows comparisons with male (or female) workers who have been previously employed on the same job.

Given that it is shown by the complainant that work is 'like' or 'equivalent', what might constitute a material difference? In the Handley v. Mono case in 1978, the Employment Appeal Tribunal decided that part-time work could constitute a material difference. But there were very special circumstances here. For instance, the difference in hours was substantial, all full-time workers (who included women) were treated alike regardless of sex, the complainant was entitled to enhanced over-time rates after working fewer hours than full-timers, and her machine was idle while she was not at work, thereby reducing her overall value to the company. Again, in National Coal Board v. Sherwin and Spruce in 1978, the Employment Appeal Tribunal considered that the time at which work was done was immaterial if it was like work. Thus, the disadvantage of night work could be compensated by the payment of a night-shift premium rather than a higher basic rate. However, it was suggested that if the same work done at night involved genuine differences, such as additional duties or responsibilities, this might amount to a material difference. Age may justify higher pay if it affects ability to work. Thus, in White v. Scot Bowyers Ltd. in 1976, it was held that the age difference of three years between a man and a woman justified a 6-percent difference in salaries. Yet in West v. Burroughs Machines Ltd. in 1977, an age gap of 33 years was held not to justify a 20-percent pay differential because the man concerned was no more experienced at the work he was then doing than the complainant. An important question is how far market forces are allowed to influence relative pay under the legislation. In the case of Fletcher v. Clay Cross (Quarry Services Ltd.) in 1977, the Employment Appeal Tribunal found that where an employer pays a worker more for doing the same work than other employees because the person concerned had been earning more in his previous employment and would not have accepted employment for less, this was a material difference, genuinely due to some other factor than sex. However, the Court of Appeal later held that such a view would render the Equal Pay Act unworkable. Thus, it appears that market forces do not constitute a material difference within the Act, which has significant implications for employers' recruitment policies.

The extent to which women may claim comparison with men may be considerably widened where a system of job evaluation has been implemented. If job evaluation is undertaken it must not be weighted unfairly in favor of one sex or the other, nor may one group be paid more than another where they are rated as equal under such a scheme. However, tribunals are not entitled to consider whether, in their view, job evaluation should have been conducted differently (i.e. based on different factors). Nor may women argue that female attributes such as dexterity should have been awarded higher points relative to male attributes such as strength. In the <u>Johnson v. Bridon Fibres and Plastics</u> case in 1976, points allocation was held to be a matter for negotiation between the employer and trade unions. However, the case of <u>O'Brien and Others v. Sim-Chem Ltd.</u> in 1979, a failure to include trade unions or women in the development of a job evaluation scheme was held to imply a lack of impartiality. This decision of the Court of Appeal was later overturned by the House of Lords.

In Britain pay discrimination based on race is covered under the Race Relations Act of 1976. The Act has been in operation for a very short time only; so far no equal-pay cases have been brought forward under it.

Comparing equal-pay legislation in Canada, the United States, and Britain, a high degree of commonality is to be found among them. The features common to the three countries are summarised as follows:

(1) Equal work is defined as 'same', 'similar', or 'substantially similar' work (excepting federal legislation in Canada)
(2) Criteria for comparing work are spelled out (excepting Britain): skill, effort, responsibility, and working conditions
(3) Legislation applies to situations where both men and women are employed in the same or similar jobs
(4) Legislation applies at the establishment level
(5) Pay differentials between men and women are permitted if such differentials are based on seniority, merit, productivity, or any factor other than sex.

Equal-pay legislation has been in effect for well over 15 years in Canada and the United States but for only five years in Britain. But even in the first two countries, very limited empirical evidence exists on the impact of such legislation on pay inequities.[30] The evidence provided by such studies, along with that provided by gross trends in female/male and non-white/white earning ratios over time, point to only a limited impact of legislation.

Perhaps the restrictive nature of equal-pay legislation partly accounts for this lack of impact. As has been pointed out, the legislation (except at the federal level in Canada) applies to cases in which the same or broadly similar work is performed by men and women within the same establishment. First, it leaves open the possibility of differential pay rates based on minor differences in job duties. For example, in the same plant a male machine operator may be assigned minor maintenance chores while his female counterpart is responsible for clean-up duties— the former carrying a slightly different title and having the higher valued 'extra' responsibility. This practise may also be justified under the 'exceptions' provided in the legislation, which in most cases contains a general exception permitting differentials between male and female pay based on any factor other than sex. In other cases, specific exceptions are listed which include seniority, experience, and merit. The general exception may have the effect of allowing employers, as previously mentioned, to pay female employees less than men by marginally adjusting the job duties. Some of the specific exceptions, though otherwise justified, may also work against female employees. For example, owing to prevailing notions of their role in society, women are more prone than men to have discontinuous work patterns, thus lowering their seniority and experience.

Second, the legislation also limits work and pay comparisons to employees within the same establishment. If this were defined narrowly, the employer could put all his female employees in one building and pay them less than all the male employees in the next building.

Finally, the present legislation is applicable only where both men and women are employed in a given job so that their pay levels can be compared. If only women are employed in a job—as is true in several cases—employers can continue to pay them less than men in the occupation as a whole. In fact, employers may even be encouraged to segregate females into selected jobs in order to evade the equal-pay legislation.

Comparing equal-pay legislation in Canada, the United States, and Britain to the ILO Equal Remuneration Convention (No. 100), two differences are noticeable. One, the Convention does not include the word 'establishment' or 'firm' anywhere, and thus presumably allows comparisons to be made between organisations. As was discussed above, in none of the three countries is this so. Two, the Convention employs the standard of 'work of equal value' instead of 'same or broadly similar work', as is the case in the three countries (except at the federal level in Canada). The 'work of equal value' standard allows comparisons between similar jobs but also, more importantly, between dissimilar jobs. Since men and women continue to have markedly different occupational distributions,[31] there is mounting pressure, particularly in Canada and the United States,[32] to adopt the value standard in equal-pay laws.[33] While the rationale for the value standard is obvious, its operativeness is not. The value standard requires a single job evaluation scheme encompassing all jobs. Certainly at the present level of knowledge and practise, the viability of such a scheme does not appear promising. More research, creative thought, and commitment are needed to move towards this goal.

NOTES

1. The author is Associate Professor, Faculty of Business, McMaster University, Hamilton, Canada. This chapter was specially written for this book.
2. Equality between two jobs can be established with reference to either their respective content and requirements or their respective value to the organisation.
3. Concern with pay inequality between whites and non-whites is of more recent origin.
4. For example, see the following articles:
E. Rathbone, 'The Remuneration of Women's Services', Economic Journal, vol. 27 (1917) pp. 55-68;
M. G. Fawcett, 'Equal Pay for Equal Work', Economic Journal, vol. 28, (1918) pp. 1-6; and
F. Y. Edgeworth, 'Equal Pay to Men and Women for Equal Work', Economic Journal, vol. 32 (1922) pp. 431-457.
5. Fawcett, 'Equal Pay', p. 1.
6. N. C. Agarwal and H. C. Jain, 'Pay discrimination against women in Canada: Issues and policies', International Labour Review, vol. 117 (1978), pp. 169-178.
7. For a good conceptual analysis of these factors, see G. T. Milkovich, Wage Differentials and Comparable Worth: The Emerging Debate. Buffalo: State University of New York at Buffalo, 1979, pp. 1-47.
8. S. Ostry, The Female Worker in Canada. Ottawa: Dominion Bureau and Statistics, 1968, pp. 40-45.
9. This involves re-estimating female (or non-white) earnings using the coefficients from the male (or white) regression equation. The difference between the earnings females (or non-whites) would expect if their word-productivity characteristics were paid for as if they were males (or whites) and the actual earnings of females (or non-whites) is treated as a measure of discrimination. For a discussion of this methodology, see A. S. Blinder, 'Wage discrimination: Reduced form and structural estimates', Journal of Human Resources, vol. 8 (1973) pp. 436-455.

10. While every effort has been made to include as many studies as possible, these tables should not be viewed as being exhaustive.

11. J. S. Adams, 'Wage inequalities, productivity and work quality', Industrial Relations, vol. 3 (1963) pp. 9-16.

See also J. S. Adams, 'Injustice in social exchange' in L. Berkowitz, ed., Advances in Experimental Social Psychology. New York: Academic Press, 1965, pp. 267-299.

12. R. N. Oaxaca, 'Theory and measurement in the economics of discrimination', in L. J. Hausman, O. Ashenfelter, B. Rustin, R. Schubert, and D. Slaiman, eds., Equal Rights and Industrial Relations. Madison: Industrial Relations Research Association, 1977, pp. 1-30.

13. B. R. Bergmann, 'Occupational segregation, wages and profits when employers discriminate by race and sex', Eastern Economic Journal, vol. 1 (1974) pp. 103-110.

14. Milkovich, Wage Differentials, p. 35.

15. For an excellent discussion of the external labour market approach to wage determination, see A. M. Cartter, Theory of Wage and Employment, Illinois: Richard Irwin, 1959, pp. 11-76.

16. For a detailed review of the internal labour market approach, see Chapter 3.

17. Such an influence would be felt in the entry level jobs, which the firm fills from the external labour market.

18. International Labour Office, Job Evaluation. Geneva: Studies and Reports, New Series, No. 56, International Labour Office, 1960, p. 8.

19. D. W. Belcher, Compensation Administration. Englewood Cliffs, N.J.: Prentice-Hall, 1974, p. 8.

20. J. L. Otis and R. H. Leukart, Job Evaluation. Englewood Cliffs, N.J.: Prentice-Hall 1954, p. 106.

21. C. H. Lawshe and R. F. Wilson, 'Studies in job evaluation: The reliability of two point rating systems', Journal of Applied Psychology, vol. 31 (1947) pp. 355-365.

J. H. Myers, 'An experimental investigation of point job evaluation systems', Journal of Applied Psychology, vol. 42 (1958) pp. 357-361.

A. W. Charles, 'Installing single factor job evaluation', Compensation Review, vol. 3 (1971) pp. 9-21.

22. C. H. Stone and D. Yoder, Job Analysis. Long Beach: California State College, 1970, p. 20. Mimeographed.

23. International Labour Office, Equal Remuneration, General Survey by the Committee of Experts on the Application of Convention and Recommendations. Geneva: International Labour Office, 1975, p. 55.

24. For a more detailed explanation of the distribution of power between the federal and provincial governments, see International Labour Office, 'Equality of opportunity and pluralism in a federal system: The Canadian experiment', International Labour Review, vol. 95 (1967) pp. 381-416.

25. Federal, Alberta, Manitoba, Northwest Territories, Nova Scotia, Ontario, Saskatchewan, and Yukon Territories.

26. A thorough discussion of court decisions in Canada is provided in an unpublished paper by B. M. Knoppers and L. L. Ward, 'Equal pay and Quebec's charter in human rights and freedom', Faculty of Law, McGill University, Montreal, 1978, pp. 17-40.

27. D. Elisburg, 'Equal pay in the United States: The development and implementation of the Equal Pay Act of 1963', in Proceedings of the Equal Pay/Equal Opportunities Conference. Toronto: Ontario Ministry of Labour, 1979, pp. 25-39.

28. For a thorough discussion of leading court decisions on equal pay in the United States, see ibid., pp. 30-35.

29. B. Seear, 'Equal pay and equal opportunity in Great Britain', in Proceedings of the Equal Pay/Equal Opportunity Conference. Toronto: Ontario Ministry of Labour, 1979, pp. 17-24.

30. For Canada, see M. Gunderson, 'Time-pattern of male-female wage differentials: Ontario 1946-1971', Industrial Relations/Relations Industrielles, vol. 31 (1976) pp. 57-71. For the United States, see E. Lazear, 'Male-female wage differentials: Has the government had any effect?', in C. L. Lloyd, E. S. Andrews, and C. L. Gilvoy, eds., Women in the Labor Market. New York: Columbia University Press, 1979, p. 331-351.

31. Whether these differences are due to employment discrimination or reflect true preferences of the two groups is not relevant here. For detailed information on occupational distribution of the labour force by sex and race, see Chapter 1.

32. In Britain, too, arguments were put forward in favour of the equal-value standard prior to the drafting of the Bill on equal pay and its consideration and passage by the Parliament. For a discussion on this point, see C. A. Larsen, 'Equal pay for women in the United Kingdom', International Labour Review, vol. 103 (1971) pp. 1-11.

33. As mentioned earlier, the federal government in Canada legislated the value standard in 1977. But federal legislation in Canada applies to only about 10 percent of the labour force.

6

TRADE UNIONS AND
DISCRIMINATION

INTRODUCTION

Many studies of discrimination assume implicitly or explicitly that discriminatory behaviour originates with the employer, but such behaviour may stem equally from consumers or from employees and their representatives, the trade unions.[1] One reason for such behaviour is that white men, who form the majority of union members, dislike associating with coloured employees or women in the workplace, particularly where minorities or women gain access to supervisory posts. A second, and probably more potent, reason is that minorities and women are seen as a potential threat to job and income security through their effect on the supply of labour. Under such circumstances, taste based models of employer discrimination suggest that wage differences between minority or female employees and white males may be necessary if the former are to obtain employment. Similar models of employee discrimination lead, in contrast, to the prediction that in the absence of employer discrimination wage differentials between the groups will, in the long run, disappear and the labour force will be, as far as possible, segregated.[2] It is clear, therefore, from this perspective, that the emphasis should be placed on segregation rather than wage differences when attempting to identify union discriminatory practises and this is germane to the various empirical studies of the phenomenon referred to below. However, if the view is taken that unions protect the interests of minority workers relative to the employer, we might expect to find a positive effect of union membership on earnings relative to non-union members, and it is therefore relevant to consider wage as well as occupational differences in employment.

In general, unions are founded on the basis of an egalitarian ideology. This may be taken to imply that the movement should not discriminate against particular groups of employees. Thus, Marshall reports that from the beginning, in the United States, Samuel Gompers and other leaders of the American Federation of Labor were committed to the organisation of workers without regard to race or religion, though circumstances eventually led to various compromises which weakened this philosophy.[3] Similarly, in Britain the Trade Union Congress (TUC) dealt with a number of resolutions concerning equal pay at its annual congress, from the late 19th century on, but these appear to have been subordinated to other policy objectives. Indeed, it appears that union policies towards minority workers are to a large extent the product of union environment. Industrial structure determines the racial or sex employment pattern, which may be taken as given by 'conservative' unions. The form of union organisation, whether on a craft or industrial basis, is also crucial. This leads Northrup[4] to conclude, again for the United States, that unions have largely been a passive agent in the advancement of Negroes in employment, but that equally, other than a few industries, they have not been a major hindrance to such progress as has occurred. This contrasts with Hill's interpretation[5] that 'the tradition of racial discrimination within trade unions is the great historic failure of organised labour.' Before examining these points in detail, however, it is necessary to review the legislation in the United States, Canada, and Britain insofar as it relates to trade unions and to examine the extent to which unions have been successful in recruiting minority workers into membership.

THE LAW AND TRADE UNIONS

The United States

The United States, relative to Canada and Britain, has a more comprehensive and complex body of statutes, presidential executive policies, and administrative regulations designed to prevent or eliminate discrimination in employment by employers and trade unions. These include:

(1) Laws and administrative guidelines such as the Civil Rights Act of 1964, as amended in 1972; the presidential Executive Orders; and the regulations and guidelines issues by the Equal Employment Opportunities Commission (EEOC) and

the Office of Federal Contract Compliance Programs (OFCCP), the agencies charged with administering the Civil Rights Act and the Executive Orders, respectively.

(2) The labour relations statutes, as well as the administrative decisions of the National Labor Relations Board (NLRB), which administers these statutes. Trade unions have been affected, far more than employers, by provisions of the National Labor Relations Act (NLRA). This is because trade unions acquire certain legal rights and duties as a result of the NLRA and the Railway Labor Act (RLA). For instance, unions which acquire the privilege of exclusive bargaining rights under these statutes have the duty to represent all members of the bargaining unit fairly.

(3) Judicial interpretations[6] and consent decrees have also considerably expanded the scope and effectiveness of anti-discrimination legislation in the United States.

(4) Fair Employment Practices laws in the State, several of the early Civil Rights Acts, such as the Civil Rights Act of 1866, as well as the U.S. Constitution (the due process clause of the 5th Amendment and the equal protection clause) can also be used by a complainant to redress a grievance.

In effect, an aggrieved party can file a charge of unfair employment practises with the appropriate state agency and ultimately with the EEOC. If the matter is not settled at the state or federal administrative levels, the employee may bring suit in a federal court. He need not exhaust the remedies provided for in the collective agreement before going to court. Even if he chooses to do so, and if his charge of employment discrimination is rejected by an arbitrator, he is not disqualified from filing a lawsuit under Title VII of the Civil Rights Act. Thus, labour/management agreements or any other agreements cannot set aside an employee's right to sue under Title VII. In most cases, an individual can either pursue these actions concurrently or await a decision which, if unfavourable, can be relitigated in a new action (Aaron, May 1976; 1978).[7]

One important qualification is included in Section 703(h) of Title VII, which provides, in part, 'Notwithstanding any other provision of this title, it shall not be an unlawful employment practice for an employer to apply different . . . terms, conditions, or privileges of employment pursuant to a bona fide seniority . . . system. . . .' This provision was included in the statute in order to make it clear that Title VII would not undermine 'vested rights' of seniority (Congressional Record 110, 6986, remarks of Senator Clark). As Aaron has stated, 'such assurance was probably necessary to obtain the powerful support of organized labor' in the passage of the Act (Aaron, 1976).[8] Seniority is sacrosanct to American unions, much more so, for instance, than in Britain. A seniority provision is embodied in virtually every collective agreement.

Canada

Two major pieces of legislation—labour relations laws and human rights statutes—specifically prohibit discrimination by trade unions. Some of the more prominent provisions of these laws are discussed below.

Labour Relations Laws

The Canada Labour Code, as amended in June 1978, prohibits trade unions from discriminating in membership (Section 134(2)), referrals for employment (Section 161.1), and a variety of other actions. The code requires the trade unions to observe 'the duty of fair representation' of all employees in the bargaining unit (Section 136.1). The unions are prohibited from requiring an employer to terminate the employment of an employee because of expulsion or suspension from membership in the trade union, except for failure to pay membership dues, initiation fee, etc. (Section 185). Similarly, a trade union is prohibited from expelling or suspending from membership, denying membership to, or taking disciplinary action or imposing a penalty in a discriminatory manner or discriminating against a person for testifying or making a disclosure or for filing a complaint against a union (Section 185).

Where a union denies membership to any employee or class of employees in a bargaining unit due to a discriminatory policy or practise, such a union would be refused certification if such discrimination were to be demonstrated. If already certified, it would be decertified after the fact and its collective agreement annulled (Section 134.2).

The Canada Labour Code provides that after June 1, 1978, unions which operate a hiring hall must establish rules regarding the assigning of work to employers via a hiring hall and post these rules in the hiring hall (Section 161.1). These rules must be applied fairly and without discrimination. In case of violation, the Canada Labour Relations Board is empowered to issue an ordinance to comply, to remedy or counteract any consequence adverse to the fulfilment of the objectives of Part V of the Code.

Similar provisions exist in several provincial labour relations statutes. For example, Ontario's Labour Relations Act contains provisions prohibiting unions from discriminating against minority groups and women in membership or referral for employment and imposes a duty of fair representation of all the employees in the bargaining unit (Section 60). The Act provides for refusal of union certification (Section 12) and annulment of a collective agreement by the Ontario Labour Relations Board if discrimination is demonstrated (Section 40(b)). Similarly, unions are prohibited from discriminating in the selection, referral, assignment, designation, or scheduling of persons for employment (Section 60(a)). Other provinces, including Nova Scotia and British Columbia, also have some of these provisions in their labour relations legislation.

Human Rights Legislation

All jurisdictions in Canada have human rights legislation and prescribe grounds upon which discrimination is prohibited. All the statutes forbid discrimination by a trade union on the prohibited grounds as specified under each of the Acts. The federal and provincial Acts forbid a trade union to exclude any person from full membership, to expel or suspend or otherwise discriminate against any of its members, or to discriminate against any person in regard to employment by an employer. The federal statute, in addition, states that discriminatory policy, practises, or agreements affecting recruitment, referral, hiring, promotion, training, apprenticeship, or any other matter relating to employment or prospective employment are forbidden.

The labour relations legislation is generally administered by the labour relations board in each jurisdiction, while the human rights legislation is the responsibility of the human rights commission in each jurisdiction. In Canada problems of restriction of union membership on prohibited grounds, such as race or colour, appear to have arisen, or at least reached the courts or labour relations boards, on relatively few occasions.

Britain

Trade unions in Britain have complete immunity for actions in tort following the Trades Disputes Act 1906, at least insofar as an act is done in contemplation or furtherance of a trade dispute. Thus, questions of the legal responsibility of unions for the acts of their officials do not often arise in practise. However, as far as discrimination is concerned, unions, like employers, are regulated by the Sex Discrimination Act (SDA) of 1975 and the Race Relations Act (RRA) of 1976. Section 17 of the SDA and Section 11 of the RRA define a trade union as an organisation of workers, an organisation of employers, or any other organisation whose members carry on a particular profession or trade for the purpose of which the organisation exists.

The SDA and RRA make it unlawful for a trade union to discriminate against a person who is not a member of account of sex, marriage, or race in the terms on which it is prepared to admit that person into membership or by refusing or deliberately omitting to accept an application for membership. Further, it is unlawful for a trade union to discriminate in relation to denial of access to benefits, deprivation of membership, or any other detriment. Both the Commission of Racial Equality (CRE) and the Equal Opportunities Commission (EOC) are empowered to carry out formal investigations when they consider that an organisation may be discriminating against a particular group; in 1979 the EOC announced that it intended to conduct an enquiry into the attitudes and practises of trade unions. In particular, it was to conduct a formal investigation into the Society of Graphical and Allied Trades (a printing union) with respect to allegedly less favourable membership conditions for women and pressures on employers to discriminate.

Section 49 of the SDA states that if a trade union is wholly or mainly elected nothing in Section 12 shall make unlawful any provision which ensures that a minimum number of persons of one sex are members of that body, either by reserving seats on the body for members of that sex or by making extra seats on that body available (by election or co-option or otherwise) for members of that sex on occasions when their number is below what is regarded as a reasonable minimum. This, however, does not make lawful any discrimination in the arrangements for determining entitlement to vote in an election of members of the body or otherwise to choose representatives to serve on that body, nor does it permit discrimination in any arrangements concerning membership in the organisation itself.

In addition to these provisions, Section 4 of the SDA and Section 2 of the RRA cover discrimination by way of victimisation. The 'discriminator' discriminates against the 'person victimised' by treating that person less favourably than others for having brought proceedings against the discriminator or any other person under the legislation or given evidence in this connection.

Legislation in the three countries relating to trade unions and discrimination has, then, followed the particular industrial relations traditions and practises of each country. In the United States and Canada general human-rights legislation has been applied to this area and federal laws have been backed up by state or provincial laws. In the United States explicit provision has been made to protect seniority provisions, and in Canada to enforce rules relating to hiring halls. In Britain, in contrast with its tradition of voluntarism or minimal regulation of industrial relations by the law, the legal framework has been restricted in comparison with those of the other two countries.

MINORITY GROUP MEMBERSHIP IN TRADE UNIONS

The United States

While in absolute terms there has been no substantial decline in trade unionism in the United States in terms of the degree of unionisation in the whole labour force, membership has declined over a period of 20 years from 26 percent to 20 percent in 1976. The growth in the percentage of union membership comprising blacks and women has, therefore, gone against the trend. It should also be noted that these figures exclude the membership of employee associations, on which data have been collected only since 1968 but suggest that they are growing. Also excluded are members of single-firm and local unaffiliated unions and those who are not union members but have their terms and conditions of employment determined by union-negotiated collective agreements (see Chamberlin, Cullen, and Lewin, 1980).[9]

In analysing disaggregated figures of unionisation, particularly in cross-section, attention must be paid to possible deficiencies in the data. Thus, the EEOC notes in relation to its own data on minority membership in 15 building trade unions that some locals fail to report, the number of minority workers in union membership is exaggerated, and non-construction workers and apprentices are included.

Ashenfelter and Godwin (1972)[10] provide time-series data back to 1886 for black workers (see Table 6.1). These show clearly that up to 1930 the percentage of the black labour force unionised was negligible, but that since that year the proportion has grown to equal that of white workers by 1967 and is projected to exceed the figure for whites by a comfortable one-third by 1980, as Table 6.2 seems to confirm. Since the bulk of unionisation in the United States was in the crafts prior to 1930, these figures are consistent with the view that industrial unions are less discriminatory than craft unions in relation to entry. Ashen-

TABLE 6.1

Estimates of the Extent of Unionization Among Black and White Workers, 1886-1967, Selected Years

Year	Total Unionists	Black Unionists	% of Black Labour Force Unionised	White Unionists	% of White Labour Force Unionised	Black Unionists as % of Total Unionists
1886	960,241	60,000	2.4	900,241	4.2	6.2
1890	540,454	3,523	.1	536,931	2.8	.7
1900	868,000	32,619	.9	835,381	3.5	3.8
1910	2,146,000	68,753	1.4	2,077,247	6.4	3.2
1926-28	3,500,000	61,000	1.1	3,439,000	7.9	1.7
1930	3,416,000	56,000	1.0	3,360,000	7.9	1.6
1940	8,717,000	600,000	10.7	8,117,000	17.3	6.9
1944	14,146,000	1,250,000	21.4	12,896,000	25.8	8.8
1955	16,802,000	1,500,000	21.3	15,302,000	26.0	8.9
1967	17,790,040	1,989,270	23.0	15,800,770	23.0	11.2
1980 (projected)	21,698,000	3,385,000	28.5	18,313,000	21.3	15.6

Source: Orley C. Ashenfelter and Lamond Godwin, 'Estimates of the Extent of Unionization Among Black and White Workers, 1886-1967, Selected Years', in Proceedings of the Twenty-fourth Annual Winter Meeting, Industrial Relations Research Association (Madison, Wi.: The Association, 1972), Table 1, p. 219.

151

TABLE 6.2

Fraction of Workers Unionised by Race and Sex,
United States, 1967, 1973, 1975, and 1976

	All Workers	Male Workers		Female Workers	
		White	Black	White	Black
1967[a]	.23	.31	.32	.12	.13
1973[b]	.26	.33	.37	.14	.22
1975	.25	.31	.37	.14	.22
1976	.22	.29		.14	

[a]1967 data are based on the Survey of Economic Opportunity and refer only to private sector workers.

[b]1973, 1975, and 1976 data are based on the U.S. Current Population Survey and include both private and government sector workers. The 1973 Survey indicates whether the worker is a union member and the 1975 Survey whether covered by a collective agreement. However, there is a 90 percent overlap between the two.

Sources:

Ashenfelter, 'Union relative wage effects: New evidence and a survey of their implications for wage inflation', Princeton University Working Paper no. 89, Industrial Relations Section, August 1976.

Antos, Chandler, and Mellow, 'Sex differences in union membership', Industrial and Labor Relations Review, vol. 33, no. 2, January 1980.

felter (1972)[11] also demonstrates that black membership in 12 craft unions in 1967 can be explained in terms of black employment as a percentage of total employment in 1890, which preceded strong unionisation. The three unions with the highest percentage of black membership in 1967, namely Common Laborers Union (30.5), Plasterers and Cement Masons Union (30.0), and Bricklayers Union (9.6), were those with the highest percentages of black employment in 1890 (20.0 percent, 10.3 percent, and 6.1 percent, respectively). The coefficient of determination between the two series was 0.96, which is significant at the 0.001 level.

Data on unionisation among blacks and women compared with white males for four years (1967, 1973, 1975, and 1976) are presented in Table 6.2, which refers to the number employed. They suggest that, at least up to 1975, black and female union-isation increased relative to that of white males, though female unionisation remains well below that of men. In 1976 women represented 20.0 percent of total union membership as opposed to 16.6 percent in 1954, but this is well below their representa-tion in the total labour force, and the proportion of women organised in unions (excluding employee associations) was lower in 1976 than in any year since 1952 (Chamberlin, Cullen, and Lewin, 1980).[12] However, as Bloch (1977)[13] notes, to some extent this may reflect the shifting race/sex composition of the workforce across occupations and industries and also the growth of union membership in sectors (such as the government sector, excluded in the 1967 survey), which were not previously union-ised. This idea has been tested by Antos, Chandler, and Mellow (1980)[14] who estimate union membership equations by logit analy-sis with data taken from the 1976 Current Population Survey, based on a human-capital model with age, education, race, sex, occupation, and industry as explanatory variables. Non-whites made up 13 percent of union members and 10 percent of non-union members in 1976, and holding the above factors constant, it was also found that being non-white has a positive effect on the probability of union membership. Women were 26 percent of union members and 48 percent of non-union members in the sample, but almost 57 percent of the male/female unionisation differential is eliminated by controlling for occupational and industrial status, and a further small amount when education and age are allowed for. Putting it another way, if the female occupational and industrial pattern were altered to conform to the male, there would be an increase of roughly 50 percent in the number of female union members. The investigators note that part of the unmeasured gap could represent discrimination and accept that segmentation of the market may mean that differ-ences in occupation and industry represent indirect discrimina-tion.

A breakdown of the 1967 figures by occupational group (see Ashenfelter, 1973)[15] shows that in the case of men, white blue-collar workers are much more likely to be unionised than their black equivalents, while the reverse is true for sales, clerical, managerial, and professional workers. Similarly, for women unionisation among sales, clerical, and professional workers is much higher for blacks. A rather more comprehensive breakdown of unionisation by occupation, sex, and race (for 1970) is provided in Table 6.3, which is derived from U.S. Department of Labor data. This tends to confirm the above observations, though the differences are less marked. The EEOC study concludes from a historical analysis of the position of blacks and women in unions that there has been minimal progress in the entry of blacks into the skilled building trade unions, where discrimination has traditionally been most marked, over the period 1900 to 1972; that in recent years the proportion of women in unions has actually declined (as outlined above); and that there is still considerable sex segregation among union members.

In addition to membership in unions, representation of minority groups in the government of unions is important. As Chamberlain, Cullen, and Lewin note, unions, including those with substantial or even majority female memberships, are dominated by male leaderships. Le Grande (1978)[16] shows that in the United States in 1976 only 57 official positions in unions were held by women and there were only 47 women officials, though this is an improvement over the situation in 1956 (33 and 29, respectively). In 1976 there were only two women in the elective office of president and seven secretary-treasurers, while a further 48 held appointive positions. A similar situation holds for black workers. The U.S. Commission on Civil Rights (1976)[17] reports that only five out of 177 national unions had minority male presidents and that minority males were poorly represented in other executive positions.

Canada

As there are no data on union membership by race in Canada, it is necessary here to concentrate on female representation in the unions. Female union membership in 1977 was 28.6 percent of total union membership (885,504), as opposed to 27 percent (750,637) in 1976. These figures represent a considerable increase from the 16.4 percent rate in 1962, when Statistics Canada began collecting data from trade unions under the provisions of the Corporations and Labour Unions Returns Act (CALURA).

Since 1962, women have been joining both the labour force and the trade unions much more rapidly than their male counterparts. Moreover, union activity of Canadian women has risen even more than their increased labour force participation. For instance, the rise in union membership of women was 202 percent from 1962 to 1976 (160 percent of this in the ten years between

TABLE 6.3

Wage and Salary Workers in Labour Unions and Membership Rates by Occupation, Sex, and Race in the United States, 1970 (All workers, including part-time and seasonal employees)

Occupation of Longest Job Held in 1970	All Races		Male				Female			
			White		Black, Asian American and Native American		White		Black, Asian American and Native American	
	Number in Labour Unions	Percent in Labour Unions	Number in Labour Unions	Percent in Labour Unions	Number in Labour Unions	Percent in Labour Unions	Number in Labour Unions	Percent in Labour Unions	Number in Labour Unions	Percent in Labour Unions
All occupations	17,192	20.4	12,009	27.6	1,496	29.0	3,053	9.8	634	13.8
Professional, technical, and kindred workers	1,032	9.0	586	9.6	43	12.0	351	7.7	53	12.2
Managers, officials, and proprietors, except farm	514	7.5	440	8.1	23	15.8	43	3.6	8	—*
Clerical and kindred workers	2,058	13.1	930	28.7	131	32.8	845	7.6	152	16.1
Salesworkers	261	4.9	145	5.4	8	9.6	101	4.1	8	6.6
Craft and kindred workers, supervisors of blue collar workers	4,328	42.7	3,996	44.0	243	40.2	79	19.0	11	—
Operatives and kindred workers	6,093	40.4	4,007	47.2	592	41.8	1,246	28.5	248	31.6
Non-farm labourers	1,471	28.9	1,172	30.1	285	27.6	47	17.1	17	—
Service workers, including private household	1,409	10.9	769	20.2	167	19.9	337	5.3	137	6.9

*Negligible.

Source: U.S. Department of Labor, Bureau of Labor Statistics, Selected Earnings and Demographic Characteristics of Union Members, 1970.

1966 and 1976), contrasted with a rise of about 115 percent in the female labour force[18] (see Table 6.4). The 27-percent rate of unionised women fell considerably short of the 37.5-percent female proportion of the workforce in 1976, however.

The majority of Canadian workers do not belong to a union, and proportionately fewer women than men are unionised. As Table 6.5 shows, there were 8,263,000 paid workers and 3,041,941 union members in Canada in 1976. Only 36.8 percent of these workers were union members—42.9 percent of men and 26.8 percent of women in the paid workforce. There is, therefore, a considerable scope for increased unionisation of the female workforce in Canada. In addition, industries with a relatively lower degree of unionisation, such as services, trade, and finance, are predominantly female; the proportion of women is 40 percent or greater in each of these industries, which account for over 70 percent of all female employment (see Table 6.5). The potential for female employment and membership is increasing much more rapidly in these sectors than in the more highly unionised sectors; for instance, female employment increased 70 percent more rapidly than that of men between 1962 and 1975.[19] Increased unionisation of women will not be without difficulties. The predominantly female industries are difficult to organise for a variety of reasons, including the small size of most firms[20] and the lack of militancy and union consciousness among white-collar workers.[21] The difficulty of organising in these sectors is confirmed by the fact that male unionisation is also low in services, trade, and finance, as shown in Table 6.5.

If unionisation of female workers is to expand and to be effective in representing women, those women must take a more active role in the management of the unions. As Table 6.6 indicates, women are not represented on the executive boards of Canadian unions in proportion to their overall membership; women constituted 9-12 percent of the executive board members of unions from 1971 to 1976, even though they constituted 23-27 percent of all union members during the same period. This lower representation in the management of unions can be accounted for by numerous reasons, including women immigrant members having language problems, most women belonging to unions with a predominantly male membership,[22] and women's membership being concentrated in a few organisations.[23]

Table 6.6 shows that national unions have consistently had the highest percentage of women board members relative to international and government unions: women board members in national unions ranged from almost 13 percent to 17 percent from 1971 to 1976. In 1977 the national unions increased their share of

TABLE 6.4

Changes in the Labour Force and Union Activity by Sex in Canada, 1962 and 1976

| | Women | | | | | | Men | | | | | |
| | 1962 | | 1976 | | Percent | | 1962 | | 1976 | | Percent | |
	Number	Per-cent	Number	Per-cent	Increase 1962–1976		Number	Per-cent	Number	Per-cent	Increase 1962–1976	
Labour force	1,788,000	27.1	3,837,000	37.6	+114.6		4,819,000	72.9	6,369,000	62.4	+32.2	
Union members	248,884	16.4	750,637	27.0	+201.6		1,266,021	83.6	2,028,085	73.0	+60.2	

Note: The figures under the Corporations and Labour Unions Returns Act, unlike the survey carried out by the Canada Department of Labour, do not include those for independent local unions. The total union member-ship reported by the CALURA report in 1976 was 2,778,722, compared with 3,041,941 reported by Labour Canada. The CALURA figures are reported as of December 31 and the Labour Canada figures as of January 1.

Sources: For Labour force: Canada Yearbook 1965 and 1978/79, Statistics Canada, Ottawa. For Union activity: Corporations and Labour Unions Returns Act (CALURA), 1976, Part II, Statistics Canada, Ottawa, August 1978.

TABLE 6.5

Paid Workers[a] and Union Members in Selected Industries,[b] and Union Members as Percentage of Paid Workers, by Sex, and Women Union Members as Percentage of Total Union Members, Canada, January 1976

Industry	Women			Men			Total Union Members	Women Union Members as Percentage of Total Union Members (percent)
	Paid Workers (thousands)	Union Members	Union Members as Percentage of Paid Workers (percent)	Paid Workers (thousands)	Union Members	Union Members as Percentage of Paid Workers (percent)		
Agriculture	24	270	1.1	82	2,734	3.3	3,004	9.0
Manufacturing	446	161,237	36.2	1,364	704,960	51.7	866,197	18.6
Construction	37	3,716	10.0	407	300,539	73.8	304,255	1.2
Trade	596	43,867	7.4	891	87,824	9.9	131,691	33.3
Community, business and personal services	1,388	417,292	30.1	917	336,520	36.7	753,812	55.4
Transportation, communication and other utilities	164	74,858	45.6	626	365,235	58.3	440,093	17.0
Public administration	205	129,763	63.3	459	306,632	66.8	436,395	29.7
Finance, insurance, real estate	260	5,635	2.2	196	3,607	1.8	9,242	61.0
All industries[c]	3,131	839,849	26.8	5,132	2,202,092	42.9	3,041,941	27.6

[a]Includes any employed person who worked for salary, wages, tips, piece rates, commission or payment in kind. Working owners, working shareholders, or executives of an incorporated business are paid workers.

[b]Excluded are certain industries with very few women workers: forestry, fishing and trapping, and mines, quarries and oil wells.

[c]Including those categories not shown separately in the table.

Sources: Paid workers: Unpublished data from Statistics Canada, Labour Force Survey Division. Union members: Unpublished data from Labour Canada, Labour Organisations Section. Reprinted from Women in the Labour Force: Facts & Figures, Ottawa: Labour Canada, 1976 edition, Table 2, p. 7.

TABLE 6.6

Women Executive Board Members as Percentage of
Total Executive Board Members, by Type of Union,
in Canada, 1971-1977

Type of Union	1971	1972	1973	1974	1975	1976	1977
Total Executive Board Members							
International*	116	132	170	170	142	158	112
National	389	460	417	417	541	589	636
Government	209	413	352	352	483	402	443
Total	714	1005	939	939	1166	1149	1191
Women Executive Board Members							
International*	6	5	5	5	6	8	5
National	49	65	57	57	74	99	155
Government	13	24	19	19	36	29	39
Total	68	94	81	81	116	136	199
Women as Percent of Total							
International*	5.2	3.8	2.9	2.9	4.2	5.1	4.5
National	12.6	14.1	13.7	13.7	13.7	16.8	24.4
Government	6.2	5.8	5.4	5.4	7.5	7.2	8.8
Total	9.5	9.4	8.6	8.6	9.9	11.8	16.7

*Figures relate to Canadian board members only.
Source: Corporations and Labour Unions Returns Act Administration, Statistics Canada; personal correspondence.

female board members to 24 percent. This in part reflects the fact that national unions have more women members than other unions. In 1976, of the total women members reported, 44.9 percent were in national unions, while 34.5 percent belonged to international unions and 20.6 percent were in government employees organisations.[24]

Britain

In comparing British and North American experience with respect to co-worker discrimination against minority groups, two features must be stressed at the outset. First, the extent of unionisation is approximately twice as great in Britain as in North America, and therefore the potential for influencing the welfare of minority group workers is that much the greater. Second, racial minorities in Britain form a much smaller proportion of the total working population, include a much higher ratio of immigrant workers, and may have their employment prospects diminished by language problems to a much greater extent than minorities in North America. For women the comparisons between Britain and North America are much closer.

According to Smith (1976),[25] members of racial minority groups comprised 2.5 percent of the population of Britain in 1971 and 1.8-2.12 percent of adults (750,000), and nearly all of these were themselves immigrants. Immigration statistics reveal that by 1976 the non-white population of Britain had reached 1.6 million, or 2.9 percent of the total population. Smith (1977)[26] shows that no less than 70 percent of Pakistani women speak English slightly or not at all; the corresponding figure for Indian women is 60 percent, for African-Asian women 41 percent, for male Pakistanis 43 percent, for male Indians 26 percent, and for male African-Asians 19 percent. In Daniel's 1968 survey every informant mentioned language as the greatest difficulty connected with the employment of immigrant workers and a factor which tended to confine them to lower levels of manual work. These factors give rise to problems of interpretation.

Thus, as Smith (1976)[27] notes, 'the question arises how far the lower job levels of the minorities are the result of inferior academic or job qualifications, and how far of other factors, such as racial discrimination and the difficulty of adapting to the work situation in a new country'. Immigrant workers are also less likely to be familiar with the conventions of union organisation and likely to be more difficult to organise because of problems of communication. Particularly in times of depressed economic activity, they are likely to be seen by indigenous workers as a threat to income and job security.

Smith (1974)[28] also questions whether minority groups have participated as fully as they might in union activities. It is not known how many members of racial minorities hold official union positions, as no unions maintain statistics on the racial composition of their membership, but it appears that there are virtually no full-time officers. Smith reports that 'in 1972 the Transport and General Workers Union took in the first full-time official in the country who was not white. Such a situation could hardly exist without some racial discrimination on the part of the unions at a high level'.[29] Brooks (1975)[30] finds in the case of London Transport that immigrant participation in union activities is less than that of indigenous workers and that considerably more of the immigrants are less interested in union offices. While a majority of immigrants had never been to a branch meeting and felt that they were in a sense excluded from the union, there was little evidence of separate industrial organisation on the part of immigrant groups.

The survey by Smith (1976)[31] suggests that trade union membership is, if anything, higher among minority groups than among the white population (see Table 6.7). While to some extent industrial distribution of employment is favourable to unionisation of immigrants, correcting for this reduces union membership for men only from 60 percent to 57 percent (as opposed to 47 percent for white men). Again, distribution by plant does not appear to be significant, so that 'the high level of union membership among minority men tends to resist attempts to explain it away'. It is, indeed, remarkable that 60 percent of Asian men who speak no English at all are members of a trade union, though it is not known how far this is due to the existence of the closed shop. Smith suggests that one-third of minority men who are union members belong to the Transport and General Workers Union, while the Amalgamated Union of Engineering Workers and the National Union of Railwaymen (NUR) also have higher than average concentrations of minority men. Brooks (1975)[32] finds similarly on the railways that immigrant union membership is slightly higher than that for the native population. Allen, Bentley, and Bornat (1977)[33] find in Bradford, however, that only 16.2 percent of coloured workers are unionised, compared with 46.0 percent of white workers, though 'unionisation is not uniformly high for white workers not uniformly low for coloured workers'. The explanation of this finding, which appears to be at variance with that of other studies, as the investigators note, is probably that in Bradford coloured workers are heavily concentrated in industries and occupations where the unions have been traditionally weak. Thus, in the textile industry coloured workers are concentrated in combing and spinning rather than in dyeing and finishing, where unionisation is relatively high.

As far as women are concerned, in some unions their absolute numbers are much more substantial than is the case for racial

TABLE 6.7

Percent Trade Union Membership by Country of Origin

Men		Women	
White	47	West Indian	39
West Indian	64	Total Asian	31
Pakistani/Bangladeshi	59	Asian membership	
Indian	63	by religion	
African-Asian	51	Moslem	18
		Hindu	37
		Sikh	33

Source: D. J. Smith, 1976. The fact of racial disadvantage: A national survey, Political and Economic Planning, vol. XLII, Broadsheet no. 560 (February 1976).

minority groups. While the degree of unionisation is much lower for women than for men, it is female unionisation that has been growing rapidly in recent years, reflecting the increased employment opportunities for women. In 1978 eleven unions (Footwear Leather and Allied Trades Union; National Union of Hosiery and Knitwear Workers; Tailors and Garment Workers Union; Shop, Distributive and Allied Workers; Tobacco Workers Union; Confederation of Health Service Employees; Health Visitors Association; National Union of Public Employees; National Union of Teachers; Civil and Public Services Association; and Association of Professional, Executive, Clerical and Computer Staff), some of them among the largest unions in the country, had a majority of female members, although official posts in these unions are invariably dominated by men. As Table 6.8 shows, between 1967 and 1977 female union membership in toto increased by over two-thirds at a time when male membership increased by only 13 percent, but the difference in union representation still remains substantial. Further, as Table 6.9 illustrates, in Britain representation of women as full-time officials, on National Executive Committees, and as TUC delegates is small and well below what one would expect on the basis of women's share of total union membership. Whatever the cause, it is clear that issues central to women are unlikely to receive high priority in the union decision-making process until these facts alter.

TABLE 6.8

Trade Union Membership in Britain

	Total Labour Force (thousands)		Trade Union Membership (thousands)		Percent of Potential Membership		Cumulative Percent Increase on Actual Membership	
	Men	Women	Men	Women	Men	Women	Men	Women
1967	14,927.6	8,397.4	7,908	2,286	53.0	27.2	—a	—
1968	14,866.4	8,429.7	7,836	2,364	53.0	28.0	-0.9	3.4
1969	14,657.2	8,508.6	7,972	2,507	54.4	29.5	0.8	9.7
1970	14,527.0	8,517.8	8,444	2,743	58.1	32.2	6.8	20.0
1971	14,381.8	8,476.1	8,382	2,753	58.3	32.5	6.0	20.4
1972	14,372.9	8,795.7	8,452	2,907	58.8	33.1	6.9	27.2
1973	14,252.0	9,033.5	8,450	3,006	59.3	33.3	6.9	31.5
1974	14,231.9	9,354.2	8,586	3,178	60.3	34.0	8.6	39.0
1975b	14,393.5	9,458.3	8,729	3,464	60.6	36.6	10.4	51.5
1975	14,393.5	9,458.3	8,600	3,427	59.7	36.2	8.8	49.9
1976	14,461.0	9,618.6	8,825	3,561	61.0	37.0	11.6	55.8
1977	14,437.7	9,741.1	8,953	3,753	62.0	38.5	13.2	64.2

aNot applicable.
bChanges have been made in the way union statistics are collected. Both the old and new figures are given for 1975.
Source: Equal Opportunities Commission, Third Annual Report, 1978, HMSO, 1979.

TABLE 6.9

Representation of Women in Certain Trade Unions in Britain, September 1976

Union	Women as Percent of Membership	Full-Time Officials	National Executive Committee Members	TUC Delegates
APEX[b]	55	1 (3)[a]	4 (8)	3 (7)
CATU[c]	53	0 (3)	2 (9)	2 (4)
COHSE[d]	70	5 (28)	1 (19)	0 (5)
CPSA[e]	68	4 (19)	8 (17)	8 (20)
NUHKW[f]	73	2 (22)	2 (18)	1 (8)
NUPE[g]	65	2 (79)	6 (16)	4 (21)
NUT[h]	75	2 (19)	4 (36)	1 (23)
NUTGW[i]	88	6 (35)	5 (13)	5 (13)

TWU[j]	65	3 (5)	1 (12)	1 (3)
USDAW[k]	59	4 (78)	1 (10)	5 (15)

[a]Figures in parentheses are the number of women needed in each kind of position to match their share of the union membership.

[b]Association of Professional and Executive Staff

[c]Ceramic and Allied Trade Union

[d]Confederation of Health Service Employees

[e]Civil and Public Services Association

[f]National Union of Hosiery and Knitwear Workers

[g]National Union of Public Employees

[h]National Union of Teachers

[i]National Union of Tailors and Garment Workers

[j]Tobacco Workers Union

[k]Union of Shop, Distributive and Allied Workers

Source: Low Pay Unit Bulletin, no. 14 (April 1977).

165

There are, then, similarities in the three countries with respect to the representation of minorities in unions, though comparison is made difficult by the lack of detailed statistics on racial composition of memberships of unions in Britain and Canada. In each country there has been a significant increase in female participation in the labour force and a growth in the number of female union members, though their proportion of union members is much lower than that of men. In both North America and Britain, on the other hand, racial minorities appear to have a higher degree of unionisation than their white equivalents. Women and racial minorities are significantly underrepresented in the government of unions. The context has, however, been different, for while in Britain unionisation has reached unprecedented levels (over 50 percent of the workforce) in the post-war period, white male unionisation has actually fallen in the United States and Canada.

These factors still leave the question of whether, on balance, unions have assisted or hindered the progress of minority and female workers. It is to this question we must now turn, recognising that it is necessary to distinguish between different types of union (notably craft and industrial) and different levels of union government (namely national and local) before it is possible to come to an unequivocal conclusion.

TYPE OF UNION

As Ashenfelter[34] points out, at the extremes we may distinguish between those unions which attempt to influence pay and conditions by limiting the available supply of labour (e.g. craft unions) and those which attempt to do so by means of a bargained settlement based on a strike threat (e.g. industrial unions). In the former case, it is necessary to determine some basis for exclusion from membership; this may be effected by distinguishing group characteristics such as race and sex, which in certain circumstances may result in the exclusion of substantial numbers of potential members. This exclusion may be achieved indirectly by limiting membership predominantly to friends and relatives of incumbent members.[35] In the alternative case, where power depends on the ability to organise a substantial proportion of the total labour force, any attempt to limit membership will reduce the potency of the strike threat; discrimination is therefore more difficult to implement. Here minority groups are dependent on the strength of employers' motives to hire them and on their ability to threaten the wage rates and job control procedures

of unionists.[36] As Bloch[37] notes, the conflict between improvement in pay and conditions of union members and the organisation
of minority groups is greatest when unemployment is high, since
in that case unemployed non-unionist minority workers can be
substituted for union members in the event of a strike. Historically there are instances of blacks being employed as strike
breakers in a number of industries in the United States, including
the automobile, iron and steel, coal, and clothing industries
(though cases of female labour being used in this way are less
clearly documented). Thus we would hypothesise that craft
unions, or indeed any organisation or profession in which admission involves the approval of a licensing body, [38] are likely to
be more discriminatory than industrial unions.

Within the craft sector in North America it is, however,
necessary to distinguish between referral[39] and non-referral
unions. In certain industries such as construction, transportation (including maritime and longshore), printing and publishing,
hotels and restaurants, food and kindred products, and apparel
and retail trades, employers depend primarily on unions for
their supply of labour. While it is suggested that referral unions
comprise less than 15 percent of organised labour in the United
States, [40] the total membership (referral and non-referral) of
the major international unions in the above industries was estimated at 8.8 million in 1970.[41] In such industries unions often
operate 'hiring halls' which are limited to union members and
operate as private employment agencies for workers and those
employers who have signed agreements to hire labour solely
through this mechanism. Here denial of union membership is
equivalent to denial of opportunities for employment. Wolkinson
(1973)[42] notes that in some instances a local union will operate
an exclusive job referral system under which the employer is
obliged by contract to obtain his entire workforce through the
union (as occurs in the printing industry in Britain), while in
others a non-exclusive referral system operates, under which
an employer hires a proportion of his workforce himself and
obtains the balance through the local union. The United States
Commission on Civil Rights points out that in 1970 the proportion
of minority males in highly paid occupations such as carpentry,
construction crafts, and printing was markedly below their
proportion among all union members, and a similar situation is
found with respect to white and non-white women. However,
it is difficult to determine precisely how far such differences
represent the policies of the unions as such and how far they
represent self-selection on the part of minority workers themselves.

Unfortunately, the data used by Ashenfelter to test for the effect of craft unions on discrimination in the United States is not available for Britain, but as Jain and Young (1978-1979)[43] note, a number of detailed investigations of union practises at the plant level have tended to support the hypothesis that craft union restrictions have limited the opportunities available to immigrant workers. Thus, Patterson (1968)[44] reports that union pressure in printing and engineering toolrooms led to a policy of rejecting immigrant labour. However, it appears that resistance to immigrant labour has been no less marked among the general unions, perhaps reflecting the fact that much of this potential labour is relatively unskilled. Daniel (1968)[45] reports that 44 percent of those from racial minority groups in his survey who were members of general unions claimed to have experienced employment discrimination, as opposed to 39 percent in craft and industrial unions and 35 percent in the case of non-union members.[46]

In considering union race or sex practises it is also necessary to distinguish between national and local representation. As Marshall (1974)[47] points out, the motive for equality strengthens as we move from the local to the national level because the latter has broader political objectives. Further, whereas the national union perceives that power is a function of size of membership, at the local level it is seen to depend more narrowly on control of labour supply within the local labour market. This is clearly illustrated in U.S. construction unions, where, due to the fact that collective bargaining is a local function, economic power is concentrated in the local or district councils. In order to maintain wage levels at a high level, local union leaders, according to Glover and Marshall (1977),[48] often attempt to restrict the number of skilled craft workers, while national leaders have, in contrast, attempted to strengthen the union through membership drives. In these situations the authority of the union leadership becomes crucial, and here, Ashenfelter (1972)[49] suggests, three factors are significant. First, the nature of the political mechanism by which the leadership remains in power will influence the extent to which the views of the white or male majority and the black or female minority influence the race or sex policy of the union. Second, the nature of the economic mechanism by which the leadership attempts to satisfy the pecuniary and non-pecuniary expectations of the membership will determine the effect of the above policy on the minority workforce through such features as exclusion from or inclusion in union membership and opportunities for upgrading or promotion. Third, the actual or potential size of the minority group membership of the union will determine precisely what the policy will be. The likelihood of implementation of an anti-discriminatory union policy is likely to be positively correlated with the size of the minority group relative to the majority for two reasons. The stronger feelings of black or female workers towards such policies compared with those of whites or males may create a such disproportionate effect on policy through log-rolling tactics[50] and unequal treatment that there is a greater danger of union labour being substituted by non-unionists. Also, to some extent the likelihood of egalitarian policies may be influenced by the representation of women and minorities in leadership positions. Where these groups are small relative to the majority, however, there is little likelihood that individuals from among them will be elected to key positions in the union, as has been shown to be the case earlier.

In Britain there are also striking differences in attitude between national, local, and plant union policies. Up to 1974 the TUC tended to adopt a policy of non-intervention (despite a general policy of opposition to racial discrimination) on the grounds that the most serious problem was that of the failure of immigrant workers to integrate sufficiently with indigenous workers (Miles and Phizacklea (1978)).[51] However, following certain disputes with racial aspects (referred to below), from 1974 a more positive approach was adopted. In 1975 the General Council formed a special sub-committee, the Equal Rights Committee, to focus attention on minority groups which may be discriminated against because of factors such as race, sex, or religion. Specific tasks for this body were to include the preparation of union recruitment literature in minority languages and the examination of union rule books to ensure that these did not put minority groups at a disadvantage unnecessarily. Hepple (1968)[52] supports the view put forward in the United States that there is a conflict between national union policies and the actions of local branches. Full-time union officials are likely to identify their interests as being synonymous with the well being of the union and, particularly in the case of general unions, as being better served by a policy of inclusiveness. Branch officials and shop stewards may see, however, that immigrant workers are a possible threat to their own living standards. 'It appears that a frequent if unsatisfactory compromise is to re-affirm union policy while making little effort to implement it' (Jain and Young 1978).[53] Thus, Smith (1977)[54] reports that while unions had seldom made formal representations against racial minorities, they had seldom made positive representations on their behalf either, and 25 percent of plants said that there were complaints from white workers when members of racial minorities were first hired, though this opposition generally abated subsequently.

Thus, both North American and British experience suggests that patterns of discrimination differ between craft and industrial unions. This is not unexpected, as the former are generally organised horizontally and the latter vertically. In contrast to craft unions, which have certainly in some cases prevented blacks and other minorities from becoming members of the union, industrial unions may discriminate against them after they have been admitted into the collective-bargaining unit. Such unions may actively prevent the participation of non-whites and minorities in union leadership positions and fail to process their grievances.

DIFFERENCES BY REGION, OCCUPATION, AND INDUSTRY

The United States

While suggesting that employers' practises are likely to have more influence than union practises on Negro employment patterns in the United States, since the latter's membership is no more than a third of the non-agricultural labour force, Norgren and Hill (1964)[55] suggest that unions have been important determinants of Negro employment patterns (and, it can similarly be argued, of sex employment patterns) in particular geographical areas, occupations, and industries.

Much has been made in the literature of differences in treatment of the races between the North and the South. It is held that unions which developed under the influence of the traditions of the South are likely to find it difficult to adopt egalitarian policies and hence are likely to discriminate (Northrup (1971)).[56] Again Norgren and Hill (1964) argue that:

the predominant pattern of union racial practices in the South is one of widespread discrimination, characterised by pervasive exclusion of Negroes in the craft-oriented industries, and of job segregation in the industries organised by industrial unions. Thus, one must conclude that, on balance, unions have impeded rather than enhanced the Southern Negro's occupational progress.

Marshall (1965),[57] however, points out that historically in the
North, where unions were stronger and coloured craft workers
fewer, it was almost impossible for Negroes from the South to
gain employment, while skilled openings were available to them
in the South. Union/non-union wage differentials do appear to
be larger for black males (though not for black females) in the
South, but Oaxaca (1975)[58] points out, this does not necessarily
reflect non-discriminatory practises or otherwise on the part of
the unions in the South. Rather, it could reflect the fact that
non-union wages, being less frequently determined by national
standards, are lower than in other parts of the country. Neither
would we expect the effect of unions to be constant across occupations and industries. Craft unions in particular will, as noted
earlier, restrict entry to skilled trades, thereby having a depressing effect on the wages of the unskilled relative to the
wages of the skilled but possibly a favourable effect on the earnings of those minority workers who are able to surmount the
entry barriers into the skilled trades. Inter-industry earnings
differentials will themselves be influenced by the skill structure
within each industry. It is the construction industry that has
caught the attention of academics above all other industries, but
even here it has been noted that the position of bricklayers,
plasterers, and finishers differs from that of plumbers, pipe
fitters, and electricians (Ashenfelter (1973)).[59] The former
group contained a significant number of black workers prior
to unionisation, while the trades in the latter group, being unionised from their formation at a later stage of technological development, are much more discriminatory. It is estimated that the
building trades contain three-fifths of all referral union
membership—about 1.5 million workers in total. Both Dubinsky
(1973)[60] and Wolkinson (1973)[61] point out that the membership
procedures of the building trades lend themselves to discriminatory practises. Most of the unions in the industry admit members
through a fraternal system that requires sponsorship by two or
more members and a majority vote in favour of admission by the
membership of the local union. In effect this works to the benefit
of relatives and friends of those in the industry, and since few
blacks are members, they tend to be excluded from the informal
selection system. Wolkinson also notes that the printing industry
parallels the construction industry in its use of hiring halls,
which are in its case referred to as 'out of work rooms', in which
unemployed craft workers obtain information on job openings.
In other industries the situation may be less extreme. In the
automobile industry, for example, Negroes have perhaps made
their major advances (Northrup 1971),[62] while in the steel indus-

try Negroes hold a high proportion of skilled jobs in some areas
but are excluded from others. The situation may also vary over
time. In the building trades, despite relatively small changes
in the racial composition of construction union membership,
Glover and Marshall find that on a national scale minorities have
made significant gains in building trades apprenticeships. In
the coal industry, in contrast, mechanisation has caused a loss
of jobs for Negroes, since few of them have had the opportunity
of working on machines. For example, Northrup notes that
while Negroes once held approximately 25 percent of the jobs
in the Southern Appalachian region, the figure has dwindled
to a low level in many states. This experience points out the
importance of examining current entry to new job openings as
well as mean employment level of minority groups, and also of
conducting time-series as well as cross-section analyses.

Britain

Although racial minorities make up a very small proportion
of the labour force in Britain, it should be borne in mind that
they tend to be very concentrated geographically in cities such
as London, Birmingham, and Bradford and that immigrants have
in the past entered jobs which proved to be unattractive to
indigenous labour. Hence they tend to be concentrated indus-
trailly in industries such as textiles, health, and transport
and occupationally in unskilled or semi-skilled tasks.[63]
Table 6.10, which summarises the positions of a sample of
3292 Asians and West Indians and 1239 white men in 1974, suggests that the gap between Pakistani and white men with respect
to mean level of skill is particularly wide. It seems that members
of racial minorities with equivalent academic qualifications find
it particularly difficult to obtain management, professional, or
white-collar jobs, but differences are much less marked between
the racial minorities and indigenous workers at the skilled manual
level (Smith 1976).[64] Regional location influences this picture.
Thus, it appears that only 6 percent of Asian men in the areas
of highest concentration are doing non-manual jobs, compared
with 46 percent of those in the areas of lowest concentration.
As Table 6.11 suggests, a much higher proportion of the minority
than of the white population is employed in the manufacturing
industry, in part no doubt reflecting the relative abundance
of unskilled and semi-skilled jobs in this sector. There is also
a tendency for minority men to be employed in larger plants
than whites, which should make it easier, on the average, for
unions to recruit this group into union membership.

TABLE 6.10

Job Level Analysed by Country of Origin—Men

Job Level	White (percent)		West Indian (percent)		Pakistani/ Bangladeshi (percent)		Indian (percent)		African/ Asian (percent)	
Professional/management	23	} 40	2	} 8	4	} 8	8	} 20	10	} 30
White-collar	17		6		4		12		20	
Skilled manual	42		59		33		44		44	
Semi-skilled manual	12	} 18	23	} 32	38	} 58	27	} 36	24	} 26
Unskilled manual	6		9		20		9		2	
Not classified	1		1		1		—*		—	

*Equals nil.
Source: D. J. Smith, The fact of racial disadvantage: A national survey, Political and Economic Planning, vol. XLII, Broadsheet no. 560 (February 1976).

173

TABLE 6.11

Type of Industry Analysed by Country of Origin—Men and Women

Industry	West Indian (percent)	Pakistani/ Bangladeshi (percent)	Indian (percent)	Asian African (percent)	General Population (percent)
Shipbuilding and vehicles	7	12	12	6	4
Textiles	1	26	10	6	2
Construction	7	1	4	7	7
Transport and communication	10	5	12	11	7
Distributive trades	3	7	9	15	13
Professional and scientific services	9	2	6	3	12

Note: Table includes selected industries only.
Source: D. J. Smith, The fact of racial disadvantage: A national survey, Political and Economic Planning, vol. XLII, Broadsheet no. 560 (February 1976).

As for women, approximately half of their number are engaged in three major service industries—professional and scientific services, the distributive trades, and miscellaneous services, where traditionally unions have been weak (Table 6.6). This is consistent with the picture in North America. These industries tend to use skills analogous to those used in household activities, involving light rather than heavy physical demands, requiring a high degree of manual dexterity, or involving considerable contact with female consumers. As for occupational distribution (Table 6.7), two-thirds of women are found in non-manual occupations, as opposed to one-third of men. The vast bulk of female employees are found in a limited number of occupations where women are engaged in part-time work (defined as working less than 30 hours per week); this group, with a relatively weak work attachment, is particularly difficult to attract into union membership. Thus, while for women geographical segregation is much less marked than for racial minorities, both in North America and Britain, occupationally and industrially they tend to be crowded into a few sectors of employment.

PATTERNS OF UNION DISCRIMINATION

Complete Exclusion and Restriction of Supply

As Dodge (1972)[65] notes, there are three ways in which the supply of labour may be restricted in order to maintain a wage differential in one occupation over another demanding similar skills. First, unions may negotiate higher than equilibrium wages in an occupation and prevent employers from offering lower wages despite the existence of a queue of qualified applicants. Second, unions may control hiring through 'hiring halls' as outlined above. Third, government sanctioned licencing bodies may impose qualifications for entry into an occupation which are higher than performance of the job requires. Each of these methods implies some form of rationing; which type may depend on whether it is the employer, the union, or a licencing body which actually carries out the rationing function. Dodge notes that possible forms of rationing include nepotism, requirements for high levels of education and training, tests of ability on entry, and entry fees. Broadly, we may distinguish between price and non-price rationing devices. In the former an admission fee is received from each new member, so that there is an incentive for the union to expand membership further than otherwise would be the case, the equilibrium admission fee from the point of view of labour adjustment being that which equals the difference between the net present value of the income stream received by a union member over the relevant period and what the same member would receive in the next best paid occupation. Non-price rationing may take the form of nepotism. In practice, Becker (1959)[66] notes, while price rationing would seem to be the most rational policy for a union to adopt, it is rarely used. This may be symptomatic of discriminatory behaviour, since if price-rationing is adopted the union must pay for any discrimination. Suppose a union wishes to admit an additional number of white men but some applicants are black or female. It would then be necessary to lower the admission fee to ensure sufficient white male mambers, and the difference between the actual and the non-discriminatory fee would measure the cost of discrimination against minority groups in unions that restrict entry by means of non-price rather than price rationing devices.

Occupational licencing in the United States began in the 19th century and, according to Rottenberg (1962),[67] covered more than 80 occupations by the 1950s, including doctors, nurses, pharmacists, funeral directors, embalmers, beauticians, barbers, real estate brokers, salesmen, engineers, and plumbers. If licencing standards are imposed on new entrants but not on incumbents, this will create windfall gains for workers already employed and encourage the continual raising of entry standards. Thus, in the case of barbering it is suggested that the educational requirement is longer than the skill and knowledge relevant to the craft would imply, including as it does skills relevant to other crafts. The effect of these restrictions will be to limit opportunities for minority workers, since they are likely to possess, on average, lower educational qualifications than the rest of the population. Further, employees already in such occupations will resist any attempts to remove such indirect discrimination, since such action would imply a capital loss to themselves.

Historically, certain unions have excluded coloured workers by means of limitations in their constitutions. Norgren and Hill report that in 1930 at least 22 national unions, predominantly railroad unions but also boilermakers, machinists, and airline pilots, barred Negroes from membership by such means. After the Second World War the prevalence of such practises was greatly reduced by merger and the focus of attention on equality of opportunity, so that today no international union constitution contains any provision providing for discriminatory treatment of black workers. However, it is alleged that the locals of some national unions in industries such as railroads, construction,

printing, and metal-working frequently bar black workers from
skilled jobs by informal means, particularly in the South, where
there is a more rigid division of work into white and non-white
jobs. Wolkinson reports that 14 out of 75 EEOC cases analysed
over the period 1965-1968 involved informal union practises of
exclusion by craft unions. The methods adopted include agreements not to sponsor black applicants for membership, failure
to process their application forms, refusal to admit them to
apprenticeship programmes, and examinations designed to exclude
large numbers from craft worker status.

In Canada a number of cases have concerned attempts by
unions to exclude workers on the basis of race, creed, nationality,
ancestry, or place of origin. For instance, in T. Barbisen and
Sons v. Operative Plasterers and Cement Masons International
Association of United States and Canada Local 435, the union
insisted that the employer enter into an agreement which would
impose restrictions on hiring Italian workers. The Labour Relations Board relied on Section 12 of the Labour Relations Act in
holding the union guilty of failing to bargain in good faith.
Again, in Journal Publishing Co. of Ottawa Ltd. v. Ottawa
Mailers Union Local 60 (1970), the Board held that since the
the union's constitution required a person to be a Canadian citi-
zen or to declare his intention of becoming one in order to be
eligible for membership in the union, it was contrary to the
purpose and intent of Section 12, and therefore denied certification to the union. In a similar case, Victor Productions Ltd.
and Co. v. International Alliance of Theatrical Stage Employees
and Moving Picture Machine Operators of the United States and
Canada, Local 58, Toronto (1971), the Board cited the rationale
developed in the Journal Publishing Co. of Ottawa, Ltd. case
and denied the union's application for certification. The board
noted that the union's constitution included restriction with
regard to citizenship, age, facility with the English language,
moral character, and length of residence. Finally, in the case
of Steinberg's Ltd. v. Canadian Merchandising Employees Union,
the employer objected to the certification of the union on the
grounds that the union was not qualified because its constitution
denied membership to supporters of the Communist party. The
employer, Steinberg's Ltd., claimed that Communism is a 'creed'
and therefore discrimination on that basis is prohibited by Section
12 of the Act. The Board noted, however, that this restriction
was typical in the constitutions of international unions and held
that creed pertains to religious belief; Communism and Fascism
were political movements or parties.

In a case under the human rights legislation, M. W. Kellogg Co. v. United Association of Journeymen and Apprentices of the Plumbing and Pipefitting Industry of the United States and Canada (1968), six individuals complained that they were denied opportunity to work at the company's Clinton, Iowa, construction project on the basis of their race and colour by the union as well as the employer. On the day of the appointed hearing by a Board of Inquiry, a settlement of the complaint was negotiated between the complainants and the Human Rights Commission, on the one hand, and the local union and the company, on the other. The chairman of the Board of Inquiry found the terms of the settlement to be fair and recommended that no further action be taken with respect to the complaints.

In the settlement both the union and the employer completely and unequivocably repudiated any further act of discrimination and provided for full compensation, in the total amount of $28,600 (the difference between the total of the six complainants' actual earnings and the amount they would have earned had the employment opportunity been realised for the equivalent period of time), inclusive of any travel or living allowances paid. Additional terms of the settlement were as follows:

(1) The company and the union agreed to forward individual letters of apology to each of the six complainants, as well as to forward letters of instruction and advice to their employees and members, respectively, outlining their policy of compliance with the Ontario Human Rights Code.
(2) The company agreed to notify the Commission and the complainants of the next available job opportunities for which the latter may be qualified on a fair and equal basis, while the union agreed to refer them to available work opportunities as long as they remained members in good standing.
(3) The company and the union agreed to co-operate with the Commission in any subsequent investigations or inquiries that might be undertaken with respect to the recruitment and employment practises of the company or the employment or referral practises of the union.

One means of restricting the supply of labour which has also been an issue in Canada is the exclusion of women from employment upon marriage. In 1971, the Manitoba Human Rights Commission became aware of an article in the collective agreement between the town of Dauphin and a union representing its employees which permitted the town to terminate the employment of a woman when she married. An action was commenced by the

Attorney General against the town to restrain it from terminating a woman's employment when she married. The town agreed to remove the discriminatory provision from the collective agreement, and the action was discontinued. Women employees no longer face the prospect of losing their jobs if they marry.

There are in Britain no formal bans on the recruitment to union membership of minority workers nor any limitations on their entry into apprenticeships, although in the case of women, at least, it is known that the numbers of female apprentices in certain trades are negligible. Wright (1968)[68] suggests that resistance to the employment of coloured workers on the part of white workers has been most marked in public transport, including buses and railways, which are heavily unionised. Usually such resistance has involved threats of strike action or 'working to rule'. Where a closed shop exists, coloured workers can easily be excluded simply by refusing them union membership, usually on grounds of alleged inadequate training. Smith (1974)[69] points to the example of a factory in South-East England employing members of both the Amalgamated Union of Engineering Workers (AUEW) and the Transport and General Workers Union (T & GWU), where a quota limited Asians to 5 percent of the labour force, despite the fact that a majority of the applicants and 18 percent of the local labour force belonged to minority groups. In another area with a large Asian population only eight Asians were employed out of a workforce of 1000. While it was claimed that this was a consequence of the failure of the minority group to score highly enough in a nationally agreed aptitude test, there was believed to be a tacit agreement between management and union at the local level not to hire Asians in large numbers.

Apprenticeship Systems

It is clearly established that in North America and Britain women and coloured workers are far less well represented among apprentices than their numbers in the total labour force would lead one to expect, but against this the unions would point to a lack of qualified applicants from these groups.[70] The most detailed information available is for the United States. As an instance of poor representation, statistics on apprenticeship in referral unions in 1973 reveal that only 0.6 percent of the 250,000 apprentices were women. As far as Negroes are concerned, according to Census data there were 2190 Negro apprentices in 1950 (1.9 percent of the total) and 2191 (2.52 percent of the total) in 1960. At the latter date only in the labouring and trowel-trades section of the building trades did the proportion of Negroes reflect their representation in the total workforce of 10.6 percent. However, it should be borne in mind that only about 10 percent of the skilled workforce obtain qualifications under an apprenticeship, within the economy as a whole. Nonetheless, apprenticeships are quantitatively important in industries such as construction, printing and publishing, and precision metal-working. Dubinsky shows that in the case of the construction industry many apprentices drop out of the programme before completion but still manage to become qualified craft workers.[71] Alternatives to the conventional apprenticeship programmes are upgrading labourers who have already obtained experience in the industry, by direct admission through the 'back door' of friends and relatives, and through accelerated programmes for non-union craft workers and labourers. Marshall (1965)[72] concludes from this trend that attention should be placed more on vocational and general education than on apprenticeship as such, as far as Negro employment opportunities are concerned.

Perhaps the best examples to consider in some detail are the various construction industry trade unions in the United States. Local building-trades unions exercise a high degree of control over employment and training in the construction industry.[73] The major channels through which they exercise this control are (1) the formal apprenticeship programme or the informal on-the-job training system, (2) the hiring hall or work referral system, and (3) union membership. Four common institutional practises of building-trades unions adversely affect the opportunities of minorities to become members of unions, and of these the last two listed below affect referral and apprenticeship as well: (1) approval by the membership and nomination and endorsement by members, (2) restrictions on the size of the membership, (3) methods of recruitment, and (4) examinations. In Volger v. McCarthy (1971), the defendant union, Asbestos Workers Local 53, required applicants for membership to be sponsored by three members, to receive approval by a majority of the members, and to be related to a present member. The court enjoined the union from continuing these nepotistic and discriminatory membership practises and ordered the local to develop objective criteria for membership, including a method by which union size based on industry need could objectively be determined, and to alternate white and Negro referrals.

In United States v. Local 86, Iron Workers (1971), one of the defendant unions—Plumbers and Pipefitters Local 32—had a policy of questioning non-member applicants for referral about their experience. The local also required applicants for referral to apply for membership before they were placed on an out-of-work list. On two separate occasions, two minority applicants for referral (a pipe welder and a plumber and pipe fitter) were not questioned about their experience, nor were they told about the membership application procedures. Both were simply told no work was available. Subsequent testimony revealed that work was available in each of the applicant's respective trades. According to a court decision, Local 32 had discriminated against blacks by failing to inform them of the union's procedures for referral and membership and by providing them with false or misleading information on work conditions in the trade.[74] Other discriminatory-referral cases include Dobbins v. Local 272, IBEW (1968) and United States v. Local 357, IBEW (1972).

In United States v. Sheet Metal Workers Local 36 (1969), the Eighth Circuit court found that Local 1 and Local 36 committed unlawful employment practises by excluding Negroes from membership in the locals, from participation in the apprenticeship training programmes, and from access to the locals' employment referral systems. The court ordered the locals to modify their referral systems, as well as their examination procedure. In addition, they were asked to undertake an effective public information programme designed to make it clear that Negroes from then on would have equal opportunities for union membership and related benefits.

Similarly, other institutional practises which adversely affect minorities have been struck down by the courts. These include age limitations, education requirements, oral interviews, experience, recruitment methods, and written examinations. In United States v. Local 638, Steamfitters (1973), the court struck down age limitations to apprenticeship; in United States v. Local 10 Ironworkers (1973) and United States v. Local 1 Bricklayers (1972), the requirement of a high school diploma was judged not to be job related and to have a disproportionate effect on minority applicants; in Local 86, Ironworkers, a court eliminated the oral interview because it, along with other selection standards such as experience and references, was based on 'subjective nonreviewable determinations', since the oral interview accounted for 30 percent of the 100 points an apprentice applicant could receive; in United States v. Local 24 Plumbers (1973) and in Local 1 Bricklayers (1972), the issue of experience requirements was ruled on; in two cases, Local 638, Steamfitters, and Local 357, IBEW, the subject was recruitment methods such as word-of-mouth. A court ordered the locals to change their method of disseminating information on employment opportunities in the trade; similarly, written tests with no validity or with differential validity were prohibited in Local 638, Steamfitters.

Partly in response to court cases and affirmative-action pressures, construction industry unions and employers have been forced to adopt more objective and more formalised apprenticeship standards and selection procedures. This is especially true in the area of testing. In many cities apprenticeship tests formerly developed and administered by local joint apprenticeship committees are being administered by independent testing agencies and the efforts to validate these tests have been greatly increased.[75]

Government efforts such as outreach programmes; a variety of imposed ('Philadelphia-type') and negotiated ('hometown') city and area plans[76] (implemented under Executive Order 11246 and applied to contractors and subcontractors performing government construction work); and court cases have helped to promote increased minority membership in building-trades unions. As Glover and Marshall (1977) pointed out, on a national scale minorities have made significant gains in building-trades apprenticeships. The latest apprenticeship data show that 18.1 percent of apprentices in 1976 were minorities; 9.4 percent of all apprentices were blacks, while 8.7 percent were members of other minority groups.[77] However, the racial composition of construction union membership has changed more slowly.[78] Moreover, minority representation varies significantly by trade and by place.

It is difficult to assess the aggregate impact of apprenticeship reform, judicial action, affirmative-action plans of government contractors and unions, and voluntary compliance with the spirit of all these programmes, much more so the individual effects of any component of the overall effort; thus, although some progress has been made, it is impossible to tell just how much.[79]

Fair Representation and Failure to Adequately
Represent Minority Interests

In the United States, Section 9(a) of the National Labor Relations Act (NLRA) provides, 'Representatives designated . . . by the majority of employees in . . . [an appropriate] unit . . . shall be the exclusive representatives of all employees in such unit for the purposes of collective bargaining'. In J. I. Case Co. v. NLRB, the Supreme Court ruled that the union's exclusive bargaining status precludes the employer from negotiating with individuals or groups of employees over any matters within the scope of collective bargaining, even if the terms so negotiated are more advantageous to such employees than the terms of the collective agreement.[80] As Aaron has stated, no other country except Canada grants majority unions exclusive collective-bargaining authority.

This unique feature of granting majority unions plenary and exclusive collective-bargaining authority inevitably led to the development of another unique feature: the union's duty of fair representation (Aaron, 1978). In Steele v. Louisville and Nashville Railroad, as far back as 1944, the Supreme Court interpreted the Railway Labor Act (RLA) to require that the exclusive power delegated to unions be exercised fairly with respect to all members of the bargaining unit. The Court nullified a contract negotiated by an all-white union that deprived non-member black firemen of the jobs they held in the unit and gave them to white firemen. Thus, the 'duty of fair representation' was created not to protect employees from the excesses of the employer, but to protect them from the excesses of the union; the right to exclusive representation of all employees in a bargaining unit carries with it the concomitant duty to represent all employees fairly.

In the landmark case of Vaca v. Sipes (1967), the Supreme Court first clearly articulated the standards governing the duty of fair representation in the grievance-processing context. The Court summarised the applicable rule this way: 'A breach of the statutory duty of fair representation occurs only when a union's conduct toward a member of the collective bargaining unit is arbitrary, discriminatory, or in bad faith'.[81]

The Vaca standards provide a dual check on a union's exercise of power. First, the union's decision-making process is evaluated subjectively; the union cannot act, or fail to act, on the basis of discriminatory or bad-faith motives. Second, the union's actual decision is subjected to objective scrutiny. According to a note in the Harvard Law Review (HLR) of February 1980 the subjective and objective tests together can be utilised to judge virtually any act, or failure to act, by a union, including situations in which a union is chastised by remaining inactive with respect to employer discrimination. Administrative agencies have a role to play in the question of first representation. The RLA covers the railroad and airlines industries and is administered by the National Mediation Board (NMB), which handles questions of representation and interest disputes, and the National Railroad Adjustment Board (NRAB), which adjudicates rights disputes. As Aaron has observed, neither of the two boards has contributed anything to the solution of racial and minority problems in the two industries covered by the RLA.[82]

The NLRA is administered by the National Labor Relations Board (NLRB). Until 1962 the NLRB did not consider failure by unions to represent their members fairly to constitute an unfair labour practise. The NLRB in earlier cases (e.g. Bekins Moving and Storage Co. v. NLRB [1974]) withheld certification from unions that won representation elections but were shown to have engaged in invidious racial and other prohibited discrimination. Moreover, in one case, NLRB v. Mansion House Center Management Corp. (1974) the Court of Appeals refused to enforce an NLRB decision ordering an employer to bargain with a labour organisation that practised racial discrimination against its members. The court remanded the case to the NLRB for a new decision but clearly held that the NLRB's remedial machinery cannot be available to a union unwilling to correct past practises of discrimination.

In Bell & Howell Co. v. NLRB (1977), the NLRB held that a union's duty of fair representation includes the duty not to discriminate on the basis of sex. The NLRB further held that it would treat claims of sex discrimination in the same manner as any other allegations of invidious discrimination (Schlei and Grossman, 1979).[83] In more recent cases, the NLRB has overruled its earlier decision in Bekins. In Handy Andy, Inc. (1977), the Board held that allegations of invidious discrimination must be dealt with under unfair labour practise remedies and that certification was not to be withheld (Schlei and Grossman, 1979).

In Britain the problem of failure to adequately represent minority interests was perhaps most clearly illustrated in the Mansfield Hosiery Mills case in 1972, in which the National Union of Hosiery and Knitwear Workers was found to have failed to ensure that minority workers were adequately represented at the shop-floor level. For instance, in the all-female rough makeup section there were no Asian shop stewards, though Asians made up half the labour force. The Commission on Industrial Relations (1976) commented that this type of situation had arisen because non-Asians had refused to vote for Asians as well as because the Asian women were reluctant to offer themselves for shop steward duties. Some Asians felt that their grievances were not pursued very sympathetically by non-Asian shop stewards. The Commission noted the danger that inadequate representation might lead to the formation of breakaway unions to represent the interests of racial minorities; it put the onus on the union leadership to take active and positive measures to deal with the problem.

A similar problem arose in the first industrial tribunal finding against a trade union under the 1976 Race Relations Act (RRA), Modgill et al. v. T. I. Pel Ltd. and FTATU (April 1979). The paint spray shop of the company concerned had become 100 percent Asian, and the grievances of the workers there included the lack of a shop steward of their own, a longer working week than other departments, lower wages, and segregation. The tribunal accepted their claim that such matters constituted discrimination against them on grounds of race or colour by the Furniture, Timber and Allied Trades Union (FTATU) and the company. However, the tribunal found that the discrimination was unconscious rather than deliberate and largely a consequence of a failure of communications between the union and a particular section of its membership. In view of this and the positive steps taken by the employer and the unions to improve the situation, the remedy was a simple declaration by the tribunal of a case of discrimination.

However, on appeal the Employment Appeals Tribunal (EAT) reversed the tribunal decision, stating that 'had there been evidence of a policy to segregate, or of the fact of segregation . . . that might well have constituted a breach of the legislation, but . . . we do not consider the failure of the company to intervene and to insist on white or non-Asian workers going into the shop, contrary to the wishes of the men to introduce their friends, itself constituted the act of segregating persons on racial grounds within the meaning of the Act. Indeed a refusal to appoint other applicants because they were Asian might have amounted to discrimination'. Thus, we must distinguish congregation, which is passive, from segregation, which is an active policy; shifts consisting of a single race are not necessarily unlawful. As far as the union was concerned, the EAT, again reversing the previous ruling, said that inadequate representation or communication does not of itself amount to discrimination. What has to be shown is that different treatment has been given to one group over another, not that service is generally poor.

Discriminatory Seniority Systems and Promotion

While industrial unions, in contrast to craft unions, have traditionally recruited black workers, they may well discriminate against them after entry. This is seen particularly in relation to seniority arrangements. If whites acquire more seniority they will obtain higher earnings, better fringe benefits, easier access to overtime, preferred jobs and promoted posts, and a lower possibility of layoff through the operation of 'last-in, first-out' systems. One example of this was found in a practise that used to operate in the brewery industry in New York. Desirable jobs were allocated on the basis of seniority, but a union referral system operated in such a way that Negroes seldom accumulated sufficient seniority during the summer months to qualify for the seniority status that would protect their jobs in the winter.[84] Seniority systems have the serious disadvantage, then, of perpetuating existing unfavourable minority employment patterns. If black workers or women are the last to be hired during the recovery phase of the cycle, they will be the first to be laid off in the recession phase. Gilman[85] found that only half of the differential unemployment experience between white and coloured workers could be explained by differing characteristics of the two groups and that the unexplained residual could be the result of the operation of seniority systems. This possibility was confirmed in a case study of a redundancy in an aerospace factory, where the proportion of salaried black workers, who were not covered by a seniority system, remained constant, while the proportion of non-salaried blacks, who were so covered, fell from 14.3 percent to 9.5 percent.[86] Seniority may operate on the basis of the plant, the department, or particular jobs within a department. The last two of these may give rise to segregated seniority rosters in which coloured workers are restricted to the inferior promoted posts. This can, therefore, avoid the possibility of coloured workers' obtaining jobs which place them in a supervisory position over white workers. Of the 75 cases of discrimination analysed by Wolkinson, no less than 27 were concerned with seniority issues, of which he distinguishes three types. The simplest case is where black and white workers performing the same work are placed in separate seniority groups, with only the white groups having promoted posts. A second possibility is what he terms discriminatory progression line seniority systems, in which, while black workers perform work functionally related to that of white workers, they are again denied opportunities for promotion. The third case is that of discriminatory departmental seniority systems, in which whites are placed in departments requiring a high level of skill and blacks into those requiring a low level of skill. Obviously, plantwide seniority systems are potentially beneficial to minority workers compared with the other alternatives to which reference has been made.

Seniority Cases in the United States

In attempting to resolve the complex issues relating to seniority discrimination, the U.S. courts have resorted to the three theories proposed in a Note in the Harvard Law Review (1967).[87] Under the first, 'status quo', positions in the hierarchy already achieved would be left intact. If whites were preferred over blacks and other minorities in the past, the latter could not improve their status. The 'rightful place' approach would allow an incumbent black or affected minority worker to bid for openings in 'white' jobs comparable to those held by whites of equal tenure, on the basis of full length of service with the employer. Under the 'freedom now' theory, maintenance of the distribution of jobs established by a discriminatory system after Title VII became law constitutes an unlawful employment practise. If the adjustment of seniority rights contemplated by the 'rightful place' theory indicates that a senior minority worker would have priority over a white worker currently holding a particular job if that job were unfilled, then under 'freedom now' the minority worker would be immediately entitled to it, even though this would require displacement of the white incumbent.[88] In the early decisions, the courts took the 'rightful place' approach. Since 1977, however, the Supreme Court seems to have decided in favour of the 'status quo' theory.

Seniority in a unionised company refers to seniority within a bargaining unit. The unit describes the specific territory—occupation, craft, department, multi-plant, multi-employer, etc.—to which a collective-bargaining agreement applies. Unit seniority refers to seniority as a principal criterion of selection, promotion, layoff, recall, and so forth. For example, various separate functions in a plant (within the same bargaining unit) may be designated as departments for seniority purposes. Generally, in such a case transfers between departments are not permitted except where they involve a promotion. Transfers between departments may also result in a loss of seniority, since departmental seniority systems base employee rights not on the date of hire but on the date of assignment to that department. Thus, it becomes increasingly costly to the individual to move across departments in terms of accumulating seniority.[89]

A combination of narrow seniority units and discriminatory employment practises has been used for many years in the pulp and paper and the tobacco industry in the South, as well as the iron and steel industry in many parts of the United States, to confine blacks to less desirable jobs in these industries. Although the seniority practises in these industries were developed out of the needs of the industries and were not discriminatory per se, blacks were employed for certain jobs and seniority lines were perverted to deny them the right to bid even for the bottom jobs in seniority lines. In cases involving such practises the courts applied the 'rightful place' approach. That is, blacks who were employed before hiring became non-discriminatory were permitted to advance on the basis of plantwide seniority, instead of occupational seniority, after they were placed in a progression line.[90]

The first case to conclude that Title VII was violated by an apparently neutral seniority system because of its perpetuation of past discrimination involved the tobacco industry—Quarles v. Philip Morris, in 1968.[91] In this and other court cases in the tobacco industry (such as Robinson v. Lorillard Corporation (1970); Tobacco Workers International Union v. Robinson (1972); and Russel v. American Tobacco Company (1973)), a typical remedy was for the blacks and other minority workers freely to transfer to vacancies in the lower paying jobs within departments previously closed to them, to work in such a position for a minimal period (usually one month, because in this industry virtually all production jobs require minimal training time), and thereafter to use their full accumulated employment-date seniority in bidding for future vacancies in higher rated jobs. This was helped by maintaining ('red circling') the transferee's rate of pay at the pre-transfer level until such time as that level was matched or exceeded by the employee's advancement in the department.[92]

In the paper industry courts allowed the same 'rightful place' relief, but with some refinements. The courts recognised that the industry was characterised by a considerable degree of sophistication in terms of job skills. The courts determined residency periods in jobs in which the required training was acquired to perform satisfactorily in the higher rated jobs. In other jobs the prior industry requirement of sequential advancement within established lines of progression was relaxed to permit job skipping, since in these jobs training bore no relationship to a particular high position on the line (Pamberton, 1975),[93] as in the case of United States v. Local 189, United Papermakers, et al. (1970).

In the steel industry blacks were generally hired to do blast furnace work, and although they were permitted to work up to the top jobs in blast furnace departments, they were generally excluded from the rolling mills. The courts have put an end to this practise.

To summarise, in practise the 'rightful place' remedy did not require the wholesale eradication of departmental or job-progression bidding procedures or the merger of departments or job-progression seniority lines involving employees not previously discriminated against; plant- or companywide seniority operated when the bidders included adversely affected employees in competition with those not discriminated against. The 'rightful place' doctrine was applied so that white incumbent workers would not be bumped out of their current positions by blacks and other minorities with greater plant seniority; plant seniority was to be assessed only with respect to new job openings (Local 189, United Papermakers and Paperworkers v. United States). While white incumbents were not displaced, back pay and other benefits were awarded to the victims of discrimination. The compensation in one case included increments of pension and profit sharing.

Transfer Rights and Seniority Carry-over. There was a wide variance in the number of opportunities a member of the affected class was entitled to have to bid for or transfer to a job in another department using carry-over seniority. Decrees ranged from a single good-faith opportunity to an unlimited number of transfers.

Plantwide seniority carry-over was allowed only for bidding into entry-level and above-entry-level positions where on-the-job experience was unnecessary. Where on-the-job experience was necessary to qualify for the next higher opening, courts were flexible with respect to provisions for reasonable probationary periods, during which time plantwide seniority could not be used to bid on a higher position in the department. The latter was especially true in trucking industry cases; in the trucking industry, the entry-level job in the road service required qualifications that an individual could acquire only after a specified period in city service or in road service for another company. Therefore every employee was not necessarily qualified for all entry-level jobs on the date of hire, and less than full seniority carry-over was also consistent with the 'rightful place' remedy in this industry. Normally, seniority carry-over was granted only for the protected class and not for all employees.

Rate and Seniority Retention. The seniority system as restructured under the 'rightful place' remedy provided rate retention (red circling) for employees who were qualified only for transfer into entry-level jobs in new departments where those jobs carried lower pay rates than the jobs the transferring employees held at the time. Also, to encourage the exercise of the new interdepartmental transfer right, employees were provided with retention of seniority in the department from which they transferred for a specified period. Therefore, if an employee who could not perform the new job wished to return to the former department did not lose any seniority rights in that department. In <u>United States v. Bethlehem Steel Corporation</u>, the second circuit (1971) commented '. . . a discriminatorily assigned employee will have little incentive to transfer if he loses money or job seniority by doing so'.[94]

As has been pointed out, in the early cases, starting with <u>Quarles</u>, the court took the 'rightful place' approach. In <u>Quarles</u> the court took the position that one characteristic of a bona fide seniority system was lack of discrimination and that a racially discriminatory system established before passage of the Act was not a bona fide seniority system under the Act. In 1977, however, the Supreme Court in <u>International Brotherhood of Teamsters v. United States</u> (1977) held that a departmental seniority system was lawfully bona fide even where the employer was proved to have engaged in pre-Act discriminatory hiring and promotion policies, and despite the fact that the seniority system perpetuated into the present the effects of the pre-Act discrimination. Thus, constructive (back) seniority could not be awarded to employees who were victims of pre-Act but not of post-Act discrimination. In effect, the Supreme Court seems to have taken the 'status quo' approach as opposed to the 'rightful place' approach taken by the lower courts in <u>Quarles</u> and other early decisions.

In <u>Franks v. Bowman Transportation</u> (1976), <u>Albemarle v. Moody</u> (1975), and the <u>Teamsters</u> case, the Supreme Court subscribed to the make-whole remedy approach. In the <u>Franks</u> case the Court held that the victims of discrimination in selection decisions following the effective date of the 1964 Civil Rights Act were entitled to seniority from the date of the discriminatory action, to restore competitive and benefit seniority status in relation to job and compensation rights, respectively.[95]

In view of the fact that in the <u>Teamsters</u> case the Court rejected the reasoning of the long line of lower court cases which had held that a seniority and transfer system constituted present discrimination and violated Title VII if it perpetuated into the present the effects of pre-Act discrimination, and since it had important effects on seniority held sacred by unions, the case will be discussed in some detail. In the <u>Teamsters</u> (T.I.M.E.— D.C. Company) case, the government's first charge was that the union and company practised discrimination against blacks and Spanish-surnamed applicants and employees. It was alleged that the company discriminated against minorities in hiring for line (over-the-road) driving positions and that the departmental seniority system included in the collective-bargaining agreement with the Teamsters perpetuated this discriminatory impact.

Those Negroes and Spanish-surnamed workers who had been hired, the government alleged, were given lower paying, less desirable jobs as servicemen or local city drivers and thereafter were discriminated against with respect to promotions and transfers.[96] The Court found that the company had violated Title VII by virtually refusing to hire minorities for the more desirable and better paying line drivers' positions. Of the company's 6472 employees in early 1971, 571 (9 percent) were minorities; but of the 1828 line drivers only 15 (0.8 percent) were. The Court also noted that only once prior to 1969 had the company employed a minority line driver.[97]

Second, the Court examined the effects of the seniority system and the question of whether it met the 'bona fide' requirement of 703(h). In the collective-bargaining agreement, seniority in terms of 'benefit status' (i.e. entitlement to pay and benefits) ran from date of hire on a systemwide basis. But 'competitive status' (i.e. entitlement to promotions, immunity to layoffs, etc.) seniority dated from the beginning of an employee's tenure on a particular job at a particular terminal. Thus, competitive seniority did not accrue across jobs, thereby discouraging city drivers from bidding for line drive jobs.

The Court held that constructive (back) seniority cannot be granted to a date prior to the effective date of Title VII.[98] Thus, workers suffering from the effects of pre-Act discrimination were not entitled to relief even though the present application of the seniority system may reduce their opportunities or discourage their bidding for promotion. However, in keeping with Albemarle and Franks, the Court held that a non-applicant who could establish qualifications for a job and an interest in applying for a specific job vacancy at the time it was open might be entitled to back pay, a job when an opening occurs, and constructive seniority; this is the concept of making whole workers who have suffered from discrimination. Thus, the employer was found in violation of Title VII based on other evidence; the seniority system was not a violation on the basis of this finding.[99]

Earlier court cases had taken the view that seniority systems which were superimposed upon patterns of discriminatory job assignments, and thereby perpetuated the effect of such assignments, were illegal under Title VII. Thus, a departmental seniority system made it difficult for a black or a woman originally assigned to a 'black department' or a 'woman's job' to advance because they would lose job security and perhaps pay if they transferred to another department. This 'adverse effect' perpetuated the original discriminatory assignment. Seniority-unit restrictions on promotional opportunities were therefore held to be illegal.[100] Similarly, for layoff purposes, the restrictive seniority units were required to be modified so that minorities and women competed for the fewer jobs remaining after a layoff on the basis of their total length of service, rather than on the basis of their service in a particular segregated department.

In the Teamsters decision, however, the Supreme Court held that the 'routine operation' of a bona fide seniority system would not violate the federal law even though it perpetuated the effect of pre-Act discrimination. Workers denied a position after Title VII became effective, if their race or sex played a part in that denial, would be entitled to full relief, including seniority dating from the time the worker should have been hired or promoted. But in order to be entitled to that relief, something more must be shown than the 'routine operation' of a 'bona fide' seniority system. It is still far from clear what constitutes a 'bona fide' seniority system. What is known is that such a seniority system is one which did not have its genesis in discrimination and was not negotiated or maintained for the purpose of discrimination; only a few court cases have worked out the meaning of a 'bona fide' seniority system.

The Teamsters decision has posed another problem. There is a conflict between two rights: the contractual (i.e. collective agreement) guarantee of seniority and the legal right of equal access to jobs. Where an employer has recently taken affirmative action to include minorities and women in the company's workforce, the layoff of such junior minorities and women under a 'last in, first out' clause can amount to segregation and is certainly contrary to the underlying purpose behind the anti-discrimination laws (Blumrosen, 1980).[101] However, as Teamsters has established, a countervailing purpose is expressed in laws that afford some protection to expectations under seniority systems. The problem, as pointed out earlier, is how to adjust these two conflicting purposes.

The issue around which this problem centres may be phrased in terms of the question 'What is a seniority system?', according to Blumrosen (1980). In the U.S. statutory structure, the adverse-effect principle applies, except in the case of seniority systems. In the predominantly nonunionised private sector, employees operate under informal, and normally not contractually binding, understandings that layoffs will take place on a 'last in, first out' basis. Are those systems 'seniority systems'? Since the 'bona fide' seniority provision was put into Title VII at the behest of trade unions, a strong argument can be made, according to Blumrosen, that they are not, and that only collectively bargained seniority systems are protected.[102]

The next issue is what kind of rights are considered to fall within the definition of a 'seniority system'. For instance, some collective agreements guarantee a specified work week, such as 40 hours. Many others do not, but do contain a last in, first out layoff clause. In that situation, does the 'seniority system' encompass a guaranteed work week? A resolution of this issue is crucial to the last in, first out problem. According to Blumrosen (1980), if a guaranteed work week is not part of the statutory 'seniority system' the employer may be under the Griggs, or adverse-effect, principle when it comes to deciding how to reduce its hours of work and must adopt the alternative that will not have an adverse impact on the recently hired minorities or women. The resolution of these questions will ultimately be based on a complex balancing of the conflicting policy considerations noted above. Court and/or government intervention cannot be a permanent or desirable remedy for the affirmative action/seniority dilemma. What is needed is creative collective bargaining. The company and the union must voluntarily modify traditional systems to lessen the impact of layoffs on minorities and women.[103]

Seniority Cases in Canada

In Canada there have been seniority cases involving women. In one case a complaint was filed by two women that they were unfairly laid off by McGavin Toastmaster Ltd. in Manitoba. They claimed that men with less seniority were retained during their period of layoff and that the union refused to enforce the seniority clause in the collective-bargaining agreement for these women. The case was heard before a public inquiry in September 1971 and a Ministerial Order was issued. The Order was appealed successfully by the company and the union in the Court of Queen's Bench. The Manitoba Human Rights Commission further appealed the Queen's Bench decision to the Court of Appeal but was unsuccessful.

Seniority issues have also arisen in collective agreement provisions covering maternity protection and equal pay. Maternity protection covers more than two million workers in Canada, in all industries except construction, in establishments employing more than 500 workers. An analysis of data provided by Labour Canada reveals that the impact of increased attention by trade unions to the role of women in the economy is being felt at the bargaining table. As demonstrated in Tables 6.12 and 6.13, collective agreements are increasingly incorporating provisions on seniority during maternity leave, in the form of either retaining or accumulating seniority. The former is much more frequent

TABLE 6.12

Collective Bargaining Agreements Containing Provisions
Dealing With Seniority during Maternity Leave
for Women in Canada and Ontario

	Canada (percent)	Ontario (percent)
1972	38.1	44.9
1975	42.5	48.8
1979	46.5	50.1

Source: Labour Canada.

TABLE 6.13

Forms of Collective-Bargaining Agreement Provisions
Dealing with Seniority Clauses during Maternity Leave
for Women in Canada and Ontario

	1972 (percent)	1975 (percent)	1979 (percent)
Canada			
Seniority retained	22.9	23.6	23.8
Seniority accumulated	6.1	6.9	9.4
Seniority	9.1	12.0	13.2
Ontario			
Seniority retained	29.4	34.8	34.7
Seniority accumulated	6.8	8.4	9.9
Seniority	8.7	5.6	5.5

Source: Labour Canada.

than the latter. Also, according to Paul Malles, [104] such protection of seniority is considerably stronger for the larger agreements unit than for the smaller unit. Separate seniority units for women are becoming rare, as the data in Table 6.14 indicate.

Seniority Cases in Britain

In Britain, as in North America, it is common to find that racial minorities and women are less than proportionately represented in promoted posts, though again this may represent employer policies and inadequate endowments of human capital as much as the policies of the unions. Smith (1974)[105] reports the finding in one bus company with Transport and General Workers Union (T & GWU) representation that there were no Asian inspectors, despite the fact that over half of the platform staff of over 1000 were Asian. Wright (1968)[106] reports a case where management wanted to promote some very competent coloured workers who were assistants to white workers but were forced to crop their plan to do so because of union pressure; in another firm a 'gentleman's agreement' had been made between management and the union that coloured workers would be the first to go in the event of a redundancy. As for women, the Equal Opportunities Commission (EOC) (1978) reports that shop floor and local trade union resistance to desegregating jobs is felt to be a substantial problem by many companies, especially in printing, chemicals, and pharmaceuticals. Similarly, in the

TABLE 6.14

Collective-Bargaining Agreement Provisions on Separate Seniority Units for Women in Canada and Ontario

	Canada (percent)	Ontario (percent)
1972	4.3	7.2
1975	1.7	2.8
1979	1.5	1.4

Source: Labour Canada.

printing industry unions have opposed the compensatory training for women allowed for under the Sex Discrimination Act.

Seniority Policy Measures

Suggestions to modify the seniority system which have been put forward in the United States include front pay, inverse seniority, work sharing, and plantwide seniority.

Front Pay. The use of 'front pay' has been suggested by the United Automobile Workers (UAW) for identifiable discriminatees. Such victims would be entitled to a job, back pay (from the date they were illegally denied employment), and back seniority rights, except those usable in layoff-recall situations. Additionally, any discriminatee caught in a layoff due to the employer's original refusal to hire should be paid full wages and fringe benefits for the period of layoff.[107] As Elkiss (1980)[108] has suggested, this remedy might lessen the negative impact of a layoff on minorities; however, it has limited value, since they are still laid off. They receive money but no jobs. Moreover, many employers cannot afford front pay at a time when reduction of the workforce is mandatory.

Inverse Seniority. The practise of inverse seniority permits senior workers to elect temporary layoff at the time of a reduction in force, without jeopardising their long-term job security, in the place of junior workers who would normally be laid off. Three factors facilitate the adoption of inverse seniority plans. First, firms which face cyclical demand or have technological or economic reasons for temporary shutdowns, and which handle these situations by reductions in the workforce, are likely to adopt this concept. Second, companies which have a relatively high proportion of skilled workers and/or complex internal labour markets may find these plans attractive. Third, companies which have supplementary unemployment benefits (SUB) or guaranteed annual wage (GAW) plans are most likely to adopt these plans because they can make it financially attractive for senior workers to elect layoff without significant additional cost to the company.[109] The inverse seniority practise evolves from the collective-bargaining process and is not court or government imposed.

Work Sharing. Work sharing requires a reduction in the work week so that all employees may share the available work. The number of hours per shift could be shortened and the work spread out, so that all employees work part time as a substitute for layoff.

Trade unions object to this remedy because it would render useless any seniority system. Moreover, take-home pay would be less. Benefits would accrue to the employer, since the unemployment insurance rate is tied to the amount of benefits collected by laid-off employees.[110] This remedy has limited application. Not all operations throughout the workplace can be reduced uniformly. Skilled workers may have to be retained full time. Depending on the amount of work sharing, it may prove to be too much of a hardship.

Plantwide Seniority. The courts, some trade unions, and affirmative-action groups often have suggested that seniority be based on date of hire into the plant, not a particular department or unit. This is especially true after the Weber v. Kaiser Aluminum & Chemical Corp. case (1979), in which the Supreme Court ruled that Title VII's ban on racial discrimination does not condemn all private, voluntary, and race-conscious affirmative-action plans. Trade unions can actively seek to end unequal opportunities for minorities and women. A voluntary affirmative-action plan can be mounted which also encompasses layoff and recall on the basis of date of hire.

Segregated Union Organisation at the Local Level

Segregation may take place at the workplace or within the union organisation. By the 1940s a majority of the U.S. labour unions affiliated with the American Federation of Labor had organised segregated locals or all-black auxiliary units which excluded black workers from certain job classifications. Auxiliary locals were subordinate to their parent white locals' officials and nominally enjoyed equal status within the national union. They are more common in the South than elsewhere and in craft than in industrial unions. Norgren and Hill (1964)[111] note that in some cases Negroes have opposed the integration of segregated locals because they feel that the system provides them with some measure of job security. Nonetheless, they suggest that the primary purpose of such arrangements is to limit Negroes to a narrow range of unskilled, low paying, and non-promotable jobs. Segregated locals violate Title VII of the Civil Rights Act, and the AFL-CIO is committed to their abolition. Nonetheless, Wolkinson reports that segregated locals existed in 20 of the 75 cases examined in his study, longshore and railroad industries being involved in over half of these cases.

As far as Britain is concerned, the EOC (1978)[112] reports that it is still the case that some workplaces retain separate union branches by sex. Lewenhak (1977)[113] traces union attitudes towards women members back through time and finds that although after the Second World War unions which had still excluded women from membership gradually accepted them, in many unions it was still the case that women were not accorded equality of membership. The Tobacco Workers Union, which terminated its special women's section in 1947, tried to limit women to repetitive processes; the Amalgamated Engineering and Foundryworkers Union set up special women's sections; in 1945 the Electrical Trades Union transferred women from its 'mixed' auxiliary section to a women's section set up for 'dilutees' during the war; the Woodworkers Society admitted women in 1952, but they did not qualify for union office; and women were excluded from the Jacquard Section of the Power Loom Carpet Weavers and Textile Workers Association. Solden (1978)[114] notes that there were reasons why participation in a mixed trade union might be disadvantageous to women. In particular, their lower scales of union contributions and hence of benefits meant that women were second-class union members; this situation was reinforced by the paucity of female union officials and their inferior status resulting from occupancy of lower paying and less skilled jobs. Typically, the response to this problem was the all-women branch, the reservation of places for women on committees, and the formation of women's advisory councils.

Thus, for both North America and Britain there is evidence that unions have excluded minority workers from membership, rationed apprenticeships to members of the majority group, failed to adequately represent minority workers who have obtained membership, enforced discriminatory seniority systems in collusion with employers, and on occasion operated segregated locals and branches. However, it is also possible that unions have acted as a protection against discriminatory employers. Thus, the question remains whether on balance unions have assisted or hindered the progress of minority and female workers. It is to this question that we must now turn.

EMPIRICAL STUDIES OF THE EFFECTS OF UNIONS

There are two related approaches to estimating the effects of unions on the wages of minority groups relative to those of the majority. The first examines relative wages at the aggregate level as an accounting identity. The effect of a trade union on the black/white or male/female ratio will be determined by three factors—the difference in the percentage of each group which is unionised or subject to a collective-bargaining agreement, the difference in the percentage mark-up in each of the groups resulting from union membership, and the depressing effect of unionisation on the wages of non-union members.[115] The average level of wages may be expressed as the arithmetically weighted mean of union and non-union wages.

$$\overline{W} = \alpha W_u + (1 - \alpha) W_n, \qquad \text{(Eq. 1)}$$

where $\overline{W}$, W_u and W_n are the average wage, the union wage, and the non-union wage, respectively, and α is the proportion of the workforce paid the union wage. Applying this equation to the effects of unions on minority workers, we obtain

$$\Delta W = \alpha_w M_w - \alpha_b M_b \qquad \text{(Eq. 2)}$$

where ΔW equals the effect of unionism on relative wages, α_w and α_b represent the proportion of the white (or male) and black (or female) workforce unionised, and M_w and M_b are the proportionate differences between the wages of the union and non-union white (or male) and black (or female) workers.

In order to calculate the above however, we need to estimate the independent effect of unions on the relative earnings of the various groups. The ideal way to achieve this is to apply a Mincerian human-capital model to micro-data. Thus, the wage rate for the ith worker (or the average wage for the ith industry or occupation) is given by

$$\log W_i = aU_i + bX_i + e_i \qquad \text{(Eq. 3)}$$

where W_i is the wage, U_i is a zero-one dummy variable representing union membership status, X_i is a vector of other relevant variables (such as education, experience, region, marital status, race, and sex) and e_i a random disturbance term. The assumption of this model is that U_i is exogenous, otherwise the estimate of coefficient 'a' will be biased. Johnson[116] feels, however, that it is plausible to suppose that the wage level itself depends upon the degree of unionisation and specific training, that the propensity to quit depends negatively on the wage rate, and that unionism depends negatively on the propensity to quit. If this is the case, the estimates that follow concerning the effect of unionism on relative wages will be biased upwards. It is also important to control adequately for level of skill. As Mulvey[117] suggests, theoretical considerations imply that skilled workers will obtain a higher union mark-up than unskilled workers because the elasticity of labour demand is lower in their case. Since women and racial minorities are, on the average, less skilled than white men, their mark-up should be lower, notwithstanding the possibility that unions may discriminate against them.

The empirical studies that have been undertaken in the United States to determine the effects of unions on the relative positions of minority and majority groups can be classified according to whether they are concerned with wage differences, the degree of exclusion, or a combination of the two; whether they are made on a time series or cross-section basis; and whether they are aggregated or disaggregated according to occupation, region, or public and private sectors. Time series analyses have been carried out by Rapping (1970),[118] Ashenfelter and Godwin (1972),[119] and Moore and Raisian (1980).[120] The first of these attempts to estimate the impact of unionism on the percentage change in non-white male employment relative to the total change in male employment and unionisation. Rapping divides the economy into 22 industry groups which are dichotomised into 'unionised' and 'non-unionised' for two periods, 1910-1930 and 1930-1960, according to the extent of unionism in 1929 for the first period and 1953 for the second period. While the coefficient of the unionism dummy variable is negative, perhaps not surprisingly in view of the crudeness of the procedure, it is insignificant according to conventional standards. Therefore, there is no conclusive evidence from this study that the presence of unions has increased entry barriers based on race.[121] Ashenfelter and Godwin, as noted earlier, examine the hypothesis that industrial unionism has had a less discriminatory effect on the black/white wage ratio over the period 1900 to 1967 than has craft unionism. Evidence consistent with this hypothesis requires the effect of unionisation on the ratio to have been numerically smaller prior to the 1930s (when the bulk of unionisation was in the crafts) than later. This is indeed the case, since the study found that the presence of unionism may have reduced black wages relative to white by some 2 percent in 1930 but increased it by 1940 by as much as 3 percent. A study by Moore and Raisian (1980)[122] covering the period 1967 to 1974 shows that the relative wage effects of unionisation vary dramatically for both white and black male workers in white-collar occupations—for instance, from -8.01 percent in 1973 for black white-collar workers to +59.19 percent in 1967. However, it should be borne in mind that the number of observations for this group is small and most of the coefficients are insignificant. In contrast to

the results for white-collar workers, all 16 of the coefficients
for blue-collar workers were significant and for all years studied
the effect of unionisation was substantially greater for blacks
than for whites. However, the highest- and lowest-effect years
are opposite for the two groups, and as Moore and Raisian note,
this raises some serious questions as to whether cyclical forces
are a major cause of these year-to-year variations in union
premium estimates.[123]

Results from some of the several cross-section analyses
that have been carried out are summarised in Table 6.15. These
estimates are based on regression coefficients derived from equations such as Equation 3 above, but must be combined with the
data provided earlier on the extent of union membership in order
to derive the overall effect of unionism on race/sex wage differentials. In this respect, it should be noted that unions may
also increase the annual hours of work of their members, particularly through their impact on the probability of employment,
and that some allowance should be made for this.[124]

Oaxaca's findings, summarised in Table 6.15, are based
on results for 200 union/non-union wage differentials. Overall,
they suggest that differentials are highest among black males
and white females. Ashenfelter, however, draws the inference
that while black and white females draw approximately the same
wage advantage as white males from union membership, black
males obtain a significantly greater advantage than any of the
other groups. He also finds, unlike Moore and Raisian, that
the union/non-union wage differential increased considerably
between 1967 and 1975, which might reflect the fact that unemployment was increasing over this period and that unions have
a greater impact on the relative wages of their members in periods
of recession. Despite these sizable wage mark-up effects of
unions, the overall effect on aggregate minority/majority wage
differentials is relatively small. Ashenfelter's results from
Table 6.15, when combined with unionisation data from Table
6.2, imply that unionisation may narrow black/white wage differentials by 2.3 percent but widen the female/male differential by
2.9 percent (using 1975 data). The latter result is a consequence
of both the lower mark-up for women and the fact that they are
less likely than men to be members of trade unions.[125] Later
investigators have attempted to deal with the problem that union
membership may be determined by the level of wages, as well
as determining it, by using simultaneous-equations models. Lee
(1978)[126] estimates the union effect on wages for semi-skilled
operatives and finds results (reported in Table 6.15) compatible
with those of Ashenfelter insofar as the union wage differential

TABLE 6.15

Cross-Section Estimates of Union/Non-Union Wage Differentials by Race and Sex

Source	Year of Investigation	Categories Studied	Groups Studied				
			White Males	Black Males	White Females	Black Females	All Workers
Oaxaca (1975)	1967		11.3%	25.1%	21.6%	7.3%	15.7%
Ashenfelter (1976)	1967		9.3	21.5	14.4	5.6	11.6
Ashenfelter (1976)	1973		15.5	22.5	12.7	13.2	14.8
Ashenfelter (1976)	1975		16.3	22.5	16.6	17.1	16.8
Kiefer and Smith (1977)	1973	North	17.9	15.0	13.4	10.4	—[a]
		Border	36.6	24.0	30.7	20.7	—
		South	31.4	49.2	28.3	22.6	—
Lee (1978)	1976		16.2	28.5	2.8	12.7	
Leigh (1978)	1969		Craft / Other[b]	Craft / Other[b]			
		Craft workers	38.1 / 13.3	12.9 / 20.1			
		Operatives	29.9 / 18.3	17.8 / 27.2			
		Non-farm labourers	38.6 / 32.4	48.1 / 33.9			

202

		Adjusted[c]	Unadjusted	Adjusted[c]	Unadjusted
Leigh (1980)	1971 Young Men	37.2	24.6	28.0	22.0
	1969 Middle-Aged Men	36.2	9.2	45.2	31.5
	1971 Middle-Aged Men	45.9	13.2	105.0	37.6
Antos, Chandler, and Mellow (1980)	1976		21.0[d]		14.0[e]

[a]Data not available.

[b]The 'other' category includes industrial unions, government employee/white-collar unions, and miscellaneous unions.

[c]Adjusted for selectivity bias (i.e. the fact that wages determine union membership).

[d]White males and black males combined.

[e]White females and black females combined.

Sources:

R. L. Oaxaca, 'Estimation of union/non-union wage differentials within occupational/regional sub-groups', The Journal of Human Resources, Fall 1975.

O. Ashenfelter, 'Union relative wage effects: New evidence and a survey of their implications for wage inflation', Princeton University Working Paper 89, Industrial Relations Section, August 1976.

N. M. Kiefer and S. P. Smith, 'Union impact and wage discrimination by region', The Journal of Human Resources, Fall 1977.

L. F. Lee, 'Unionism and wage rates: A simultaneous equations model with qualitative and limited dependent variables', International Economic Review, vol. 19, no. 2 (June 1978).

D. E. Leigh, 'Racial discrimination and labor unions: Evidence from the N.L.S. sample of middle-aged men', The Journal of Human Resources, vol. XIII, no. 4 (Fall 1978).

D. E. Leigh, 'Racial differentials in union relative wage effects: A simultaneous equations approach', Journal of Labor Research, vol. 1, no. 1 (Spring 1980).

J. R. Antos, M. Chandler, and W. Mellow, 'Sex differences in union membership', Industrial Relations Review, vol. 33, no. 2 (January 1980).

is greater for black than for white males and greater for male than for female operatives. He also concludes that unionised firms tend to select highly productive workers, which explains why unionised and non-unionised firms can coexist in the same product market. Using a similar approach, Leigh (1980)[127] finds that when separate union and non-wage equations are estimated, adding selectivity variables to remove the effect of wages on union status, the estimated effect of unions is increased. That is, ordinary least squares (OLS) estimates appear to be biased downward, rather than upward as earlier studies have suggested. Leigh himself recommends caution in interpreting these results, given the large size of the coefficients, but his study, like others, shows unions to benefit black members more than white members.[128]

Perhaps more interesting than the overall results are those obtained from disaggregated data. In a regional analysis Kiefer and Smith (1977),[129] using the May 1973 U.S. Current Population Survey, find that unions have the effect of reducing racial wage differentials in the South while leaving them virtually unchanged in other regions and of increasing inter-sex wage differentials in the three regions, North, Border, and South, they considered. More specifically, for black males the presence of unionism decreases the North/South and Border/South differentials by about 7 percent and 9 percent, respectively. For women the effect on the Border/South differential is negligible, but both the North/Border and North/South differentials are increased by 2 percent. Making the comparison intra-regional, the differential for black males in the South is some 7 percent smaller than would be the case in the absence of unions, and the male/female differential within each region is at least 3 percent more (12 percent in the South) with unions than without them. The regional estimates of total effects of unionisation in this study are much larger in most cases than those of Ashenfelter and Oaxaca[130] (though not Leigh), suggesting that national estimates mask regional variations. Kiefer and Smith draw the conclusions that future investigations of the effect of unions on wages should be based on micro-economic data and should allow for regional variations in wage structures, and that policy-makers should pay regard to the possibility that different policies may be called for in different regions.

Several investigations have used data disaggregated by industry and occupation. In the latter case it has generally been observed that union and non-union wage differentials are larger for less skilled than for more skilled workers, which is consistent with the view that for blue-collar workers, unions tend to narrow skill differentials. Thus, Oaxaca (1975)[131] concludes:

> The estimated union/non-union wage differentials are
> generally the larger amongst operatives, labourers,
> and service workers. In particular, this is true for
> male labourers and white female operatives and service
> workers. These occupations are likely to be organised
> by industrial unions, whose wage policies result in
> the compression of skill differentials. Consequently,
> the wage differentials between union workers in skilled
> and unskilled occupations are smaller than the differ-
> entials amongst their non-union counterparts.

Leigh (1978),[132] again using occupational data, attempts to re-
examine Ashenfelter's 1972 and 1973 empirical analysis using
U.S. National Longitudinal Survey (NLS) data on type of union
and collective-bargaining coverage, as opposed to union membership. While Leigh's estimates are somewhat higher than those
of Ashenfelter, the pattern is in general the same. In the blue-
collar occupations (for which the results are shown in Table
6.15), blacks enjoy larger differentials than whites and there
is an inverse relationship between level of skill and size of differential, which Leigh takes to be evidence of the wage levelling
impact of industrial unions.[133]
  Among white workers it appears that craft unions have a
greater impact on relative earnings than do industrial unions,
but for black craft workers and operatives the reverse is true.
For industrial unions the effect on the black/white wage differential is positive—4.2 percent (compared to the 3.9 percent found
by Ashenfelter), while for craft unions the net effect is negative
(-1.6 percent), which reinforces Ashenfelter's conclusion that
craft unions are more discriminatory than industrial or other
non-craft unions.
  One of the earliest studies by Rapping (1960) examined
the hypothesis that the percentage of employed black males would
be lower where unionisation was higher, on account of union
policies of racial exclusion. The unionisation coefficient was
found to be negative in seven out of eight regressions, and in
most extensively organised occupational groups—craft workers
and operatives—the coefficients were highly significant. Rapping
is, however, cautious in interpreting these findings as offering
conclusive support for his hypothesis, because of imperfections
in the unionisation data, the inability to control for establishment
size, and the possibility that the relative supply of black workers

might itself be negatively correlated with the degree of unionisation. Landon and Peirce (1971),[134] also recognising that discrimination would manifest itself in exclusion (since unions would be unlikely to permit employment at sub-standard wages), used cross-section data for the building trades in 27 cities to test the hypothesis that the ratio of the wage rate for electricians to that for labourers would be correlated with the extent to which blacks were excluded from the labour market. They measured exclusion as the difference between the percentage of labourers and the percentage of craft workers who are black. Recognising that the elasticity of demand will be lower and the ease of controlling supply greater for craft workers, Landon and Peirce hypothesise that the relationship between wages and unionisation in any State will be stronger for labourers than for electricians.[135] The unionisation measure is negatively significant to a high degree in each equation in which it appears, which is consistent with the hypothesis. Also, when the degree of unionisation is held constant, the percentage of labourers who are black is positively related to a high degree to the electricians/labourers earnings differential, implying that electricians are paid more when black labourers are more numerous, or that labourers who are white are paid more. However, there is a similar positive relationship between the percentage of craft workers who are black and the electricians/labourers earnings ratio. This relationship is not consistent with the hypothesis and is not adequately explained by Landon and Peirce.[136]

We should also allow for the possibility that the construction industry may be a special case. Ashenfelter (1973)[137] found that there was a significant difference for both race groups in this industry relative to other industries as far as union/non-union wage differentials for blue-collar workers were concerned. The average union wage exceeded the non-union figure by at least 30 percent in construction for black and white groups, compared with a figure of only about 10 percent elsewhere. Further, Ashenfelter (1976)[138] finds that there were considerable differences among industries in proportionate union/non-union wage differentials, the figure for blue-collar workers in durable manufacturing being the lowest and contrasting most markedly with that for construction workers. Further, while the union differential showed an increase in virtually all industries from 1967 to 1975, the increase was much more marked in construction (13 percentage points) than in any other industry. Finally, several studies have suggested that black workers in the public sector receive relatively favourable treatment with respect to the level of their pay within particular occupational groups.

Using the U.S. National Longitudinal Surveys of older males (45-59 years of age), Shapiro (1978)[139] found that in the public sector there was no evidence that unions had a positive wage effect in the case of white- or blue-collar whites and white-collar blacks but that in the case of blue-collar black government employees there was evidence of a significant positive union effect on wages of approximately 12 percent.

The above studies concentrate simply on the question of wages and level of employment. We must also consider the effects of unions on non-wage aspects of employment which may have a differential impact on members of minority groups. Leigh (1979)[140] examines the effect of unions on two non-wage variables—the propensity of individual workers to leave their present employment and opportunities for occupational upgrading. In the former case, the union/non-union tenure differential is found to be substantially greater for black than for white men, but the union/non-union voluntary quit differential (negative) is slightly greater in absolute terms for whites than for blacks. In the latter case, black unionists have a somewhat greater incidence of upward mobility within particular firms than white unionists, but there is little difference between the two in the case of occupational downgrading. The conclusion of this study, therefore, appears to be that union-established institutional rules do not appear to be more discriminatory than the rules established in unorganised markets. Kahn and Morimune (1979)[141] find that while unionisation has no discernible effect on unemployment spells of union members or of white non-union workers, an increase in union strength substantially increases the expected unemployment spells of non-union non-white males and non-white females. Specifically, a one-percentage-point increase in unionisation in a Standard Metropolitan Statistical Area leads to a three-percent increase in expected spells of unemployment for these two groups. Finally, the response of employers to the existence of a union wage premium, as noted earlier, may be to raise hiring standards, which makes it even more difficult for minority workers to gain employment. Kalachek and Raines (1980)[142] do find that there is a tendency for unionised, but not non-unionised, firms to raise their hiring standards over time.

To conclude, the U.S. evidence appears to show that black males benefit most from unionisation, while for women of both races the presence of unions tends to widen the male/female earnings gap. In each case, however, the impact on the overall differential is relatively small. The effect of unions on the exclusion of minorities from certain occupations is not conclusively demonstrated in some of the empirical studies, but it does appear that the craft unions in particular have reduced minority earnings. Disaggregated data reveal that there are significant differences by region, with unions having a pronounced positive impact for minority men and negative impact for those women employed in the South; by industry, with the sharpest effect being felt in construction; by skill, with the less skilled being most favoured by unionisation; and between the public and private sectors, with blue-collar blacks gaining most from employment in the public sector.

In Canada and Britain empirical studies of the impact of unions on employment and earnings of minorities (particularly racial minorities) are notable for their absence. However, one Canadian study by Gunderson[143] shows that, unlike the case in the United States, unionism has a substantial relation to higher wages of females relative to those of males. Specifically, within narrowly-defined occupations within the same establishment, located in a large Canadian city, unions raised the ratio of females' to males' wages from 0.82:1 to 0.90:1, thereby closing the gap almost to half. The higher earnings associated with unionisation can also be computed from the more aggregate data, according to which female/male earnings ratio comes out to 0.42:1 for non-union workers and 0.60:1 for union workers.[144] However, although unionism here appears to have a greater impact on the wages of females than on those of males, a much smaller percentage of women are unionised, and consequently only a few get the wage benefits of unionisation. The total impact of unionisation—the product of the union impact on wages and the proportion of the labour force unionised—actually favours male wages, because their large proportion of workers organised outweighs their smaller benefit from unionisation.

As for Britain, Chiswick (1980)[145] has attempted to analyse earnings, using data drawn from the 1972 General Household Survey (GHS) within the framework of a human-capital model. Interestingly, it is found that there is little difference between the earnings of native born and of foreign born white men, controlling for personal characteristics and other factors, yet that coloured immigrants earn about 25 percent less than either native or foreign-born white men. However, the sample size is very small, with only 135 coloured men (all but eight foreign born), and the GHS contains no information on unionisation.

In an analysis of the effect of collective-bargaining structure on the earnings of men and women, Thomson, Mulvey, and

Farbman (1977), [146] using the 1973 New Earnings Survey, have, in contrast to Chiswick, a sample size of no less than 137,000 full-time adult employees. As Table 6.16 indicates, they find that women covered by agreements have consistently higher differentials over women with no agreement than do men in corresponding groups. Explanations for this phenomenon must be speculative, given the current state of knowledge, and Farbman offers a number of possibilities. First, the differential may be higher when a lower proportion of the total group is covered by a collective-bargaining agreement than when a higher proportion is covered; the former situation is true for women. Second, the spillover effect may be enhanced if women are a small percentage of the workforce in highly organised male dominated industries and a high proportion of unorganised women are concentrated in small, low paying firms. Third, unionisation and collective-bargaining coverage can eliminate monopsonistic exploitation, which is likely to be greater for women due to their relative lack of mobility. Finally, the data related to 1973, when equal pay had not yet been fully implemented, and women who were covered by collective-bargaining agreements may well have achieved equal pay sooner than those who were not so covered. In order to be more certain of the significance of these explanations, it is necessary to use multiple-regression techniques as in the U.S. studies and the paper by Nickell (1977). [147] The latter utilises not only collective-bargaining coverage data but also unionisation data. It holds constant environmental effects (employment in conurbations, on shifts, and by establishment size); growth and unemployment effects (change in employment over the previous year and percentage employed in high paying regions); labour quality variables (age, skill, and payment-by-results proportions); and other variables (percentage of female workers and degree of industrial concentration). The results for 1966 indicate a union mark-up on the order of 14 percent for women and 5 percent for men, though the latter is not significant, while the 1972 mark-up is 19 percent for women and 18 percent for men. Again, as Nickell himself notes, this does not necessarily imply that trade unions operate to the advantage of women, since the relative wage effect may be swamped by the tendency of unions to exclude women from the advantages of membership in high-wage industries.

Thus, in both Canada and Britain, unlike the United States, unions appear to improve the male/female wage differential in favour of women.

TABLE 6.16

Average Gross Hourly Earnings by All Agreements and No Agreement for Adults in Great Britain, April 1973

Agreement Coverage Sample Group	Industry Group	1 All Agreements* (pounds)	2 Differential (percent)	3 No Agreement (pounds)
Manual males	Manufacturing	0.87	+ 8.8	0.80
	Non-manufacturing	0.79	+16.2	0.68
	Public sector	0.81	+12.5	0.72
	Private sector	0.84	+12.0	0.75
	All	0.83	+12.2	0.74
Manual females	Manufacturing	0.52	+13.0	0.46
	Non-manufacturing	0.49	+28.9	0.38
	Public sector	0.50	+31.6	0.38
	Private sector	0.51	+18.6	0.43
	All	0.51	+18.6	0.43

Non-manual males	Manufacturing	1.13	-14.4	1.32
	Non-manufacturing	1.25	0.0	1.25
	Public sector	1.28	+ 6.7	1.20
	Private sector	1.13	-11.7	1.28
	All	1.21	- 4.7	1.27
Non-manual females	Manufacturing	0.57	- 1.7	0.58
	Non-manufacturing	0.76	+33.3	0.57
	Public sector	0.83	+36.1	0.61
	Private sector	0.58	+ 3.6	0.56
	All	0.73	+28.1	0.57

*All agreements include rational agreements, local agreements, and combinations of the two.

Source: Reprinted from A. W. J. Thomson, C. Mulvey, and M. Farbman, 'Bargaining structure and relative earnings in Great Britain', British Journal of Industrial Relations, vol. XV, no. 2 (July 1977).

CONCLUSIONS AND POLICY IMPLICATIONS

Each of the three countries analysed in this section has implemented legislation to control the activities of trade unions in relation to minority workers. The most extensive legislation has been in North America, with general civil- or human-rights legislation (absent in Britain) and federal or provincial laws. Britain, with its relatively voluntaristic tradition, has relied on those sections of its equality-of-opportunity legislation which refer to trade unions. The evidence cited in this chapter suggests that radical changes in the situation of minority workers are unlikely to occur as a result of the introduction of legislation alone.

As far as membership of unions is concerned, coloured workers, other things being equal, are more likely to be union members than white workers in both North America and Britain; female workers are less so. The latter fact partly reflects structural factors rather than discriminatory actions on the part of the unions, and unionisation of both blacks and women appears to be increasing relative to that of white males. This is important in view of the suggestion that discrimination declines as the size of a minority group increases. Where minorities are at a particular disadvantage is in their severe under-representation in positions of leadership within the union movement.

There are, however, dangers in treating unions as homogeneous entities. There is evidence to suggest that there are significant differences between craft and industrial unions, between national unions and unions at the local level, between unions in the South and in the North of the United States, and between union representation in cities with large immigrant communities in Britain and those elsewhere. According to Bloch (1977),[148] one tentative conclusion that emerges is that there is less discrimination against blacks and women[149] in non-referral unions in the United States than in either referral unions or the non-union sector. However, Ashenfelter (1972)[150] notes, we cannot simply infer from the facts that black unionisation is equal to that of whites and that the white/black earnings differential is lower in the unionised sector than in general trade, that unions do not discriminate against black workers (or other minorities). There is specific evidence of discrimination, and all that can be said is that the average degree of discrimination against black workers is lower in unionised than in non-unionised labour markets.

Patterns of discrimination are varied. Exclusion may be complete or partial and may rely on occupational licencing, on

limitations in the union constitution, or merely on informal practises such as the imposition of quotas on minorities, as at the
local level in Britain. A key role is played by apprenticeship
systems, and a number of court cases in the United States have
led to a requirement that apprenticeship tests be altered and
outreach programmes be established. Though the number of
minority apprentices has increased, it is difficult to assess the
aggregate impact of these measures. The union's duty to ensure
fair representation has also been upheld in a number of court
cases in the United States, and in Britain was a factor in a major
investigation by the Commission on Industrial Relations (Mansfield Hosiery Mills Ltd.)[151] and in one of the few cases involving
a trade union under the RRA. A major issue in North America
(much less so in Britain) is the existence of discriminatory seniority systems which have led to various legal approaches, such as
the 'status quo', 'rightful place', and 'freedom now' doctrines,
and to some key decisions, as in the Teamsters case. Among
the solutions put forward to deal with the problem are front pay,
inverse seniority, work sharing and plantwide seniority. Finally,
there have been instances in both North America and Britain of
segregated union organisation at the local level on the basis of
both race and sex.

Compared to the United States, little empirical work has
been undertaken in Canada and Britain on the role of unions in
diminishing or perpetuating discrimination. Attempts to estimate
the precise effects of unionism in this respect have generally
foundered on the lack of suitable statistical data to test the
various hypotheses. This is particularly true in relation to
racial minorities. We would expect unions to oppose unequal
pay for equal work relative to minority workers, since unequal
pay would encourage employers to take on minority non-union
workers in order to maximise profits. Discrimination is more
likely to manifest itself in the exclusion of minority workers
either from employment or from particular occupations. In the
United States there are a growing number of empirical studies
of union impact on minority workers using cross-section and time
series data and adopting various econometric techniques, from
OLS to simultaneous equations and logit analysis. Differences
in the sizes of estimates in different samples using different
econometric techniques, and over time, suggest that we must
be cautious in giving precise estimates of the unions' effect.
It does appear, however, that on balance unions improve the
relative wage differential for black workers and worsen it for
women. Unions have also reduced racial differentials in the
South and narrowed skill differentials. Industrial unions reduce

the wage differential that white workers enjoy over black workers, but craft unions increase it. Black workers also benefit from unionisation in the public sector to a greater extent than white workers in terms of wage differentials over non-unionised workers. There is no clear evidence that any wage advantage gained by unionised minority workers is offset by negative non-wage effects, though it does appear that unionised employers have reacted to increased wage costs by raising their living standards to the detriment of unorganised minority workers.

The policy implications that follow from this analysis are important. Unions can be an effective device for raising the wages of both males and females and for narrowing wage differentials. Consequently, the encouragement of the unionisation of the minority work force can be an important device to raise the wages of low-wage groups and to reduce the earnings gap between the races. This would be especially effective in raising the wages of low-wage families, because by bargaining for (roughly) equal absolute wage increases for different skill levels unions have a larger impact in terms of percentages on the wages of low paid workers.

The encouragement of the unionisation of low-wage workers may be especially important to counteract the spillover effect that may occur as the excess supplies of labour from the more heavily unionised workforce exert downward pressure on wages in the less unionised workforce. In essence, the unionisation of part of the workforce fosters segmentation of the labour market and overcrowding into non-unionised jobs. Extending the benefits of unionisation into the minority workforce, especially into the low-wage sectors, may be a way of breaking up such segmentation and improving the wages of low-wage workers. One criticism of the unions is that they have taken few positive initiatives to improve the position of minority workers. However, in the spirit of the legislation that has been enacted a number of industrial unions in the United States have established civil rights departments to deal with internal union racial practises and have encouraged local unions to elect fair-practise committees. Some unions, such as the United Automobile Workers and the Union of Packinghouse Workers (UPW), have negotiated collective-bargaining agreements with employers which include anti-discrimination clauses. Thus, Norgren and Hill (1964)[152] note that in the 1950s the leaders of the UPW negotiated inclusive non-discrimination clauses in the master contracts of the major packers and that by insisting on the observance of these clauses they subsequently succeeded in eliminating the segregation of workforces in many Southern plants. While the British TUC has a model clause on equality of opportunity,[153] this does not appear to have had a major impact in practise. The CRE has also issued its own Code of Practice, which lays out the responsibilities of trade unions as employers themselves and in ensuring that their staff and members do not discriminate on racial grounds.

What of the suggestions that have been made of extending the role of legal intervention? While there may be arguments in favour of extending the legislation insofar as it relates to unions, as already stated, there are limits to what the law, by itself, can achieve.[154] As Marshall (1974)[155] has observed, legislation will have a limited impact unless there is an improvement in the number of black (or female) applicants for apprenticeships, employment, or promotion who have the necessary qualifications demanded by employers and unions. He concludes that an effective strategy will need to pay particular attention to local labour market conditions and control mechanisms if local union resistance is to be overcome.

One possibility already discussed in the text is the use of 'inverse seniority' policies which provide financial inducements to senior employees to accept layoff before their junior colleagues. This would provide greater security for junior employees (including disproportionate numbers of minorities and women) and more incentive for firms to train such workers. However, union leaders may fear that any form of preferential hiring will destroy seniority, which is regarded as sacrosanct by many unions and their members (Marshall, 1965).[156] Another alternative is the implementation of imposed plans at the local level. One example is the 'Revised Philadelphia Plan' in the United States, which was instituted by the Department of Labor in 1969. It required all builders on construction contracts for more than $500,000 to commit themselves to specific goals for minority manpower utilisation in six specified trades where non-white employment was particularly low. As Glover and Marshall (1977)[157] note, this plan was far from a complete success, since it was to last only for a specified period of time, excluded women, and did not apply to privately funded projects. Clearly, a whole range of measures is required if the taint of discrimination is to be removed from the union movement.

NOTES

1. O. Ashenfelter, in 'Racial discrimination in trade unions', Journal of Political Economy, vol. 80 (May/June 1972), points out: 'Very little evidence of union effects on labour market dis-

crimination has been incorporated into this discussion. It may, in fact, be argued that this is one of the most important contemporary social and economic questions raised by the presence of trade unionism in the U.S. economy'.

2. For a demonstration of this phenomenon, see B. Chiplin and P. J. Sloane, Sex Discrimination in the Labour Market. London: Macmillan, 1976.

3. R. Marshall, The Negro and Organized Labour. New York: John Wiley, 1965.

4. H. Northrup, Organized Labor and the Negro. New York: Kraus Report, 1971.

5. H. Hill, 'The racial practises of organised labour—The age of Gompers and after', in A. M. Ross and H. Hill, eds., Employment, Race and Poverty. New York: Harcourt, Brace and World, 1967.

6. As Hill has observed, the judicial system of the United States has been the major institution of government responsible for social change, and that judiciary not only responded to emerging social forces but also helped create them. See Herbert Hill, Black Labor and the American Legal System: Race, Work, and the Law, vol. 1. Washington, D.C.: BNA, 1977.

7. Benjamin Aaron, 'Employer and union responses to anti-discrimination legislation'. Paper presented at the Conference on International Trends in Industrial Relations, McGill University, Montreal, 1976.

Benjamin Aaron, 'Discrimination based on race, color, ethnicity and national origin', in Folke Schmidt, ed., Discrimination in Employment. Stockholm, Sweden: Almqvist & Wiksell International, 1978.

8. Benjamin Aaron, 'Employer and union responses', p. 12.

9. N. Chamberlain, D. Cullen, and D. Lewin, The Labor Sector. New York: McGraw-Hill, 1980.

10. O. Ashenfelter and L. I. Godwin, 'Some evidence on the effect of unionism on the average wage of black workers relative to white workers, 1900-1967', in G. G. Somers, ed., Proceedings of the Twenty-fourth Annual Winter Meeting, December 27-28, 1971, New Orleans. Madison: Industrial Relations Research Association, 1972.

11. O. Ashenfelter, 'Racial discrimination'.

12. Chamberlain, Cullen, and Lewin, The Labor Sector.

13. F. E. Bloch, 'Discrimination in non-referral unions', in L. J. Hausman et al., eds., Equal Rights and Industrial Relations. Madison: Industrial Relations Research Association, 1977.

14. J. R. Antos, M. Chandler, and W. Mellow, 'Sex differences in union membership', Industrial and Labour Relations Review, vol. 33, no. 2 (January 1980).

15. O. Ashenfelter, 'Discrimination and trade unions', in O. Ashenfelter and A. Rees, eds., Discrimination in Labor Markets. New Jersey: Princeton University Press, 1973.

16. L. H. LeGrande, 'Women in labour organisations: Their ranks are increasing', Monthly Labour Review, vol. 101, no. 8 (August 1978).

17. U.S. Commission on Civil Rights, The Challenge Ahead: Equal Opportunity in Referral Unions. U.S. Commission on Civil Rights, Washington, D.C., May 1976.

18. The more rapid rate of unionisation for women than for men can in part be explained by the expansion of the tertiary, or service-oriented, sector of the economy, where recent union organisation has been concentrated. The primary and heavy manufacturing industries, employing a large proportion of males, were already well organised.

As a matter of fact, most of the increase in union membership since the middle 1960s is accounted for by the unionisation of government employees or by the transformation of government employee associations into collective-bargaining agents. This has particularly expanded the ranks of women union members. See G. S. Bain, Union Growth and Public Policy in Canada. Ottawa: Labour Canada, October 1978.

19. G. S. Bain, Union Growth.

20. As pointed out earlier, over 70 percent of all female employees are concentrated in trade, finance, and service industries. These industries are for the most part dominated by small establishments. Even in the manufacturing industry, only 21 percent of women work in establishments with 500 or more employees, compared with 35 percent of males, and almost 50 percent of women work in establishments of less than 200 employees, compared with 40 percent of males.

The proportion of women is thus significantly related to employment concentration as a measure of establishment size. The extent to which the employment of workers is concentrated in large establishments in a particular industry is a highly significant determinant not only of the proportion of women workers but also of unionisation in that industry. This is because trade unions tend to concentrate their recruiting efforts on large businesses. Larger groups of employees are generally more favourably disposed towards trade unionism, easier to recruit, and less expensive to recruit and administer. Moreover, collective-bargaining agreements covering large groups of employees have a greater impact on the general level of salaries and conditions than those covering small groups, and the union is able to wield more power. See G. S. Bain, Union Growth.

21. White-collar workers represent more than 50 percent of the labour force. Their numbers have increased twice as fast as those of manual workers between 1962 and 1975. However, white-collar workers are not as well organised as the latter, even though employment in white-collar sectors is expanding much more rapidly than in the well organised blue-collar sectors.

There is a dearth of data on the extent of white-collar unionism in Canada. Information on white-collar employees covered by collective-bargaining agreements does provide some indication of the degree of organisation; (in general, these figures overstate the number of union members, since both union and non-union members in a bargaining unit may be covered by a collective agreement). The Survey of Working Conditions in Canadian Industry by Labour Canada reveals that 36 percent of white-collar employees (defined in the survey as 'office workers') were covered by collective-bargaining agreements in 1977, in contrast to 73 percent of non-office workers in the same year. In 1977, 89 percent of white-collar workers were covered by collective-bargaining agreements in public administration, 43 percent in transportation, communication, and other utilities, 29 percent in the service sector, and 10 percent in manufacturing. See W. D. Wood and P. Kumar, eds., The Current Industrial Relations Scene in Canada 1979. Kingston: Queens University, Industrial Relations Centre, July 1979.

22. In 1962, 67.8 percent of women union members were in unions with a majority of male members. By 1976, 57.4 percent were still in this category. Thus, while there has been some change since 1962, the overall picture has remained the same. See Corporations and Labour Unions Returns Act Reports, Part II, for 1962 and 1976 (Canadian Government Publishers).

23. Women represented more than 50 percent of all union members in 35 out of 179 labour organisations (reporting to Statistics Canada), with a combined membership strength of 319 out of 726, or 43.9 percent of all women members).

24. See the 1976 Corporations and Labour Unions Returns Act Report, Part II.

Also see Wood and Kumar, eds., The Current Industrial Relations Scene 1979.

25. D. J. Smith, The Fact of Racial Disadvantage: A National Survey. Political and Economic Planning, Vol. XLII, Broadsheet No. 560 (February 1976).

26. D. J. Smith, Racial Disadvantage in Britain. Harmondsworth: Penguin Books, 1977.
27. D. J. Smith, The Fact of Racial Disadvantage.
28. D. J. Smith, Racial Disadvantage in Employment.
Political and Economic Planning, Vol. XL, Broadsheet 544 (1974).
29. Similarly, in a survey covering approximately 1000
racial minority workers in Bradford, S. Allen, S. Bentley, and
J. Bornat (Work, Race and Immigration, Bradford: University
of Bradford, 1977) found that there were only 13 part-time
coloured union officials and that there were no coloured officials
in branches in which coloured workers were in a minority.
30. D. Brooks, Race and Labour in London Transport.
London: Oxford University Press, 1975.
31. D. J. Smith, The Fact of Racial Discrimination.
32. D. Brooks, Race and Labour.
33. S. Allen, S. Bentley, and J. Bornat, Work, Race and
Immigration.
34. O. Ashenfelter and A. Rees, Discrimination in Labor
Markets.
35. See, for instance, P. H. Norgren and S. E. Hill,
Towards Fair Employment. New York: Columbia University
Press, 1964.
36. R. Marshall, 'The economics of racial discrimination:
A survey', Journal of Economic Literature, vol. 12, no. 3
(September 1974).
37. F. E. Bloch, 'Discrimination in non-referral unions'.
38. A. A. Alchian and R. A. Kessel, 'Competition, monopoly
and the pursuit of money', in National Bureau of Economic Research, Aspects of Labour Economics. Princeton, New Jersey:
Princeton University Press, 1962.
39. M. H. Ligget's, 'Unions and Title VII: Remedies for
insiders and outsiders', in G. G. Somers, ed., Proceedings of
the Late Twenty-Fourth Annual Winter Meeting, December 27/28,
1971, Madison: Industrial Relations Research Association, 1972,
gives the following legal definition of a referral union. 'A referral union is a local union which itself or through an agent
(a) operates a hiring hall or hiring office, or (b) has an arrange-
ment under which one or more employers are required to hire
or consider for employment persons referred by the union, or
any agent of the union, or (c) has 10 percent or more of its
members employed by employers who customarily and regularly
look to the union, or any agent of the union, for employees to
be hired on a casual or temporary basis, for a specified period
of time or the duration of a specified job'.

40. F. E. Bloch, 'Discrimination in non-referral unions'. More precise estimates are given by Herbert Hemmerman of the EEOC (in G. G. Somers, Equal Rights), who states that in 1969 there were about 3600 referral unions with a total of 2.5 million members in referral bargaining units. This was equivalent to, rather than more than one-seventh of, all union members in the United States, or 3 percent of the total labour force.

41. Commission on Civil Rights, The Challenge Ahead: Equal Opportunities in Referral Unions. Washington, D.C.: U.S. Government Printing Office, May 1976.

42. B. Wolkinson, Blacks, Unions and the EEOC. Lexington, Mass.: Lexington Books, 1973.

43. A. Young and H. C. Jain, 'Racial Discrimination in the U.K. Labour Market: Theory and Evidence', Industrial Relations Journal, vol. 9, no. 4 (Winter 1978/9).

44. S. Patterson, Immigrants in Industry. London: Oxford University Press, 1968.

45. W. W. Daniel, Racial Discrimination in England. Harmondsworth: Penguin Books, 1968.

46. We lack detailed information on membership by type of union, but S. Allen, S. Bentley, and J. Bornat (Work, Race and Immigration) present figures showing that in their sample 975 coloured workers (14.7 percent of the total potential coloured workforce) were members of general and industrial unions, while only four such workers were members of craft unions and only two members of white-collar unions.

47. R. Marshall, 'Economics of racial discrimination'.

48. R. W. Glover and R. Marshall, 'The response of unions in the construction industry to anti-discrimination efforts', in Leonard J. Hausman et al., eds., Equal Rights and Industrial Relations, Madison: Industrial Relations Research Association, 1977.

49. O. Ashenfelter, 'Racial discrimination'.

50. This would occur where groups have to vote for a package of policies rather than for individual policies and the positive benefit of other policies are seen to outweigh the disadvantages of egalitarian policies by the majority group. See G. Tullock, The Vote Motive. Hobart Paperback no. 9. London: Institute of Economic Affairs, 1976.

51. R. Miles and A. Phizacklea, 'The TUC and Black Workers 1975-76', British Journal of Industrial Relations, vol. XVI, no. 2 (July 1978).

52. B. Hepple, Race, Jobs and the Law. London: Allen & Unwin, 1968.

53. Jain and Young, 'Racial discrimination'.

54. Smith, Racial Disadvantage.
55. Norgren and Hill, Towards Fair Employment.
56. Northrup, Organized Labor.
Indeed, as Ashenfelter ('Discrimination and trade unions')
notes, under conditions in which racial antagonisms are high
and black workers form a large proportion of the total workforce,
it may not be easy to form an effective union organisation, and
this may explain the current low level of unionisation among
white workers in the South.
57. Marshall, The Negro.
58. R. L. Oaxaca, 'Estimation of union/non-union wage
differentials within occupational/regional sub-groups', The
Journal of Human Resources (Fall 1965).
59. Ashenfelter and Rees, Discrimination in Labor Markets.
60. I. Dubinsky, Reform in Trade Union Discrimination
in the Construction Industry. New York: Praeger, 1973.
61. Wolkinson, Blacks, Unions and the EEOC.
62. Northrup, Organized Labor.
63. K. Mayhew and B. Rosewell, 'Immigrants and occupational crowding in Great Britain', Bulletin of the Oxford Institute
of Economics and Statistics, vol. 40 (1978). The authors examine
the effect of geographical distribution on industrial (and hence
occupational) concentration of racial minority workers and conclude that the impact is negligible. However, they note that
such an exercise carried out at the sub-regional level might
yield different results. They find that West Indians are 6 percent and Irish and Pakistanis 10 percent more crowded than the
resident population and that the occupations in which immigrants
are found reflect lower class, pay, and level of skill than the
ten most common occupations for the population as a whole.
64. Smith, The Fact of Racial Disadvantage.
65. D. A. Dodge, 'Occupational wage differentials, occupational licensing and returns to investment in education: An
exploratory analysis', in S. Ostry, ed., Canadian Higher Education in the Seventies. Ottawa: Information Canada, 1972.
66. G. S. Becker, 'Union restriction on entry', in Philip D.
Bradley, ed., The Public Stake in Union Power. Charlottesville:
University Press of Virginia, 1959.
67. S. Rottenberg, 'The Economics of Occupational
Licencing', in National Bureau of Economic Research, Aspects
of Labour Economics.
68. P. L. Wright, The Coloured Worker in British Industry.
London: Oxford University Press, 1968.
69. Smith, Racial Disadvantage.

70. Marshall (The Negro) points out that the fact apprentices are by convention paid 50 percent of the craft rate is
itself a deterrent to non-whites who cannot depend on family
support to the same extent as most whites. He notes that when
unemployment falls many non-whites drop out of apprenticeships
in order to take up better paid jobs without the requirement
for lengthy training.

71. One study in California revealed a drop-out rate of
50 percent, 37 percent of whom eventually became craft workers.
Strauss refers to a finding that only one-third of all journeymen
participated at all in apprenticeships and that a majority of those
who did failed to complete the programme. G. Strauss, 'Apprenticeship on evaluation of the need', in A. M. Ross, ed., Employment Policy and the Labour Market. Berkeley and Los Angeles:
University of California Press, 1965.

72. R. Marshall, The Negro.

73. Building-trades unions seek to control employment in
their respective trades because of the fluctuating pattern of
employment in the construction industry. The volume of construction work at any given time is greatly influenced by seasonal
and economic changes (e.g. monetary and fiscal policies or reces-
sions). As a result of these factors, employment in the industry
fluctuates and job insecurity ensues. By controlling certain
critical employment channels, building trade unions can restrict
the number of journeymen entering the trade and thereby increase
job security and ensure high wages for their members. See
The Challenge Ahead: Equal Opportunity in Referral Unions,
U.S. Commission on Civil Rights. Washington, D.C.: May 1976,
p. 61.

74. B. L. Schlei and P. Grossman, Employment Discrimination Law. Washington, D.C.: Bureau of National Affairs, 1976.

75. Glover and Marshall, 'The response of unions'.

76. The 'revised Philadelphia plan' was instituted by the
U.S. Department of Labor in September 1969. It required all
bidders on construction contracts for more than $500,000 to
commit themselves to specify goals for minority manpower utilisation for six specific trades (ironworkers, plumbers and pipe
fitters, steam fitters, electricians, sheetmetal workers, and
elevator constructors) in which non-white participation averaged
less than 1.6 percent. The revised plan established goals and
timetables based on empirical data regarding the extent of minority representation in the trades and the availability of non-white
craft workers in the local labour market. Although the revised
Philadelphia plan provoked the strong opposition of the AFL-CIO,
contractor groups, and several congressmen, its legality was

subsequently affirmed by the Attorney General's opinion and a court decision (Contractors Association of Eastern Pennsylvania v. Schultz [1970]). The plan has been replicated in several other cities, including Atlanta, San Francisco, Washington, St. Louis, and Camden, New Jersey (Glover and Marshall, 'The response of unions').

Partly spurred by the threat of imposed plans and partly encouraged by persuasion and funding from federal Department of Labor officials, negotiated or 'hometown' plans have been developed and have been approved in 70 areas.

Apprenticeship outreach programmes are focussed on increasing the participation of minorities and women in apprenticeship in 30 states and Puerto Rico.

77. R. B. Freeman and J. L. Medoff, 'The two faces of unionism', The Public Interest (Fall 1979).

78. This is partly because the influence of national building trades over their local unions has been generally limited to persuasion. With few exceptions, national leaders have been unwilling to use their ultimate power of compulsion—placing locals under trusteeship—for fear of risking a split in the union due to internal conflict among rank-and-file members. Glover and Marshall, 'The response of unions'.

79. As both Glover and Marshall ('The response of unions') and H. G. Foster ('Industrial relations in construction: 1970-71', Industrial Relations [February 1980]) have indicated, government agencies have failed to develop the necessary base by which to measure the growth of minority employment in unionised and non-unionised construction.

80. Benjamin Aaron, 'Discrimination based on race'.

81. Harvard Law Review, 'Union liability for employer discrimination', Harvard Law Review, vol. 90, no. 4 (February 1980).

82. Benjamin Aaron, 'Discrimination based on race'.

83. B. L. Schlei et al., Employment Discrimination Law: 1979 Supplement. Washington, D.C.: Bureau of National Affairs, 1979.

84. See G. E. Lang, 'Discrimination in the hiring hall: A case study of pressures to promote integration in New York's brewery industry', in Discrimination and Low Incomes, New York State Commission against Discrimination, 1959.

85. H. Gilman, 'Employment discrimination and unemployment', American Economic Review, vol. 53 (1965).

86. A. V. Adams, J. Krislov, and D. R. Lairson, 'Plant-wide seniority, black employment and employer affirmative action', Industrial and Labour Relations Review, vol. 26 (1973).

87. Harvard Law Review, 'Title VII, seniority discrimination and the incumbent Negro', Harvard Law Review, vol. 80 (1967).

88. Benjamin Aaron, 'Employer and union responses'.

89. The reasons for departmental rather than plantwide seniority are numerous. An organisation may believe departmental seniority will be to its advantage in retaining workers with particular skills in major functional departments during a cutback. Organisations may also find that departmental seniority exists because different bargaining agents represent different groups of employees. If an employee transfers from one bargaining unit to another, the union representing the receiving unit is unlikely to want to grant seniority from the date of hiring. See John Fossum, Labor Relations, Development, Structure, Process. Dallas: Business Publications, 1979.

90. G. F. Bloom and H. R. Northrup, Economics of Labor Relations. Homewood, Ill.: Richard D. Irwin, 1977, pp. 187–188.

91. On the basis of a literal reading of the pertinent provisions of the Act, it was originally contended that if an employer ceased any and all discriminatory practises with respect to hiring, transfer, or promotion on the effective date of the Act and had a seniority system which was neutral on its face, such system was protected under Section 703(h) as 'a bona fide seniority . . . system'. B. L. Schlei and P. Grossman, Employment Discrimination Law, pp. 29–30.

In Quarles, after a careful review of the legislative history, Judge D. Butzner, Jr., concluded: 'Section 703(h) expressly states that seniority system must be bona fide. The purpose of the Act is to eliminate racial discrimination in covered employment. Obviously one characteristic of a bona fide seniority system must be lack of discrimination. Nothing in Section 703(h), or in its legislative history, suggests that a racially discriminatory system established before the Act is a bona fide seniority system under the Act'. Quoted in B. L. Schlei and P. Grossman, Employment Discrimination Law.

92. J. Pamberton, Equal Employment Opportunity: Responsibilities, Rights, Remedies. New York: Practicing Law Institute, 1975.

93. J. Pamberton, Equal Employment.

94. B. L. Schlei and P. Grossman, Employment Discrimination Law.

95. In a brief to the Supreme Court when it was considering the Franks case, the United Auto Workers (UAW) argued that innocent bystanders would be penalised by a retroactive seniority award. The UAW took the position that earned seniority rights should be preserved and that instead of a grant of retroactive

seniority, the employer should be required to compensate for discrimination financially. Thus, if an employee was the most qualified among 1972 applicants and was denied employment, and a court required that the applicant be hired in 1978 due to discriminatory selection policies, at that point, under the UAW scheme, that employee would receive back pay from 1972 but seniority from 1978. This would not disturb the seniority status or economic benefits of other workers; this would also hold true for layoffs. The Supreme Court, however, did not accept this argument. Under both Franks and Albemarle v. Moody, the worker who was discriminated against would be entitled to seniority from 1972 and back pay since 1972, less earnings received in other jobs. J. Fossum, Labor Relations, pp. 433-434.

96. Over-the-road drivers were engaged in long-distance hauling between company terminals and composed a separate bargaining unit at the company. Other distinct bargaining units included servicemen (who service trucks, unhook tractors and trailers, and perform similar tasks) and city operators, composed of dockmen, hostlers, and city drivers (who pick up and deliver freight within the immediate area of a particular terminal). All of these employees were represented by the Teamsters Union. B. L. Schlei and P. Grossman, Employment Discrimination Law: 1979.

97. J. Fossum, Labor Relations, p. 435.

98. In this case, the Supreme Court applied certain criteria and concluded that the seniority system was bona fide. It applied equally to all races and locked in whites as well as blacks. It was therefore neutral. Also, the placing of line drivers in a separate bargaining unit was 'rational' and in accord with industry practise and consistent with the NLRB precedent. The seniority system did not have its beginning in racial discrimination and was negotiated free from illegal purpose; that is, there was not intentional discrimination in the form of a seniority system. Most of these criteria involved an analysis of the intent of the employer and the neutrality of the system, as required by Section 703(h). The Court found that the union did not violate the law by agreeing to maintain the seniority system (P. Weiner, 'Seniority systems in the post-Teamsters era', Labour Law Journal (September 1979), pp. 545-558).

99. Weiner, 'Seniority systems'.

100. A. W. Blumrosen, 'Promotions, layoffs and seniority under the anti-discrimination laws of the United States', in Harish C. Jain and Diane Carroll, eds., Proceedings of the Conference on Race and Sex Equality in the Workplace: A

Challenge and an Opportunity. Ottawa: Minister of Supply and Services Canada, 1980.

101. Blumrosen, 'Promotions'.

102. Ibid.

103. Helen Elkiss, 'Modifying seniority systems which perpetuate past discrimination', Labor Law Journal (January 1980).

104. Paul Malles, Canadian Labour Standards in Law, Agreement and Practice. Economic Council of Canada. Ottawa: Minister of Supply and Services Canada, 1976.

105. Smith, Racial Disadvantage.

106. Wright, The Coloured Worker.

107. Elkiss, 'Modifying seniority systems'.

108. Ibid.

109. S. Friedman, D. Bumstead, and R. Lund, 'The potential of inverse seniority as an approach to the conflict between seniority and equal employment opportunity'. Paper presented at the 1975 meeting of the Industrial Relations Research Association, 1975.

110. Elkiss, 'Modifying seniority systems'.

111. Norgren and Hill, Towards Fair Employment.

112. Equal Opportunities Commission (EOC). Equality between the Sexes in Industry: How Far Have We Come?, EOC, 1978.

113. Sheila Lewenhak, Women and Trade Unions. London: Ernest Benn Ltd., 1977.

114. N. C. Solden, Women in British Trade Unions 1874–1976. Dublin: Gill and Macmillan, 1978.

115. Evidence on the third of these is not generally available, but as Ashenfelter and Godwin ('Some evidence') note, its effect on the overall wage differential is not likely to be great. Suppose, taking an extreme example, that half of the male workforce are union members but none of the females are; that unions raise wages by 20 percent; and that women earn 60 percent of what men earn in the absence of unions. Then the effect of unionism would be to reduce the female/male earnings ratio to 54 percent (or = $0.60 - 0.10 \times 0.60$).

116. G. E. Johnson, 'Economic analysis of trade unionism', American Economic Review, vol. 65, no. 2 (May 1975).

117. C. Mulvey, The Economic Analysis of Trade Unions, Glasgow Social and Economic Research Studies 5. Oxford: Martin Robertson, 1978.

118. L. A. Rapping, 'Union-induced racial entry barriers', Journal of Human Resources, vol. 4 (1970).

119. Ashenfelter and Godwin, 'Some evidence'.

120. W. J. Moore and J. Raisian, 'Cyclical sensitivity of union/non-union relative wage effects', Journal of Labour Research, vol. 1, no. 1 (Spring 1980).

121. Rapping claims that black employment in the union sector is 23 percent smaller than it would be in the absence of unionism, but this statement is inadmissible in view of the insignificance of the coefficient.

122. Moore and Raisian, 'Cyclical sensitivity'.

123. However, some patterns did emerge when industry rather than overall unemployment rates were used by the investigators. It appears that for some groups of workers real wages move in a counter-cyclical pattern, while for others wage patterns are rigid over the business cycle.

124. F. E. Bloch (Discrimination in non-referral unions') reports the results of the study, which revealed that the effect of union membership on the probability of being employed was positive for each of four race/sex groups, apart from white males, but significant only for black females.

125 Antos, Chandler, and Mellow ('Sex differences') ask a different question: what reduction in the male/female wage differential would result if unionisation of females increased to equal the rate for males? The answer is, only a small decline in the differential (-9 percent).

126. L. F. Lee, 'Unionism and wage rates: A simultaneous equations model with qualitative and limited dependent variables', International Economic Review, vol. 19, no. 2 (June 1978).

127. D. E. Leigh, 'Racial differentials in union relative wage effects: A simultaneous equations approach', Journal of Labor Research, vol. 1, no. 1 (Spring 1980).

128. Leigh also finds that the decision to join a union is more sensitive to relative wages in the case of white than of black males and interprets the black/white differential to indicate that organised employers use race as a criterion in rationing jobs in the union sector.

129. N. M. Kiefer and S. P. Smith, 'Union impact and wage discrimination by region', The Journal of Human Resources, vol. XII, no. 4 (Fall 1977).

130. Oaxaca found that unionism increased the differential by 1.3 percent for white women and 6 percent for black women. R. L. Oaxaca, 'Male-female wage differentials in urban labour markets', International Economic Review, vol. 14 (October 1973).

131. Oaxaca, 'Union/non-union wage differentials'.

132. D. E. Leigh, 'Racial discrimination and labour unions: Evidence from the NLS sample of middle-aged men', Journal of Human Resources, vol. XIII, no. 4 (Fall 1978).

133. The question of the effect of unions on earnings inequality has been tested by Hyclak, equality being measured in terms of Gini coefficients of annual earnings for male and female workers in 77 SMSAs. The results indicate, other factors held constant, that for all male and black workers separately, earnings are more equally distributed in unionised cities but for all women and black women there is no significant effect on earnings distribution. T. Hyclak, 'The effect of unions on earnings inequality in local labour markets', Industrial and Labour Relations Review, vol. 33, no. 1 (October 1979).

134. Landon and Peirce, 'Discrimination, monopsony and union power in the building trades: A cross-section analysis', in Proceedings of the Twenty-Fourth Annual Meeting, Madison: Industrial Relations Research Association, 1971.

135. This despite the fact that in an earlier study (S. B. Sokotka, 'Union influence on wages: The construction industry', Journal of Political Economy (1953)) no correlation had been observed between the percentage of labourers unionised and their earnings.

136. They merely note that a relatively large percentage of black craft workers in an area does not necessarily imply a large percentage in the union but that there could be omitted variable bias, so that it is not discrimination that has been captured by this variable.

137. Ashenfelter, 'Discrimination and trade unions'.

138. O. Ashenfelter, 'Union relative wage effects: New evidence and a survey of their implications for wage inflation', Princeton University Working Paper 89, Industrial Relations Section, August 1976.

139. D. Shapiro, 'Relative wage effects of unions in the public and private sectors', Industrial and Labour Relations Review, vol. 31, no. 2 (January 1978).

140. D. E. Leigh, 'Unions and non-wage racial discrimination', Industrial and Labor Relations Review, vol. 32, no. 4 (July 1979).

141. L. M. Kahn and K. Morimune, 'Unions and employment stability: A sequential logit approach', International Economic Review, vol. 20, no. 1 (February 1979).

142. E. Kalachek and F. Raines, 'Trade unions and hiring standards', Journal of Labor Research, vol. 1, no. 1 (Spring 1980).

143. Morley Gunderson, 'Male-female wage differentials and the impact of equal pay legislation', Review of Economics and Statistics, vol. 57 (November 1975) pp. 467-468.

144. Computed from data given in Earnings and Work Histories of the 1972 Canadian Labour Force, No. 13-557. (Ottawa Information Canada, 1976).

See also Appendix, Table XII, in Morley Gunderson and Harish Jain, 'Low pay and female employment in Canada with selected references to the U.S.', in P. J. Sloane, ed., Women and Low Pay, London: Macmillan, 1980.

145. B. R. Chiswick, 'The earnings of white and coloured male immigrants in Britain', Economica, vol. 47 (1980).

146. A. W. J. Thomson, C. Mulvey, and M. Farbman, 'Bargaining structure and relative earnings in Great Britain', British Journal of Industrial Relations, vol. XV, no. 2 (July 1977).

147. S. J. Nickell, 'Trade unions and the position of women in the wage structure', British Journal of Industrial Relations, vol. XV, no. 2 (1977).

148. Bloch, 'Discrimination in non-referral unions'.

149. Nonetheless, it remains true that the net effect of unionisation in toto is adverse as far as the pay of women relative to men is concerned.

150. Ashenfelter, 'Racial discrimination'.

151. Commission on Industrial Relations, Mansfield Hosiery Mills Ltd., Report No. 76, HMSO, 1974.

152. Norgren and Hill, Towards Fair Employment.

153. This clause could be included in procedure agreements; it states: 'The parties to this agreement are committed to the development of positive policies to promote equal opportunity in employment regardless of workers' sex, marital status, creed, colour, race or ethnic origins. The principle will apply in respect of all conditions of work, including pay, hours of work, holiday entitlement, overtime and shiftwork, work allocation, guaranteed earnings, sick pay, pensions, recruitment, training, promotion and redundancy (nothing in this clause is designed to undermine the protection for women workers in the Factories Act)'.

154. There have been relatively few cases under the compliance activity in the United States against unions (less than 10 percent of the total, in fact). Under the Canadian and British legislation too, only a small proportion of cases have been brought against unions.

155. Marshall, 'Economics of racial discrimination'.

156. Marshall, The Negro.

157. Glover and Marshall, 'The response of unions'.

7

CONCLUSIONS AND
POLICY IMPLICATIONS

The concept of discrimination embraces many forms and
degrees of discrimination. Pressure groups concerned with
equality of opportunity tend to regard majority and minority
workers as basically equal in terms of their abilities to undertake
various tasks and hence tend to see any difference in net market
advantages between the groups as an aberration. Human-capital
theorists, on the other hand, start from the assumption that
personal endowments differ not only between groups but also
within them, which inevitably gives rise to certain differences
in outcomes. Given that differences in levels of earnings and
in distribution of jobs do exist, it is difficult to establish at
all precisely the extent to which they are accounted for by
prejudice or inequitable treatment, rather than by economic
determinants, and to what extent they are attributable to particular actors in the system—employers, trade unions, employees,
consumers, governments, or even members of minority groups
themselves. It must be remembered that levels of earnings are
determined by both the demand for and the supply of labour
and that equal-opportunity policies focussing on the former
will be less effective if their presence is used as an excuse for
doing nothing in terms of equipping minority workers with
appropriate labour market skills.

Socio-psychological studies have been useful in pointing
out that minority group values and beliefs may well influence
behaviour with regard to job satisfaction and job choice. In
turn, interviewers for job vacancies may hold stereotyped views
of the attributes of particular minority groups which act to the
disadvantage of members of these groups. In particular, equity

theory suggests that individuals will respond to perceived under-
payment, as a consequence of discrimination, by lowering performance.

Economic analysis is useful in pointing out where we might
expect, under certain specified conditions, discrimination to be
more extensive. Examples which have been suggested include
less competitive industries, labour intensive activities, small
firms, and higher level jobs. While the approach adopted to
explain discrimination against different distinctive groups in
the labour market is broadly comparable, it is recognised that
special features apply in the case of sex and marital-status
discrimination caused largely by the household division of labour,
factors which are not relevant to racial discrimination. While
Becker argued, using an international trade model, that the
effect of discrimination would be to make the majority as well
as the minority against whom the discrimination was directed,
worse off in economic terms, monopoly power models suggest
that the perpetrators may actually gain from the discrimination.
This is important for policy, since resistance to legislation and
evasive action may be intensified as a consequence. Human-
capital models enable estimates of discrimination to be derived
which might be used in the case of an individual organisation
to establish whether or not there was discrimination against a
particular group. However, it would be wrong to suppose that
the economic measures of discrimination are always consistent
with legal definitions. For instance, both majority and minority
groups may be equally rewarded for the possession of a certain
attribute, such as experience, but the attribute may not be
closely related to the job and hence may constitute indirect
discrimination. Indeed, the economists' approach illustrates
the pitfalls in attempting to establish the existence of discrimination in a legal context.

The advantage of adopting a comparative approach, as in
this study, is that it may make it possible to establish more
clearly the extent to which certain factors are immutable, and
to which the relative position of minorities is influenced by institutional arrangements, though obviously it would be ideal to
consider more than three countries in this respect. While Canada
and Britain have tended to follow the example of the United States
in implementing laws to defend the positions of minority groups
in the labour market, U.S. law is in many respects more extensive and interventionist, particularly with regard to affirmative
action. A basic question is that of which groups should be
covered by the legislation, for if particular groups are not included, the protection provided to others may make the relative

position of the former even worse. On the other hand, the law gives support to those who do not wish to discriminate but are forced by circumstances to do so. A further question is that of which forms of behaviour should be made unlawful and what defences should be acceptable against a charge of discrimination. If the law were, for example, to outlaw discrimination based on productivity differences between groups (or statistical discrimination), the economy would have to bear certain costs as a consequence. Finally, there is the problem of enforcement and the question of the imposition of appropriate penalties. In the United States consent decrees have imposed massive financial penalties on particular organisations, while in Britain greater stress is placed on conciliation and the educative role of the Commission for Racial Equality (CRE) and the Equal Opportunities Commission (EOC) rather than on punitive measures, except as a last resort. Despite these initiatives, it appears that there have not been unambiguous and substantial gains at the macro-level in terms of gross earnings differentials between majority and minority workers as a consequence of the legislation. Between 1950 and 1970 in the United States non-white/white annual income ratios rose from 0.54:1 to 0.60:1 for males and from 0.40:1 to 0.92:1 for females,[1] but against this increase it appears that part of the gain is attributable to the fact that black workers are being offered fewer jobs in which training is provided,[2] so that any improvement in lifetime earnings will be less marked. Further, differentials in unemployment[3] and labour force participation have widened since the 1950s, and the situation of minorities may have deteriorated since that date as a consequence of the recession. The astonishing improvement in the position of black women must also be considered in the light of the fact that earnings of white females relative to white males have been falling (from 65.3 percent in 1955 to 57.7 percent in 1977).[4] For Canada and Britain we lack detailed time series of earnings by race, but in Canada the median female/male earnings ratio declined from 0.61:1 in 1960 to 0.57:1 in 1974 and in Britain the female/male weekly earnings ratio rose from 0.50:1 in 1966 to 0.57:1 in 1975 (before falling back somewhat), though incomes policy seems to have had more to do with the improvement in Britain than has equal opportunities legislation.[5] The above does not necessarily imply that equal-opportunity legislation has had no effect in the three countries but merely that it has not been sufficient by itself to lead to a substantial narrowing of the gross differential for all minority groups. This points to the need for supportive policies such as improvements in education and training for minority groups, the achievement of sustained high levels of employment, and for women, a more equal division of labour in the household in the long run.

As far as employers are concerned, the role of barriers to entry and to advancement within the organisation may have strengthened as a result of the development of internal labour markets in line with the growth in firm size and rising capital intensity. Internal labour markets pose problems for minority groups because they imply that preferential treatment may be given to incumbents with regard to promoted posts and that acquired seniority rights may be limited to majority workers. Added to this, minority workers may be relegated to the secondary sector of dual labour markets, where in response to low returns they may develop poor work habits, making them less desirable employees, and to some extent exclude themselves from applying for primary jobs through a process of self-selection. In regard to barriers to entry, employers may use sex or race as a cheap screen, which may be discriminatory for certain members of minority groups who would turn out to be desirable employees if only they were offered a job. Similarly, excessive use of credentialism (job selection based on educational qualifications) may imply that hiring standards are set in excess of job require- ments, thus excluding minority workers from certain occupations to a disproportionate extent. Similar problems may arise with respect to employment tests and interviews insofar as they are not properly validated against actual job performance and with respect to channels of recruitment where they are sufficiently narrow to arbitrarily exclude minorities. Employers should also guard against the possibility that they hold misguided or stereo- typed views on the relative performance or value of the various groups. For example, misconceptions may be important in relation to barriers to advancement, where there is no experience of minority workers being employed in senior positions. Married women in particular will be adversely affected through discon- tinuous work experience in obtaining job advancement, so it is important to assess accurately the significance of experience for determining actual performance of workers in particular jobs. Thus, entry and training requirements should be carefully estab- lished and maintained only if they are truly necessary employment or promotion pre-requisites.

In the United States, the Equal Employment Opportunity Commission (EEOC) employee selection guidelines have been legally enforceable in the courts in the past. The new (1978) uniform guidelines issued by several federal agencies now include the adverse impact four-fifths rule, the bottom-line concept, and alternative procedures, as discussed in Chapter 4. The

Canadian guidelines issued by several human rights commissions that pertain to prohibited pre-employment enquiries and the British Codes of Practice provided by the CRE and the EOC remain to be tested in courts.

Application-blank information has been the object of considerable attention by courts in the United States, and many States have passed laws that prohibit asking for or using certain types of information on application blanks, such as age, sex, race, child-care arrangements, etc., because such items may identify characteristics of the applicant which may lead to discriminatory decision-making.

In all cases in the three countries it would seem sensible for employers to clearly lay down equal-opportunity policies in order to ensure that they are not discriminating by default of appropriate action and to give them some safeguard in the event their policies are challenged in the courts. For instance, organisations must issue clear instructions regarding the employment interview through their personnel departments. Interviews should be structured as much as possible, and only questions with direct relevance to the job should be asked.

Organisations should keep in mind that over the years substantial validity evidence has been accumulated for many of the predictors. Generally, among employment tests ability tests and work sample tests—relative to personality and interest tests— have the most favourable validity evidence. The use of references and recommendations and of interviews generally has been found to be less valid for predicting job success. Choices of predictors to be used in staffing systems should be governed by the nature of the job and the validity of the predictors. Staffing systems can be improved considerably by standardisation (to obtain reliable information) and by the validation process.[6]

It has to be acknowledged, however, that small firms on both sides of the Atlantic have been largely untouched by the legislation, and, as mentioned above, there is reason to suppose that discrimination may be more widespread in small than in large firms, at least to the extent that the discriminators do not bear the costs of discrimination and smallness does not imply a greater degree of competition in the product market. A further problem in small firms may be the absence of specialised personnel departments to advise on the implementation of such policies.

In addition to the problems in the staffing systems, considerable earnings differentials exist between whites and non-whites. Lower earnings for women and non-whites can be explained by (1) lower education, skill, and experience levels, which may reflect unequal opportunities for acquiring such human capital; (2) lower paying jobs for a given level of human capital, which may be caused by employment discrimination; and (3) a lower pay level for a given job, which may result from pay discrimination. Research evidence, reviewed in Chapter 5, suggests that of these three pay discrimination is much less important than the other two in explaining lower earning levels of women and non-whites. This is so because unequal pay rates for the same or broadly similar jobs is the most blatant form of discrimination and is subject to equal pay legislation. With more effective enforcement and possible broadening of such legislation (e.g. adoption of an equal-value standard), such discrimination can be reduced even further.

Job evaluation may be seen as one means of ensuring that jobs, and hence pay, are ranked in an equitable manner, though there is no guarantee, as pointed out in Chapter 5, that the implementation of such procedures will ensure pay equity. In this respect the British approach is of interest, as the Equal Pay Act defines the area of equality as extending to job-evaluated positions within the employment unit. Indeed, the role of job evaluation in the application of equal pay may be intensified if the pressures currently being felt in each of the three countries for an extension of the requirement for equality from the individual employment unit to comparisons between organisations, and towards the concept of equal pay for 'work of equal value', as opposed to 'the same or broadly similar work', are successful. Even if pay discrimination were completely eliminated, however, earnings differentials would continue to exist due to unequal opportunities to acquire human capital and to enter higher paying occupations.

It is clear that trade unions can be a force for good or evil as far as discrimination against minority groups is concerned. Trade union leaders may see minority workers as potential union members, while their members may regard such groups as a threat to their jobs and a downward influence on their relative earnings. Certainly discrimination does appear to be more marked at the local level within the trade union movement, and it is at this level that racially segregated union organisations have existed in the United States and sexually segregated branches in Britain. At the macro-level minority union membership has been growing, and racial minorities are indeed represented out of proportion in unions in the United States and Britain, though the reverse is true for women. However, as in managerial posts in other organisations, minorities and women are severely under-represented in positions of power in the union movement and therefore may lack the capacity to ensure that union policies

work in favour of minority and women workers. Patterns of
union discrimination have included complete exclusion and limita-
tion of supply, restricted apprenticeship systems, lack of fair
representation, and discriminatory seniority and promotion
systems. Occupational licencing, which parallels credentialism
on the employers' side, is particularly important in the United
States. The same is true of apprenticeship systems, where a
number of court cases have led to more objective and formalised
apprenticeship standards and selection procedures, particularly
in the construction industry. Further, the view has been expressed in a number of court hearings in the United States that
exclusive collective-bargaining authority implies responsibility
for fair representation of all, including the minority members
of the bargaining unit. Although the law in this area is evolving
day by day in the United States, making it hard to offer any
firm generalisation about the status of seniority as a bona fide
criterion for allocating job opportunities or economic benefits,
it seems clear as of now that job or department seniority units
are legal as long as they are created and administered in a non-
discriminatory fashion. In addition, workers cannot be compensated either through back pay or through constructive seniority
for discrimination that occurred prior to the U.S. Civil Rights
Act, but those discriminated against after the passage of the
Act in 1965 may be entitled to both back pay and constructive
seniority. The Weber case makes it clear that employers and
unions may voluntarily undertake affirmative-action programmes
to modify their employment practises, such as seniority rules,
in order to eliminate the effects of past discrimination.[7]

Cases on the above issues involving trade unions have
been comparatively rare in Canada and Britain, despite the fact
that the degree of unionisation is approximately twice as great
in Britain. Both North American and British experience suggest
that problems of discrimination differ between craft and industrial unions, the latter being more receptive to minority applicants
but quite likely to treat them as second-class members. There
are also differences across industries and occupations (women
in particular being highly concentrated industrially and occupationally in terms of union membership), and also geographically,
racial distinctions being stronger in the Southern States of the
United States and the majority of racial minority union members
in Britain being found in large conurbations with a more than
proportionate share of large establishments. Yet in aggregate
the quantitative effects of unions on relative earnings appear
to be small. Ashenfelter's results for 1975 imply, for instance,
that unionisation narrows black/white wage differentials by 2.3

percent (though it increases them by 1.6 percent in the case of craft unions) but widens the female/male differential by 2.9 percent. However, differential effects by occupation, industry, and region and over time make interpretation difficult. Unfortunately, due to lack of appropriate data comparable studies in Canada and Britain are few in number. Unlike the case in the United States, however, it does appear that unions in both these countries have had a favourable effect in narrowing the female/male wage differential. Potentially, encouragement of unionisation can be an important device for improving the relative position of minority workers. At the same time safeguards are required to ensure that unions carry out their declared function of protecting the interests of workers regardless of race or sex. This may imply the formation of civil rights departments within the unions, the insertion of anti-discrimination clauses in collective-bargaining agreements, and a focus on control mechanisms at the local level. For instance, it should become essential for a union to negotiate as broad a protection clause against invidious discrimination as possible to ensure that the non-discriminatory clause is made clearly applicable to every aspect of employment. This will have the effect of giving this clause a specific purpose and, at least in North America, will ensure that questions relating to any breach thereof will permit this clause to be advanced at arbitration. The main point is that collective bargaining can be a powerful tool for preventing discrimination.[8]

What, then, are the lessons for governments and policy-makers? First, it appears that in periods of recession neither employers nor trade unions are likely to give priority to equality of opportunity, a fact that has been stressed in particular by the British EOC. Members of minority groups themselves are more likely to be more concerned with the preservation of their existing job than with the terms on which it is undertaken. This may be one reason why, for instance, the number of sex discrimination cases in Britain has declined. Another reason for this might be the fact that discrimination is frequently difficult to prove, which itself may deter individuals from taking up legal remedies. If this is so, collective action through enforcement agencies, as in the formal investigation system available to the CRE and EOC in Britain, or systemwide enforcement, as under consent decrees and class-action suits in the United States, becomes crucial. Governments can influence employment practises by acting as model employers themselves as far as equality of opportunity is concerned and by imposing affirmative-action requirements on potential government contractors. Whether Canada and Britain should go as far down this road as the United

States has is, at the least, debatable, given the inefficiencies inherent in implied targets or quotas. This problem is exacerbated by defective methods of workforce analysis and by the lack of available statistics to determine relevant labour market areas and hence degrees of under-utilisation of minority employees. [9]

In Canada and Britain there are particular problems for policy-makers because of the absence of appropriate data at the macro-level to determine the success or otherwise of policies. This is especially so in the case of race, for which there is an absence of longitudinal earnings data and also of union membership data. In the United States this problem is much less serious. Earnings series differentiated by marital status with various cross-classifications would also aid interpretation. A major problem for policy is to determine areas where discrimination appears to be particularly significant and to devise appropriate remedies. These might include, for instance, seniority policy measures such as the implementation of front pay, inverse seniority, work sharing, and plantwide seniority, or outreach programmes such as the Philadelphia plan. While there are major problems attached to initiatives such as these, policies which are tailored to specific circumstances may in the long run be more successful than a broad-brush approach. It is by no means certain that it is appropriate to apply the same law, without any modification, both to racial minorities and to women, though this does not necessarily imply that separate enforcement agencies are required for the two groups.

If there is a simple lesson to be learned, it is that too much should not be expected of the law as applied to questions of inequality of opportunity. Divisions in the labour force and attitudes towards them built up over a long period of time cannot be changed easily in the short run. Employers and trade unions cannot be expected to rectify the results of past discrimination overnight. Nor are labour markets insulated from the wider social and economic framework. Thus, labour market policies alone are likely to be inadequate in resolving the problems, perceived or real, of minority workers.

NOTES

1. For a more detailed discussion, see M. Reich, 'The persistence of racial inequality in urban areas and industries, 1950-70', American Economic Association, Papers and Proceedings, vol. 70, no. 2 (May 1980).

2. On this point, see E. Lazear, 'The narrowing of black-white wage differentials is illusory', American Economic Review, vol. 69 (September 1979).

3. For instance, in the United States the ratios of unemployment rates (for age 16 and over) for black males and black females over that of white males were 2.7:1 and 3.2:1, respectively, in 1976, 2.2:1 and 2.6:1 in 1977, 2.7:1 and 3.4:1 in 1978, and 2.7:1 and 3.4:1 in 1979. Thus, since 1976 the unemployment rate of black males has remained close to three times higher than that of white males. Unemployment has been worse for black females, whose rate has been more than three times higher than that of white males. (Ratios computed from Employment and Earnings, July 1978 and July 1979.)

4. For fuller details, see Cynthia B. Lloyd and Beth T. Niemi, The Economics of Sex Differentials. New York: Columbia University Press, 1979, chapter 4.

5. See P. J. Sloane, ed., Women and Low Pay. London: Macmillan, 1980.

6. See Herbert G. Henman III, Donald P. Schwab, John A. Fossum, and Lee D. Dyer, Personnel/Human Resource Management. Homewood, Ill.: Richard D. Irwin, 1980, p. 292.

7. Thomas A. Kochan, Collective Bargaining and Industrial Relations: From Theory to Policy and Practice. Homewood, Ill.: Richard D. Irwin, 1980, pp. 368-369, 496.

8. Kenneth P. Swan, 'Collective Bargaining and Discrimination'. Paper presented at the Canadian Association of University Teachers, September 1980.

9. Lester conducted a detailed analysis of employment procedures and processes for professional and managerial position (for instance, university faculty, executives in sizable business organisations, and professional and managerial workers in federal programs covered by the U.S. Civil Service) and the anti-bias regulation from 1972 to 1979 in the United States. His study indicates that the method of calculating under-utilisation and numerical goals can have a significant upward bias. According to Lester, in the case of a university faculty, this occurs when the percentage of women in the total current qualified supply is used as the standard or norm for judging the proper sex composition of an existing workforce, most of whom were hired or promoted a decade or more earlier, when much smaller percentages of qualified female supply prevailed. In addition, Lester points out that the required method of workforce analysis is defective because it makes no allowance for the effects of women's career choices and of the allocation of their time between career demands and demands of family and children on the supply of

well qualified female labour for both tenured professorships in major universities and top executive positions in business corporations. Moreover, until the late 1960s state laws in the United States served as a constraint on women's career opportunities and progress in professional and executive positions in industry that require, at least occasionally, long hours and night work.

For these reasons, Lester correctly stresses the usefulness of longitudinal analysis, particularly for analysing the promotion and pay patterns of high-level professional and executive workers. Richard A. Lester, <u>Reasoning about Discrimination: The Analysis of Professional and Executive Work in Federal Anti-Bias Programs.</u> Princeton: Princeton University Press, 1980.

INDEX

ABOUT THE AUTHORS

HARISH C. JAIN is Professor in the Personnel and Industrial Relations Area, Faculty of Business, McMaster University, Hamilton, Canada. He has published widely in the equal employment and human resource management areas. Professor Jain is the author of a comparative study entitled Disadvantaged groups on the labour market and measures to assist them (Organization for Economic Cooperation and Development, Paris, 1979), in addition to being the editor of the Contemporary Issues in Canadian Personnel Administration (1974), and co-editor of Race and Sex Equality in the Workplace: A Challenge and an Opportunity (Labour Canada, 1980), and co-editor of Behavioural Issues in Management: The Canadian Context (1977). His articles have appeared in the Industrial Relations Journal, Relations Industrielles, International Labour Review, Academy of Management Review, Canadian Journal of Behavioural Science, and Human Communication Research, among other professional journals.

Professor Jain was previously a research consultant with the Organization for Economic Cooperation and Development, Royal Commission on Distribution of Income and Wealth in the United Kingdom, Canadian Employment and Immigration Department, Canada Department of Labour, Saskatchewan Public Service Commission, and the Ontario Human Rights Commission.

PETER J. SLOANE is Professor of Economics and Management and Dean of the School of Social, Planning and Management Sciences, Paisley College, Scotland. He is also a Member of the U.K. Social Science Research Council and of the Economics Board of the Council for National Academic Awards.

Professor Sloane has published widely in the areas of labour economics and industrial relations. He is the author of Changing Patterns of Working Hours, HMSO, 1975, Sex Discrimination in the Labour Market, (jointly with B. Chiplin), 1976, Sport in the Market?, Institute of Economic Affairs, 1980, and editor of Women and Low Pay, 1980. He has published papers in a range of journals, including Journal of Economic Studies, British Journal of Industrial Relations, Industrial Relations Journal, Scottish Journal of Political Economy, Applied Economics, Department of Employment Gazette, The Journal of Industrial Relations, Bulletin of Economic Research, Economic Journal, International Labour Review, International Journal of Social Economics, and Economica. He was previously Lecturer in Political Economy, University of Aberdeen; Lecturer in Industrial Economics, University of Nottingham; Economic Adviser, Unit for Manpower Studies, Department of Employment; and Visiting Professor, Faculty of Business, McMaster University. He has also acted as consultant to the National Board for Prices and Incomes, Office of Manpower Economics, Commission on Industrial Relations, Royal Commission on the Distribution of Income and Wealth, Social Science Research Council, International Labour Office, Commission of the European Communities, Organisation for Economic Cooperation and Development and the World Bank.

TE DUE